Information Politics

Digital Barricades:
Interventions in Digital Culture and Politics

Series editors:
Professor Jodi Dean, Hobart and William Smith Colleges
Dr Joss Hands, Anglia Ruskin University
Professor Tim Jordan, University of Sussex

Also available

Cyber-Proletariat: Global Labour in the Digital Vortex
Nick Dyer-Witheford

Information Politics

Liberation and Exploitation
in the Digital Society

Tim Jordan

PLUTO  PRESS

First published 2015 by Pluto Press
345 Archway Road, London N6 5AA

www.plutobooks.com

British Library Cataloguing in Publication Data
A catalogue record for this book is available from the British Library

ISBN   978 0 7453 3367 0   Hardback
ISBN   978 0 7453 3366 3   Paperback
ISBN   978 1 7837 1296 0   PDF eBook
ISBN   978 1 7837 1298 4   Kindle eBook
ISBN   978 1 7837 1297 7   EPUB eBook

10   9   8   7   6   5   4   3   2   1

Typeset by Stanford DTP Services, Northampton, England Text
design by Melanie Patrick

Contents

Series Preface

Crisis and conflict open up opportunities for liberation. In the early twenty-first century, these moments are marked by struggles enacted over and across the boundaries of the virtual, the digital, the actual and the real. Digital cultures and politics connect people even as they simultaneously place them under surveillance and allow their lives to be mined for advertising. This series aims to intervene in such cultural and political conjunctures. It will feature critical explorations of the new terrains and practices of resistance, producing critical and informed explorations of the possibilities for revolt and liberation.

Emerging research on digital cultures and politics investigates the effects of the widespread digitisation of increasing numbers of cultural objects, the new channels of communication swirling around us and the changing means of producing, remixing and distributing digital objects. This research tends to oscillate between agendas of hope, that make remarkable claims for increased participation, and agendas of fear, that assume expanded repression and commodification. To avoid the opposites of hope and fear, the books in this series aggregate around the idea of the barricade. As sources of enclosure as well as defences for liberated space, barricades are erected where struggles are fierce and the stakes are high. They are necessarily partisan divides, different politicisations and deployments of a common surface. In this sense, new media objects, their networked circuits and settings, as well as their material, informational, and biological carriers all act as digital barricades.

Jodi Dean, Joss Hands and Tim Jordan

Acknowledgements

If this book has a beginning point then for me it was in the mid 1990s when I was fortunate enough to be interviewing John Gilmore, co-founder of the Electronic Frontier Foundation, key cypherpunk, early employee of Sun Microsystems, early Free Software advocate and coder, passionate civil libertarian, multi-millionaire, and who will be remembered for many many years as the coiner of the slogan 'the internet treats censorship as damage and routes around it'. During that interview I came to two conclusions. First, that John Gilmore knew far, far more, ridiculously more, about the nature, consequences and meaning of the digital and the internet than I did. Second, that I disagreed with his views.

From that beginning I feel looking back that I have for years now had as one part of my intellectual life the long effort to articulate the meaning of a politics native to the internet and the digital. And to do this in a way that is well based enough to argue with the views of those like Gilmore, while recognising that their views, particularly their libertarian views, are not simple ideologism but are based on a close understanding of changes in information in our societies. So if this book is any one person's fault it is Gilmore's!

Since then I have been privileged to work with a whole range of other academics and activists in trying to understand what this book argues is the rise of a new politics of information. I cannot name them all here and would unquestionably forget some if I tried, so I simply offer a general and heartfelt thanks to all those I've agreed/disagreed/argued with in person, in print or in the virtual during 20 years of research on the internet and on the politics of liberation.

Quite a few people were more directly inspirational for this book rather than just in the intellectual career behind it. Here I want to thank: all those in the culture digitally network (www.culturedigitally.org), especially the organisers Tarleton Gillespie and Hector Postigo; my recent colleagues at King's College London especially Paolo Gerbaudo, Btihaj Ajana, Mark Coté, Tobias Blanke, Christina Scharff, Bridget Conor, Melissa Nisbett, Paul Sweetman, Andrew Prescott; my recent PhD students who have been invaluable in keeping me on my toes, Paula Serafini, Photini Vrikki, Xiaojin Chen and Jeremy Matthews; MA students on the MA Digital Culture and Society at King's College London, especially Daniel Holland, Tyler Handley, Bentley Yaffe and Nikki Cheong; my colleagues in the Being in the Zone network that offered a brilliant counterpoint to the obsessions with information in this book, and particularly Kath Woodward and Mark Banks; several colleagues and some friends I've been fortunate to discuss some of these ideas with: Richard Collins, Dave Hesmondhalgh, Ros Gill, Melissa Gregg, Ron Deibert, Gabriella Coleman and Stefania Milan; my friends in the guild AS provide great friendship as well as living the virtual life, particularly Nico, Rahman, Liam, Rodolphe and Anders.

Finally there are three more particular debts I want to acknowledge. The editors of the Digital Barricades books series, Joss Hands, Jodi Dean and David Castle, have been brilliant at supporting this project and saving the world from the 'networtocol'. My long-time friend and fellow academic Kim Humphery remains the best possible person anyone could meet in their first university philosophy tutorial. Third, the participants in the Platform Politics Conference in Cambridge in 2011 heard the first, not terribly coherent, attempt to articulate these ideas of an information politics; thanks very much to Joss Hands and Jussi Parikka for inviting me to it and to all the participants for the excellent discussions.

Finally, I owe a debt beyond words to my family, with all the Cornwall-Joneses in the UK and all the Jordans (and Cornwall-Joneses) in Australia, but most of all to my wonderful daughters Matilda and Joanna.

Introduction:
Information as a Politics

Information as a politics of exploitation and liberation is now central to the twenty-first century. The signs of this are around us: the privacy implications of Google and Facebook; the endless 'terms of service' that we do not read but which all too often claim rights over our information; the clouds that never rain; automated blocking of websites put in place by ISPs; the centrifuges in Iran spinning out of control to explode because of the Stuxnet worm; Green Dam and the great firewall in China; the NSA spying on everyone. All these, and more, are signs of an information politics at the core of living in the twenty-first century.

Sometimes examples and events link together, such as when some proclaimed an 'information war' in 2010–11. At that time, there was the controversy of US State Department cables leaked by WikiLeaks and then US government retaliation by proxy when companies such as MasterCard withdrew their services to WikiLeaks. Online retaliation against these attacks soon followed, with attempts to close down MasterCard's and other companies' websites. A second front was opened when, a little later, web-pages were blacked out around the world in protest against legislation, going under various names such as SOPA/PIPA/ACTA, that was held to be creating greater censorship of the internet. Around the same time, hackers within the movement Anonymous created 'digital care packages' that offered the promise of secure communication to Tunisian protesters as the Arab Spring switched into high gear. In 2010 and 2011, the drumbeats could be heard behind these events, calling up the spectre of war in the information sphere. From John Perry Barlow's tweet, 'The first serious infowar is now engaged. The field of battle is WikiLeaks. You are the troops. #WikiLeaks' (Barlow 2010), to the pronouncements of Anonymous, the idea took hold that conflict in the infosphere had been let loose. Soon battles were joined, offensives launched – such as LulzSec's '50 days of lulz' campaign – defeats inflicted and victories claimed.

A proclaimed 'information war' is one symbol of the rise in importance of a politics of information, but even without the martial theme attention is often grabbed by talk about networks, search and social media. It may be the publicity given to a new technological device being released – Google Glass, the latest iPhone – or it may be a debate about the effect of trolling and bullying online. A huge cybercrime might be splashed across the front pages of websites and newspapers. Taken together these are not just instances of an information society but are examples of the rise of a political antagonism of information. I argue in this book for the recognition and analysis of a type of antagonistic politics that arises wherever digital media and cultural objects are combined with the distributive and communicative powers of the internet. I make this argument all the while being sure that this information politics does not supersede and is not disconnected from other struggles, such as the ongoing bitter struggle of capital and labour, the revisions of life in which male and female are both produced and in which their freedoms and servilities are created, the racisms that rebound into the twenty-first century making scandals like 'ethnic cleansing' part of our vocabulary, or any of the other vital struggles through which we may create our liberations or be subjected into subservience. My claim, and the purpose behind this book, is that information has become one of these ongoing conflicts of exploitation and liberation as part of a multiple politics.

None of these political antagonisms offer up their internal dynamics for understanding without an analysis that both focuses on their specific nature and connects that nature to the dynamics flowing from other kinds of exploitations. The analytic complexity that must be navigated is to abstract the forces of a politics in a way that both honours the specificity of a particular struggle but does not also then assume that this struggle is either the only kind of politics or is the dominant form of politics that integrates all others. Such complexities are familiar in the history of resistance and liberation, one need only remember the mutual but also vexed relationship between feminism and socialism to recognise that this problem of thought has occurred before (Rowbotham, Segal and Wainwright 1979). Abstractly examining a politics of a particular form of exploitation and liberation, so that its nature can be understood, and then connecting that nature back to the politics of other exploitations is the double move that is needed. Only in this way can we understand the meaning of the deep inflection in the nature of 'information' and of exploitation and liberation that has been wrought by the connection of digitisation and the digital to the internet.

It is important even at this early stage to be clear that my analysis, because it is framed within many forms of power and exploitation, is *not* arguing that information politics is the new 'master' or all-encompassing frame of political conflict that will reconcile and integrate all forms of exploitation and liberation. Rather, I am arguing that there are many forms of exploitation, and so also of liberation, among which we should now count 'information'. No one form of exploitation should be expected to encompass all others, instead multiple analyses of exploitation and power are needed. Amid this multiple exploration my arguments seek to locate the specificity of information as a form of exploitation and liberation in the twenty-first century, while also at no point denying the importance of many other exploitations and liberations. How these different political antagonisms inter-relate and may or may not connect is a further issue that will be examined in the following.

But too much has been said already! What is a 'political antagonism'? And if there are several such antagonisms, what does it mean to talk of many political antagonisms constituting the politics of liberation? Moreover, what is referred to by 'digitisation, the digital and the internet'? With so much thought and analysis already devoted to them, surely they could be more clearly defined? This first chapter will answer such questions by framing information as a politics in the following way. First, a brief outline of political antagonisms as the field of repression and liberation will be given. Second, the problem of understanding information as a political antagonism will be outlined in two parts; first, by defining information and, second, by outlining the particular information conjuncture formed by digitisation, digital and the internet. Finally in this chapter, I will preview the whole argument of the book by presenting it condensed into eight principles. These will present a first broad map of the information politics that the following chapters will examine and establish in detail, in four parts. First, an abstract theory of the dynamics of information politics will be given across three chapters linking the concepts of recursion, devices and networks and protocols. Second, particular recurring patterns of these dynamics will be examined, again in three chapters, as platforms specifically looking at clouds, securitisation and social media. Third, particular case studies will give concrete examples of information politics in three chapters exploring the relations between information and other political antagonisms. The three case studies will be the iPad, a moment of death in online gaming, and the hacktivist movement. Finally, I will propose a theory of information liberation and exploitation that draws the preceding analyses together.

The Politics of Many

The first stage of my argument is to outline the politics of many forms of exploitation and liberation. This can be seen in a political moment, such as a demonstration, where there will be many kinds of politics at play. In any protest different values are being contested, even as all contribute in some way to the broad banner that demonstration marches under: there may be local chapters of trade unions; green groups of various types, some locally based and some of the global-NGO type; splinter groups and anarchists; sub-cultures defined by music or clothes; and, since around 2010, it will not seem unusual to see the flag of online activist movement Anonymous flying proudly as feet tread the streets. Such a multiplicity will be taken for granted by nearly everyone familiar with protest.

In such moments there will be many assertions of the 'opposition'; almost certainly capitalism will be challenged by different groups, the need for a green revolution may be asserted, colonialism or racism will be attacked depending on the protest, and many hybrids of and connections between such identifications may be claimed. Analysts will often place these multiplicities into frameworks that unite and draw them together, seeking out central dynamics that allow the multiplicities to be better understood and in some cases to be brought together into one complex struggle. Moments such as a demonstration reference this ongoing conversation between the fragments and an imputed whole through which activists try to make sense of the possibilities for resistance and liberation.

The recurrence of these multiplicities, and the often contested nature of theories arguing for one form of exploitation and liberation, point to a different possibility than that of assuming there must be a conversation between fragments and whole. A path to understanding radicalism that offers an alternative, and also rich, tradition is one that refuses to draw together protests and struggles in a search for a core or fundamental conflict and instead suggests that struggles cannot be reconciled. Indeed, this tradition argues that such reconciliation is itself problematic because it requires the reduction of struggles in a way that puts them within and valued as part of one struggle. From this point of view, the assumption that there is a whole that understands liberation does not mean finding the true meaning of the fragments but removes their necessary complexity and, most importantly, removes the chance of seeing each struggle for its own dynamics. Instead of relations between fragments and whole this different tradition asserts that there is a field of struggle within which each kind of political conflict must be understood both for itself and its own meanings from which non-reductive relations to other struggles may be grasped.

If, for example, we look at a struggle such as 'don't ask, don't tell', in which gay, lesbian, bisexual and transgender members of the US military were tolerated on the condition of invisibility, we see a struggle that recurs within the politics of sexuality. This example outlines the meaning of struggle and antagonism here because the visibility, and hence normative status, of heterosexuality – particularly a kind of heterosexual masculinity – was created and maintained only at the cost of the invisibility of other sexualities. Visibility is not the only struggle in relation to sexuality, and it may have multiple meanings not always involving the equation of invisibility with oppression, but it was how the axis of struggle worked in this case (Britton and Williams 1995). The model suggested here is that one group must lose something to ensure that something else is gained by another dominant or exploiting group. This seemingly simple analytic structure can be seen recurring across radical politics: in class capital exploits workers' time; in patriarchy men benefit by extracting relations to child-rearing and domestic labour from women; in green politics rainforests do not disappear for the sheer pleasure of destruction but to fuel a pollution-dependent model of growth that disproportionately benefits certain elites.

To understand social relations as exploitation means defining the relations between groups in which one group benefits by extracting something from another group that is thereby impoverished. Such relations I will call the 'dynamics' or 'forces' that run through a political antagonism fuelling not only exploitations but also reflecting a fluidity which allows both resistance to exploitation and conceptions of a different liberated world to exist. Forms of exploitation can then only be understood within the particular dynamics of a political antagonism drawing on characteristic kinds of relations – for example, that of alienated labour in class politics, the control of women's bodies in gender, or struggles over visibility in gay, lesbian, bisexual and transgender politics. A few remarks are now needed about what is meant by dynamics and forces, which will then allow the following analysis to pose the question of what kinds of specific forces an information world generates and is generated by.

Conceptualising the nature of forces and dynamics that underpin exploitations helps to establish what is under discussion, but also opens up the danger of a theoretical framing taking on issues of such complexity and dispute that the core topic of information politics will be deferred.

The danger is worth acknowledging and sets limits on what this short discussion will claim, but the opportunity is important, for without some, even introductory, sense of what is meant by 'force' it will be difficult to understand the arguments of the following chapters. To keep the discussion appropriately brief, I will limit it to drawing on the idea of force as derived from Deleuze and Foucault's work, which will also have the advantage of being conceptually consistent with the account of information given in the next section.

Inter-relations that produce inequalities between groups are the forces that are important for this analysis. This sense of force is found in the re-interpretation of Nietzsche associated with Deleuze and Foucault:

> Humanity does not gradually progress from combat to combat until it arrives at universal reciprocity, where the rule of law finally replaces warfare; humanity installs each of its violences in a system of rules and thus proceeds from domination to domination.
>
> The nature of these rules allows violence to be inflicted on violence and the resurgence of new forces that are sufficiently strong to dominate those in power. (Foucault 1977: 151)

Forces are those relations in which dominations emerge. Tracing those forces should then offer insights into the nature of a political antagonism, and such a tracing should map out some of the abstract relations that constitute a theory of exploitation. Further, Deleuze argues for the importance of understanding in Nietzsche a general semiology in which all kinds of phenomena – things, organisms, societies, cultures – are reflections of states of forces. 'We can ask, for any given thing, what state of exterior and interior forces it presupposes. Nietzsche was responsible for creating a whole typology to distinguish active, acted and reactive forces and to analyse their combinations' (Deleuze 1983: x).

Deleuze argues for a Nietzsche that sees every body, and not just a physical human body, as constituted by a 'plurality of forces' in which some forces are dominant and others dominated. Active forces are those forces that dominate and that produce differences, a key point that will be returned to when conceptualising information, and reactive are those that are dominated. But reactive forces are not passive nor do they lose the characteristic of being forces. Reactive forces are in this sense those forces that actively obey, and in doing so they reveal that no dominant force is ever completely dominant because there is still something active in the reactive that is dominated, even where that activity is to be dominated (Deleuze 1983: 40–1). The use of such a typology can be seen in Deleuze's outline of the Nietzschean concept of *ressentiment*, which is where a reactive force appears in the place of an active and produces a particular kind of body in which being dominated takes the dominant role and forms a relationship only between reactive forces, abstracting and divorcing active forces.

> In the normal or healthy state the role of reactive forces is always to limit action. They divide, delay or hinder it by means of another action whose effects we feel. But, conversely, active forces produce a burst of creativity: they set it off at a chosen instant, at a favourable moment, in a given direction, in order to carry out a quick and precise piece of adjustment. (Deleuze 1983: 111)

Ressentiment is a body in which such creativity becomes impossible, as each side of the dominant/dominated relation of forces is seeking delay and hindrance and in which what appears to be active is reactive (Deleuze 1983: 114). Such relations are important as they make clear Deleuze's particular approach to creativity and activity through the sense in which active forces are those that make differences. This will become central in the next section when considering information as something that can only appear when a difference is made. The concept of the body can also refer only to recurrent patterns of forces as there is no relationship of active and reactive that can be identified until that relationship is ongoing and can be referred to other relationships for comparison. The Nietzschean concept of the body will be interpreted in the following as a particular dynamic of forces, with those forces understood as the quality of relations between groups which define them as active or reactive.

Nietzsche, Deleuze and Foucault's views offer a resource for defining forces as relations in which domination may occur, as well as connecting domination to recurrent patterns as bodies/dynamics and in understanding domination as becoming reactive and so without creative abilities to initiate differences. If we were to briefly consider this typology of active and reactive forces in relation to other theories of exploitation, I could draw attention to the intervention of Italian workerism that reconceptualised labour and the worker, moving the latter away from being a passive alienated subject and toward a subject capable of activity, even if that activity is refusal (Berardi 2009: 21–5; Wright 2002). Instead of conceiving of the body that is capitalism as a relation in which capital is active and labour passive, within the typology outlined here labour is reconceived as both reactive – that is, capable of activity but dominated or subjected to the active force of capital – and as potentially active, because its kind of reactivity involves activity that can turn into making a different dynamic than that of capital-labour. This inter-relationship then offers an insight into the nature of capitalism, just as the Italian workerists, and many of the Autonomists who were inspired by them, argue that capitalism is an unstable struggle between forces of capital and labour, and that this very struggle, though it involves the exploitation of value-extraction, has the potential to explode the body and produce new relations of force and a socio-economic body in which labour could be the active force.

What I wish to take forward is the sense that what needs to be examined are the dynamics, the recurrent patterns, of different forces that seek in relation to other forces to be creative or to restrain creativity. This may often be tied to the sense of struggle and battle that Deleuze draws from Nietzsche, but it may also refer to less violent imagery that also stresses differentiation and relational forces. To see this I can briefly look to other theorists who, while not particularly drawing on Deleuze's account of forces, have also taken up what might be seen as a general affirmation of creativity or differentiation in action. Most powerfully, I find in Haraway's work a critical attitude to a contemplative, internalised sense of existence and a masculine understanding of struggle and contest, while also affirming the creativity, difference-making and pure joy that is possible in the intra-actions and inter-actions of beings of all kinds (Haraway 2008: 367–8). I have elsewhere argued that – combined with Levinas' ideas about the multiple interactions of Selves and Others, which always take the form of simultaneous conversation and a hostage-taking making them always relations of both care and capture – Haraway's sense of joy and liveliness provides both an existential and cultural reading of bodies of all sorts, as can be seen in her account of relating to another species (Jordan 2013a: 32–41).

Whom and what do I touch when I touch my dog? How is becoming with a practice of becoming worldly? When species meet, the question of how to inherit histories is pressing, and how to get on together is at stake. Because I become with dogs, I am drawn into multispecies knots that they are tied into and that they retie by their reciprocal action. My premise is that touch ramifies and shapes accountability. Accountability, caring for, being affected, and entering into responsibility are not ethical abstractions; these mundane prosaic things are the result of having truck with each other ... Touch, regard, looking back, becoming with – all these make us responsible in unpredictable ways for which worlds take shape. (Haraway 2008: 35–6)

It would be misleading to see this as re-interpreting Haraway as a Deleuzean analyst of forces, particularly as Haraway is at times powerfully critical of Deleuze's thought (Haraway 2008: 27–30). Instead I hope this renders my interpretation of Deleuze, Foucault and Nietzsche's theory of forces and power into a more Haraway-like analysis that sees 'becoming-with' and dynamics as relations not just of 'force' but also of 'touch'. The world of becoming-with is also one of differences, active and reactive, but is a world in which force is only one term for such relations (Jordan 2011). Levinas' combination of care and capture addresses this range of inter-relations of forces that may occur that may sometimes be those of battle and hostage-taking and sometimes be more like conversation.

If we understand the analyst of forces as a semiologist or physician seeking the symptoms and causes that make a particular body what it is, then the following understanding of forces looks for interactions of all kinds of entities, from technological to living, through whose multifarious points of contact flow forces coloured as active or reactive and in whose relations of both joy and domination, of caring for the Other and of taking the Other hostage, we find forms of exploitation constituted. When forces or touches flow so that some benefit and because of that benefit others are impoverished, then we have a dynamic or body of exploitation. 'Benefit' must remain abstract or vague at this point because so many kinds of benefit have been embedded in exploitations; for example, labour (of several types), visibility and bodies have all been mentioned so far. This conceptualisation offers a theory of what a political antagonism is within what is assumed to be a political field of many such antagonisms. Trying to grasp the dynamics and forces, the bodies and touches, of exploitation can be done in relation to a number of political antagonisms and to understand any one such antagonism it is crucial to focus on it to be able to grasp its specificities. The aim in what follows is to find the culturally and socially embedded, historically persistent dynamics that enable exploitations and the potential for liberation and to do so in relation to information.

One of the characteristics of each political antagonism is that because each is a frame through which culture and politics is viewed, the issue is not what particular aspects of social conflict are encompassed by an antagonism but how such aspects are understood and organised in relation to other elements of social conflict. Each antagonism understands all of society but each also understands society differently. It may then seem a puzzle what each antagonism may leave out, in the sense that there is likely to be something about any element of society that is relevant to an antagonism. What is different is how each element will be understood within the frame of each antagonism. For example, within a class analysis, domestic labour may be understood as the reproduction of labour power and the maintenance of a reserve army of labour, but may be framed differently within a gender analysis as the destruction of female self-regard, as in de Beauvoir's comment that house work is an endless 'refusal of life', and an essential support to public male power in patriarchy (de Beauvoir 2010: 488). Both views of domestic labour carry truths but are framed differently by the antagonisms of class or gender. The question may then be asked of a political antagonism 'what does it *not* cover that others do?', and the answer is that it may cover all things other antagonisms may cover but not in the same way. Information is likely to be present in nearly all aspects of life, as are class, gender, race, sexuality and more, but in each case it is the nature of the view we gain by looking at an aspect of life for its role in information exploitation and liberation that is key for understanding information exploitation and liberation (Jordan and Lent 1999).

The key task of this book is to examine dynamics of forces and exploitation in the glittering towers and desperate ruins that make up our information landscape. There is no recourse to a reconciliation of such dynamics of exploitation within capitalism, patriarchy or other such antagonisms (Dyer-Witheford 1999: 186–91; Daly 1978). This is for the fundamental reason that understanding one struggle against exploitation from the viewpoint and values of another form of exploitation will necessarily mean some form of reduction of one struggle to the other. The approach followed here demands separation and concentration on the specifics of a form of exploitation, which then also turns attention to connections that are made. There is no doubt that such things as homophobia, patriarchy and capitalism are important to understanding information politics and it will be key to connect to them. No one who pays even the slightest attention can be unaware of sexist and homophobic cultures in such places as 4Chan but also of how these places have become important to internet-dependent political movements, most obviously Anonymous (Stryker

2011). Nor will the super-exploited workers making the tablets and phones on which digital culture depends be ignored (Qiu 2009). All these, and more, will make their presence felt in this analysis as they come into view through the lens of information politics; each such connection marks a moment when we can see how the politics of information is one politics, neither greater nor lesser nor dominant nor determinant, and that there are other political antagonisms of at least as much importance to projects of resisting oppression and promoting liberation. In truth, such a view of liberatory politics is often very close to any view that draws multiple antagonisms into a more unifying framework, particularly where this is a flexible framework sensitive to different political dynamics. It is important not to over-emphasise the difference between left approaches along these lines, reproducing a weary sectarianism (Jordan 2013b; Dyer-Witheford 1999: 165–91).

The analysis of a multi-pole politics of exploitation and liberation requires a double move. One move is to isolate and examine a political antagonism or dynamic of exploitation and liberation in order precisely to define its specificity. It is impossible to clearly see relations of exploitation and liberation if their analysis is constantly deferred to the analysis of other forms of exploitation and liberation; patriarchy cannot be understood in-itself if the analysis is always referred not to gender but to class, race, or sexuality. Yet patriarchy cannot be understood unless class, race, sexuality or other antagonisms are also analysed in relation to gender. This is the second necessary move, which is to see how and where the specific dynamics of a particular form of exploitation and liberation relate to, in the sense of affecting and being affected by, other such political antagonisms. Analysis must pursue this double move of specifying and tracing connections.

Here the point I raised earlier about having said too much already is reached. I can now say that politics means, for my purposes, a complex antagonism that is driven by a social and cultural relationship, understood as a dynamic of forces of care and capture, in which some benefit is gained by extracting some kind of value that is lost, and hence impoverishes others. Understanding this to be the analysis of liberation and exploitation, the second important point where I have said too much arrives: what is information politics? Earlier I mentioned the 'information war' and how this references an information politics. I have clarified the sense of politics at stake here, but what is information?

The Politics of What?

Rather like conceptualising exploitation and liberation, defining information is not straightforward no matter how familiar a word it is. Therefore when I argue something about information this is not to also claim to have said everything about it. What I aim to do in this section is to say enough about the nature of information to take forward this work's main focus on the politics of information. I will look for a starting point in communication and Serres' idea of the third man.

> To hold a dialogue is to suppose a third man and to seek to exclude him; successful communication is the exclusion of the third man. The most profound dialectical problem is not the problem of the Other, who is only a variety – or a variation – of the Same, it is the problem of the third man. (Serres 1982: 67)

Noise points us to the conditions that undermine the possibility of conversation and of passing some meaning from one entity to another and by that very fact of passing ensuring some change in each entity. Dialogue of any sort involves establishing a means by which the 'third man', or the noise that would prevent passage, is defeated and travel between conversing entities made possible. Such a concept of communication refers us not only to mathematical theories of communication, such as Shannon and Weaver's, but also to ontological theories, such as that already mentioned of Levinas, in which the relationship of Self and Other is sometimes understood as conversation and hostage-taking (Jordan 2013a: 22–41). For such transmission of meanings to occur certain technologies and cultures must create the possibilities of movement, as I have explored elsewhere (Jordan 2013a). If there is transmission then something moves, and in communication theory what is moved can be called information or, as Shannon and Weaver sometimes term it, the 'semantic content'.

Understanding communication is not the same as understanding information, but it already strongly suggests the concepts of 'difference' and of 'movement'. Difference is also key to many existing attempts to define information. Without attempting to exhaustively recount all such definitions, it is useful to note a couple of them. For example, Wilkins at the time of the British Scientific Revolution stated: 'For in general, we must note, That Whatever is capable of a competent difference, perceptible to any sense, may be a sufficient means, whereby to express the

Cogitations' (Wilkins 1694: 131). A 'competent difference' is information. The most often cited version of this kind of understanding of information is Bateson's. He begins by building on the claim that what gets on a map is a difference because in the move from territory to map there is no need to mark the map if there is no difference, of altitude or vegetation and so on, in the territory. Bateson then detaches this idea of difference from reference to a physical landscape, arguing that the world of 'forces and impacts and energy exchange' is left behind in communication for a world in which effects are brought about by differences (Bateson 1972: 455–7). Bateson notes that this world is one in which there is an infinitude of possibilities and here he makes his often quoted definition of information. 'Of this infinitude, we select a very limited number, which become information. In fact, what we mean by information – the elementary unit of information – is a *difference* which *makes a difference*' (Bateson 1972: 459). Floridi suggests that MacKay's very similar statement offers a more accurate version: 'information is a distinction that makes a difference' (McKay cited in Floridi 2010: 23[1]).

The idea that information exists only where there is a difference is the founding point being made here. If you think of a line of identical statues in a hall, then the only difference is their placement in space; the information that comes from them is that difference. Their repetition then is not about their identity with each other but their difference from each other, the statues do not repeat 'even though' they are different but repeat because they are different. Difference here emerges as a fundamental quality required for there to be something of significance, some information, that can be picked out of the infinity of things that might be mentioned about these statues. This account of repetition as a positive based on difference, rather than a negative based on identity, and the realisation that this means difference is the basis of identity and not the other way around, comes from Deleuze's analysis of difference and

---

1. Floridi's work is not detailed here as its project of creating a philosophy of information directs it away from the concerns of the present book. The most relevant part of his work is on what he terms 'semantic information' because, I argue, this semantic information is required by all other forms of information as these 'other' forms of information have to be expressed in semantic information. Floridi's definition of such information as well-formed and meaningful data (Floridi 2011: 84) defers the understanding of information to these three terms which, in my view, then repeat the issue of difference. Present concerns require less space than Floridi's arguments need for full explication and I draw on a different intellectual tradition to Floridi's by turning toward thinkers such as Deleuze and Derrida.

repetition. Deleuze argues that the 'grounding' of Being has been subject too often to a fundamental misunderstanding of difference as that which splits the same, rather than difference being that which grounds identity (Deleuze 1994, 1983; Galloway and Thacker 2007: 57):

> the mistake of the traditional accounts is to impose upon us a dubious alternative: in seeking to dispel the negative, we declare ourselves satisfied if we show that being is full positive reality which admits no non-being; conversely, in seeking to ground negation, we are satisfied if we manage to posit, in being itself or in relation to being, some sort of non-being ... The alternative is thus the following: either there is no non-being and negation is illusory and ungrounded, or there is non-being, which puts the negative in being and grounds negation. Perhaps, however, we have reason to say *both* that there is non-being *and* that the negative is illusory ... Problematic structure is part of objects themselves, allowing them to be grasped as signs, just as the questioning or problematising instance is a part of knowledge allowing its positivity and specificity to be grasped in the act of *learning*. More profoundly still, Being (what Plato calls the Idea) 'corresponds' to the essence of the problem or the question as such. It is as though there were an 'opening, a 'gap', an ontological 'fold' which relates being and the question to one another. In this relation, being is difference itself. (Deleuze 1994: 63–4)

Deleuze argues that non-Being is also based on difference, and is based not on the negative of non-identity but on the problematic and questioning produced by difference (Deleuze 1994: 64). This generative and positive sense of difference as the ground on which Being rests is obviously posed as an ontological question, however it can also be taken as an understanding of information, not unlike Wilkins' and Bateson's. Deleuze's work is important here in arguing that difference is the problem out of which and the generative basis on which information rests. Information is a difference.

Yet immediately a second problem arises because which difference is a difference that makes information? Returning to the identical statues, there is an infinity of differences that might be registered about them, such as the different place each nose is in or the different place of each head or the difference of angle from my point of view which makes me see a nose as different on different statues, and so on. The difference of place, a repetition of many other possible differences, or the difference of perspective, of a subject 'seeing' a difference based on where they are, must be picked out in some way as *the* difference that is significant and so makes a difference that forms information. Claiming that the difference between a line of absolutely identical statues is their difference in terms of space has to somehow come out of the noise of an infinity of possible differences. This is similar to Derrida's problem that similarity can never exist because if something is different it is not the same but if something has no differences then it is in fact the same object. A statue that was exactly the same as the other statues would be only one statue, the line of statues would evaporate if we removed all differences leaving only one statue. However, as soon as the line of many statues returns, how can we say they are the same statue? One is 'here' and others are over 'there' and 'there' and 'there' and so are different and cannot be repetitions because of that. What allows us to say that each statue is a repetition, in Deleuze's sense, of other statues? (Derrida 1973: 82; Jordan 2013a: 29–45)

The answer here lies in what Derrida has called 'contexts' or what Galloway and Thacker similarly argue is a 'medium', in which information is integrated into various kinds of systems and is never encountered outside such systems (Derrida 1988: 136; Galloway and Thacker 2007: 56–8). What a distinction/difference is that makes a difference is then only conceivable within such systems that are always already there. Such 'systems' are the material and social context within which any information will always already find itself – information is never 'nowhere', a generative source of things that come after it, but always comes into a pre-existing context as a difference. There are a wide variety of ways of conceiving this. For example, Galloway and Thacker argue that Deleuze's fragment defining 'societies of control' provides a definition of this context for cybernetic systems of information (Galloway and Thacker 2007: 57). The point is not this particular claim made by Galloway and Thacker but to note that there will be some such system or context, involving social, cultural, economic, technological and no doubt other factors, whether it is Deleuze's society of control or something else. Others suggest a similar conclusion. We might think of this idea of a system that encompasses and so provides an uncertain and shifting ground on which differences that provide information may be discerned as being similar to Butler's argument that 'the logic of iterability as a social logic' is what we need to be able to understand repetition and so also difference. What an iteration – involving both repetition and difference – is will only be sensible within such social logics (Butler 1997: 150; Jordan 2013a: 42–3). Or we might think of Wittgenstein's concept of language games as being a basis for a sociology of knowledge. Bloor argues this case in relation to Wittgenstein's claim that 'meaning is use':

> Meaning is generated in a step-by-step fashion as we go along. It is not progressively revealed by usage. It does not pre-exist, but is created in response to the sequence of contingencies attending each act of concept application. This is the true significance of the Wittgensteinian slogan that meaning is use. Use is not to be explained by reference to meaning, because use does not come from meaning. Rather, meaning comes from use. (Bloor 1997: 136)

Meaning as use makes sense only within existing sequences of contingencies to which new meaning adds or subtracts but always makes a difference. Such sequences of contingencies are, Bloor argues, social systems that have both performative and bootstrapped ways in which they come into existence and become both stable and forceful (Bloor 1997: 28–40, 134).

Bloor, Butler, Derrida, Galloway and Thacker and others all suggest in different ways that the resolution of difference as information is only possible within pre-existing socio-technological systems. I need not define such systems more closely and have deliberately offered a number of different understandings of what this might mean in order to focus on the abstract generality in what is common across these views. If a difference is required for information then it only 'makes a difference' if it is significant within existing social systems; the nature of such systems will require definition in their contexts but it is enough at this point to understand difference as information in this way. This 'making a difference' is what I will now call 'moving'; a difference is only information if it can 'move' within a particular system of socialities and significations. 'Movement' here is no more and no less than the ability to carry a difference within a system because that difference has significance according to that system. Information is a difference that moves.

One potential misunderstanding of this claim needs to be dealt with quickly, as it might seem that I have reduced information to communication. However, starting this analysis of the concept of information with communication was simply an initial emphasis, and it seems clear that information understood as that which moves between entities such that those entities change gives information a meaning that is different to that of transmission in communication. Whether it is a spoken word between two humans or a syn/ack interchange between routers, there is the transmission of information in communication, but this is different to the movement of a difference which already has to have happened for there to be information that can be transmitted. Movement as a constituent of information does not correspond to the requirements needed to transfer information but instead creates the conditions under which such transfers are possible. To move as a constituent part of information is entirely connected to the difference that is moved and the social and significatory system that allows such a movement. Communication and information are different things and they carry different senses of what 'move' means.

If someone asks 'we understand you say information is a difference that moves, but what is it that moves and so is information'? The answer will remain the same; it is a difference that moves, and in that movement it is that which passes and travels in certain culturally specific ways. There is no need for any more, information is a difference that moves.

A corollary to this is that information is always material, because it is always already embedded in systems that are the only way of stabilising and realising which difference is a difference that can move out of the infinity of possible differences. Such a position also suggests that the faster information moves the more it will seem to de-materialise. The handwritten letter can be touched and the letters formed by an ink pen offer a solid materiality to the information conveyed by them. The tapping of the telegraph gives an aural punctuation to the invisible – to human eyes – electricity on the wires and this tapping leads to the materiality of the telegram. In the early twenty-first century the speed and complexity of packets delivered to pixels on the screen through the 'cloud' seem to make information light and immaterial. But as will be emphasised in the following, information must always be subject to a materialist analysis because it is always material. Information is always embodied in some way, even when such embodiment has the fluidity and speed of electricity and silicon.

As a necessarily material form and as something defined in its materially embedded movement information will always be constituted within specific social and historical contexts. The key context for information as a political antagonism is that constituted by the connection of digitisation, the digital and the internet. The idea of political antagonisms as sites of exploitation has been introduced and now also the idea of information as differences that move. The final part of this chapter will frame these in their broad socio-technological historical moment when digitisation met the internet.

The Digital and the Internet

The socio-technological complex that has profoundly reshaped information in our times has become so familiar that it may seem trivial to recount its fundamental vectors: digitisation, digital and the internet. Given their familiarity I will only touch on these briefly, but wish to stress that it is in their intersection that the political antagonism of information is embedded and out of which have been born so many innovations we now daily and unthinkingly use.

The digital refers to the transformation of many different types of media-objects, such as music, video, text, picture and so on, into one type of media-object (that is, to the one type of object which can move). This is a reduction to bits of the complexity of meaning that is conveyed in media-objects and that may be materialised in paint, canvas, film negatives, audio tapes and so on. This is then a reduction that is conducted to lead to a reconstruction when the bits resolve again into the media-object, even where the media-object is also changed by the reduction and reconstruction (such as a painting going from oil paint to pixels). A song downloaded from a bit torrent on Pirate Bay is taken for its sound and cultural meaning but passes through the bits just as if it were paid for on iTunes or Amazon. Of course all media and cultural objects go, and have always had to go, through such a moment in which cultural meaning is materialised in some substance for consumption, but the digital unifies such moments and takes all different substances, all the different materialities of meaning, through the same techno-cultural moment of being in bits (Berry 2008; Lessig 2009).

Digitisation and the digital involve the creation of information in bits – manipulable, electronically stored bits that can decompose cultural objects and then ensure they are reconstructed into their individual forms. This bits-Being refers both to media-objects that are turned into digital forms and those objects that are digital from the moment they are articulated. Bits-Being, the radically fluid ontology of digitisation, connects in a profound way to the possibilities for transmission of bits that the internet brings. The information and communicative possibilities of the internet have been and continue to be analysed by a growing body of scholars, and have been experienced more and more widely, even if internet access is far from globally universal (Norris 2001; Livingston and Helspar 2007). The fundamental ability of the internet is to connect different computer networks and to pass packages of bits from anyone and to anyone who is part of a network that has implemented the connecting protocols. So much about this is encapsulated by the combination of packet-switching and the internet protocol number – two key design components of the internet – that it is worth touching briefly on these, even given that a more detailed analysis will be undertaken in Chapter 3 when examining networks and protocols (Mueller 2010, 2002; Galloway and Thacker 2007).

Packet-switching embodies the radically distributed and anti-hierarchical ideals many impute to the internet. A computer sends a message which is automatically broken up into identical length packets, each of which consists of a middle full of meaning-laden bits that are headed by information about the sender, destination and the information to reconstruct packets in the right order when all have arrived. These packets may then be sent out across the network, not necessarily travelling the same way, able to fail and be resent, and able to move equally across nodes in connected networks. At the same time, this system will fail if packets cannot each be marked with their destination, so that they arrive where they need to so they can be reconstructed, and marked with their origin, so that failed or corrupted packets may be resent. The internet protocol number answers this need (Mueller 2002: 15–30). Each computer on these interconnected networks is given a number that identifies it. Each bit sent out carries with it the mark of exactly where it came from and exactly where it should go: total authority and control. These numbers then need to be communicated and kept authoritative, and here the address space maintains a hierarchical database of numbers and their physical destinations. This is a control protocol, in Galloway's sense, of the most fundamental and authoritative kind (Galloway 2004). As distributed as packet-switching is, so IP numbers and the domain name system is centralised and hierarchical.

Centralisation and decentralisation, hierarchy and flattened network – these two go together fundamentally to create the internet over which bits may flow in ways that were previously unknown. For example, prior to the internet the idea of many-to-many communication was rarely if ever possible but now is a familiar experience.

The two innovations of the digital and the internet complement each other and together ensure something now familiar to both users and analysts in the radically changed nature of media and cultural objects. Something often commented on when this conjunction first exploded was the radically reduced costs of producing, distributing and consuming media-objects. Again this is something that has become so familiar as often not to need comment, but in uncovering the political antagonism of information after the digital met the internet, it is important to emphasise that this conjunction was accompanied by technologies so reduced in cost that previously impossible cultural pursuits became possible. Think of making a television programme in the 1960s. The cost needed to do this and then distribute it, not to speak of government regulation around television, restricted the making of such programmes to a small minority and subjected them to strict authorities. Now any gamer with an inclination, a broadband connection and computer equipment can set up their own online channel and either make programmes or just offer live-streams of their online experience.

If information is that which travels then the type of information that this book addresses is that which is inextricably part of the multiple, complex and contradictory socio-technical configuration that is sited on the connection of digitisation and the internet. The last quarter of the twentieth century experienced this change and the twenty-first century lives it.

Forces, Platforms, Battlegrounds

The conception of the politics of exploitation and liberation as multiple combined with understanding one of those poles to be information, itself understood as differences that move in the context of the connection of digitisation and the internet at the end of the twentieth and into the twenty-first century, combine to set the question this book addresses. What kind of a political antagonism is one based on information in the context of the digital and the internet? What connections to other antagonisms, other exploitations and liberations, does information as exploitation or as liberation have? To answer such questions four different phases will follow in this book, starting more abstractly before moving to the mess of the world and finishing conceptually.

In the first part of this book, a theory focusing on the particular dynamics that can be understood as constituting the forces and touches of information power will be explored. The first of these is recursion and the way information-based processes can apply their results to themselves producing startling possibilities for generating information (Recursion). The second is the way this growth of information is often controlled and codified within different devices, which may be hardware, software or anywhere in between, that bury their powers within black boxes of technologies (Technologies' Embrace). The third is the way such things as recursions and devices are (dis)organised into recurrent patterns constituted by inextricably connected networks and protocols (Network and Protocol Theory). Together recursions, devices and networks and protocols provide an understanding of the forces of information power.

The second part of the book explores how these three different dynamics that constitute information power are formed into abstract architectures or blueprints for creating recurrent and specific patterns of recursions, devices and networks and protocols. These are platforms understood as abstract architectures of information power. Three different platforms will be examined. The first is cloud computing in which the materiality of devices and networks and protocols are obscured by the magic of mobility and flexibility in information management (Clouds). The second is securitisation in which nation-states seek to collect all information and then subject it to profiling to satisfy security agencies' desire to 'master the internet' (Securitisation of the Internet). The third is social media networks in which two different understandings of public and private relations interact within enclosures of data (Social Media Networks).

The third part of the book drives these analyses into the mess of the world by undertaking three case studies. This brings together the analysis of information power with that of the architectures of platforms to see how they operate in specific conflicts. It also ensures a closer look at connections between information as a political antagonism and other forms of exploitation such as capitalism, patriarchy and so on. The first case study is of the technological device the iPad, and follows the information nature of this device to examine its class-based exploitations and its environmental significance (Battlegrounds and the iPad). The second study examines the moment in online gaming when an avatar dies and follows both the visual and gameplay significance of such moments across a number of massively multiplayer online games, connecting these to a militarised masculinity permeating such games that affects both gender and race (Death and Gaming). The third case study looks at a highly technologically mediated activist movement and traces online activism, known as 'hacktivism', to its roots and generations (Hacktivism).

Having moved from the abstraction of the nature of information to the actions of online activists, the fourth and concluding phase draws the analyses together to explore a theory of exploitation and liberation in information power (Information Exploitation and Information Liberation). The pursuit of liberation and the fight against exploitation are examined in relation to whether information is available for simultaneous complete use or is treated as a form of exclusive property; the way platforms may create open differentiations or deliver recursions to platform controllers; whether information is open, accessible and available for making or is hoarded; and finally the way information power connects to other forms of exploitation and liberation both as a set of tactics for use and as the exchange of exploitations and liberations.

With all four phases completed the political antagonism of information will have been explored and fully theorised. To preview this final theory, in the conclusion to this chapter I have articulated its key points in eight principles. These should be viewed as a kind of first map of the territory to be defined and so as something both condensed and strange.

The map of information politics offered in the eight principles that follow is condensed because these principles convey what the rest of this book will argue. That argument will follow a detailed path, addressing such disparate issues as the principles that found computing, the iconography and the legalities of cloud computing, the environmental impact of the iPad, the actions of Anonymous in Tunisia, the theory of computer protocols and more. The points outlined next are articulated from that conceptual complexity and empirical richness. The principles are then like a first map of a new terrain in that they allow one to see general features, the connections of major sections and their broad nature – mountainous, river-crossed – of the area covered. Understanding the details and the reasons why such areas connect and their meaning will require the full argument offered by the rest of this book.

The map offered in the next section should also convey something strange: it reflects an argument for a new understanding of the politics of information based on changes in information at the end of the twentieth and beginning of the twenty-first century and conceived of as a particular kind of political antagonism with a specific structure to information exploitation and information liberation. The theory draws on a wide range of existing ideas, accordingly some parts of it will be familiar, but both overall and in its specifics this should be like a map of a new land. It will include new connections between and new uses of existing theory and evidence, but also new ideas and new data.

Principles of Information Politics

1   The politics of information has always been present and always will be, but it has changed. The times now are characterised by an information flood driven on by the cultures of the digital and the internet. These new times have inverted hundreds of years of information scarcity. In times of information flood new principles of information are needed in all its aspects: its sharing, its ownership and the very meaning of what we value in information. Information has assumed a greater centrality in liberation as it has spread into all life with the rise of cultures of computing, interconnection and mobility. Information is a new politics.

2   The most significant and distinctive power of information lies in its ability for all to share simultaneously in any bit of information and for all to be able to use that bit to its full extent. Information laws, cultures and politics often continue to be dedicated to making containers that restrict this ability for all to share equally because, on the one hand, scarcity of information meant that producers – thinkers, musicians, poets, novelists, historians, scientists – were supposed to be given incentives by being able to control their information-product, while, in truth and on the other hand, church, state and capital wanted to control or profit from scarce information. Even if the desire to benefit information producers was once real in conditions of information scarcity, the cynicism of those who sought to control and profit from information always undermined this, and even if the arguments once had some purchase on social good and mutual benefit, they no longer do.

2.1   The possibility of information being available to all requires the revision of laws and property relations around information, including the cultures and economics of information, in order to move from the exclusive use of information to its availability as simultaneous complete use for all.

3   The power of simultaneous complete use of information is greatest when information is applied to itself using recursion to lead to exponential increases in information. For information to apply to itself it has to be codified and homogenised in some way such that it is possible to take the information coming from an information process and then reintroduce that information to the process. Combining recursion with information that is available for simultaneous complete use is the basis for information environments that fully benefit the communities that make information. Yet many such information environments try to define information as an exclusive property such that the results of recursions can be owned by and benefited from by a minority. The information commons means building information environments that are distributive and whose guiding principle is use and access to information, and the making of further information, for all in those environments.

4   Information is made in contexts of particular recurrent inter-relations of technologies, actors and cultures and is always material. Such recurrent patterns often have an abstract architecture that will be called a 'platform'. A platform is a particular plan for organising the production of recursions that will also define their benefits. Benefits for the few can be based on restricting simultaneous complete use, but such use can also be made available to all, ensuring all participants in a platform can themselves benefit from and continue to make new information. Ensuring information is valued as simultaneous complete use on a platform means a platform must embed within itself openness and the capacity for making for all who use the platform.

4.1   The abstract architecture of a platform must integrate openness, access and making into the activities of that platform. The abstract architecture of platforms must allow openness, access and making in the nature of each platform.

4.2   The defenders of information as exclusive property, the inglorious industries led by the recording and film industries of the West, will always assert that they are merely protecting the rights of the producers of information. Who, they will ask, will write our songs and make our movies if information products are given away? A challenge of information as simultaneous complete use is to continue developing new means of supporting producers of information and to radically critique all those industries who seek their own survival and profit ahead of the benefit information can bring to all. Information may be both released and exchanged, it may be crowd-source funded, it may be offered directly to the user from the producers with no intermediary. In short, there are many ways in which information made available to all may also support its producers.

5   The rights of the information commons is based on recursions built in platforms dedicated to simultaneous complete use of information for all on a platform. The information commons has rights to keep available the information appearing on it, because that commons is constructed out of that information. The rights of the network over those who network ensures the information commons retains the differences contributed to it and makes them available to all who access each commons. However, the rights of the network can also be exploited to produce a total archive that identifies individuals with their information.

5.1   The rights of the network must be implemented in platforms in ways that promote the information commons and that mitigate the total archive and surveillance.

6   Information politics is a politics of information but it is not the only politics of exploitation and liberation. Information politics has to be connected with the politics of other forms of exploitation and liberation.

7   The politics of information can be liberatory when information is made for simultaneous complete use and when platforms ensure an information commons that promotes openness, access and making both in its activities and in its structure as a platform.

8   The future needs information as simultaneous complete use.

Part I

Theory of Information Power

1

Recursion

Information Eats Itself

Information is a difference that moves. Information also passes between entities and in that movement both enables and is affected by change; information may make a difference from itself. We can see that if the entities that move are also able to move, are also able to flow as information, then the flow is both constant and constantly contributing to further flows. Information can eat itself in this way to produce more information and this is a key underlying dynamic of information power and politics examined in this chapter. This dynamic will be called recursion in the ability of information to contain itself. The dynamic of recursion can be theorised by understanding the significance of the point at which a difference occurs, and examples of this process can be seen underpinning major digital institutions.

For example, one of the open secrets of the growth of digital industries, though now much repeated, is Google's position as one of the largest computer manufacturers in the world. Claimed in 2006 to be the fourth largest builder of computers, Google was by 2011 claiming to be the largest of all (Levy 2011: 181; Hansell and Markoff 2006). Google keeps these computers and uses them to power itself. This fact is often repeated to demonstrate that Google needs massive computing and storage power for its search service and all the other applications it offers. An important factor underpinning this need for computing resources is that Google's search is recursive and accordingly not only takes input from those who search and use its services but continually reuses its own data to refine future searches and future identifications of the nature of its users (and hence delivery of advertisements). For example, Google claims that only 15 per cent of Google searches are new searches it has not seen, which means 85 per cent of searches can be related to other searches refining the search results. Eighty-five per cent of Google searches produce information only by being applied to previous searches and in that way creating some kind of difference to those previous searches (and so new information) (Google 2013a). This means the majority of searches are used recursively and all the differences, however minor, can be taken and applied to existing searches. This utilises differences like each query's punctuation, the length of the query, the length of time on the Google page, whether the first result is clicked on, how soon a searcher returns to try again, the searcher's characteristics and so on and so on (Levy 2011: 46–8).

Google is able to apply a past search to its present and future searches, to refine and then reapply this information. It is able to create a system in which whatever is added to it contributes not just when added but can continue to help refine searches and advertisement delivery. Any user of Google will most likely have noticed the obvious effects of this. For example, when searching for a holiday in a particular region and then finding Google offering up future advertisements for that region. To do this on top of its initial and obvious services requires massive computing power, a problem Google solved by building its own bespoke data system and in the process becoming one of the largest computer manufacturers in the world. Facebook similarly takes the information individuals need to provide about themselves in order to present themselves on the social network and turn this into a form that allows recursions. The information can be returned back within Facebook's systems to, like Google, return certain advertisements to the user and then to use further information, such as which advertisements are clicked on, to affect and create yet more information within the system. Though Google and Facebook were clearly, in 2015, large gorillas in the digital jungle, nearly all digital systems embed some form of recursion, or seek to, and this chapter examines what this means.

It is clear that the provision of information, something held by the user, is taken over in a seamless fashion by institutions like Facebook and Google and becomes part of their systems. There are here shifts when information that may be freely given up has its results appropriated. Imparting information results in a relationship that places initial activity, like a search, in a reactive state when using the very services that elicited such information in the first place. Moreover, this may become an unequal relationship in which the provision of information leads to a transfer of ownership and hence the ability to draw from a range of other actors either greater information, wanted or unwanted solicitations to spend money and more revenue from advertisers. A complex body is formed here in which a range of active and reactive forces can be seen and in which recursion is a key dynamic. For example, if Google knows that someone who searches for Walt Disney World also searches for Harry Potter World and if they see enough of these correlations then they can start to predict that anyone searching for the land of Mickey Mouse might be happy to see an advertisement for the land of Harry Potter. Even if the information provided by searchers is anonymised this effect is in play – each search that is made can be fed back into changing future searches. If this can then be connected to someone's age, gender, location and so on, perhaps by that person being logged into their Google account while they search or because on Facebook this information will already be connected, then the targeting can be even more precise. This is a key example of recursion and the way its ability to take on digital information and then use it again and again to change other similar digital actions is key to the digital world.

Differences that are moving must have a point of 'difference-from'. Without a difference registering itself as 'different-from' another difference then no significant difference – no mark on a map – can occur, as the difference always then falls back into myriad undifferentiated and unrealised possible differences or into sameness. In addition, if information can be applied to information, then information becomes exponentially more productive of further information because it contributes to itself. Recursion further results in the privileging of those who can manage recursive information processes because any information, no matter who that information might be thought to belong to, that can be drawn into a recursive process contributes to that process and to the information reach of whoever controls it.

This chapter follows the idea of information into that of recursion, or the application of information to itself. This requires addressing existing theories of recursion of which there are two key sources. The most important is the theory of computers itself, with the foundational work of Turing, Church and Gödel, though a useful beginning is in the use of recursion in linguistic theory and the work of Chomsky. This chapter will briefly examine recursion in Chomsky before turning to the basis of computation. The discussion that here leads to a theory of recursion may seem like it is based on technical matters concerning how mathematics is founded and how this relates to articulating a basis for creating electronic computers. However, this theory of recursion has immediate political and cultural ramifications when returned to the context of information politics in the twenty-first century. It should be no surprise, to anyone but the simplest technological determinist, that what seems to be a highly technical idea when embedded deep within a key technology of information turns out to have wide political implications. This chapter will then involve a shift from the concerns of linguistics and the philosophy of computation to the politics of information. This will be done by taking the theory of recursion and seeing how in digital environments it holds a dark potential for exploitation, as already prefigured in the example of Google and Facebook turning our personal information into profit by using recursions.

These are particular and striking factors about recursion that need to be understood in relation to information politics in order to understand both the extraction of information as a contributor to exploitation and the way this extraction leads to an exponential explosion in information. The latter will, in turn, lead to the second dynamic of information politics explored in the next chapter. However, before being able to grasp the meaning of exponential information increases, recursion needs to be understood.

A Theory of Recursion

A theory of recursion may be derived from two intellectual questions in which recursion plays a key role: the definition of computing and the definition of language. As noted, these may seem far from the concerns of exploitation and liberation in information technologies but they will nonetheless help articulate one of the key ideas of that politics in recursion. We can understand recursion by focusing on Church and Turing's reflections on the possibilities of computing and on Chomsky's claim that all languages are recursive. It is useful to start with Chomsky's idea of recursion in language because it introduces relevant concepts but the key discussion is to be found in Gödel, Church and Turing's work and their understanding of recursion as a foundational concept for what became computing. After examining these two conceptualisations of recursion a general theory of recursion will be outlined. The final sections of this chapter will then explore the nature of information exploitation and liberation within recursion.

Recursion appears in Chomsky's work as part of his theory of generative grammar. It is not necessary to go into this theory in detail but it is useful to see that Chomsky frames recursion within his theory in the following way: 'The use of language undoubtedly involves many factors beyond the grammar that represents fundamental properties of the speaker's knowledge of his language. It is natural to suppose that models of the speaker and hearer will incorporate "competence grammar" as a basic element ... A generative grammar is a theory of competence' (Chomsky 1975: 7). In this sense, Chomsky calls his study of language and recursion's place in it a study of a particular aspect of human intelligence. Within that study he also conceptualises recursion.[1] If we consider a sentence such as 'Chomsky believes in recursion' then we can use that sentence within another sentence or another sentence or clause within it: 'Jordan thinks that Chomsky believes in recursion' or 'Chomsky the American linguist believes in recursion'. According to Chomsky, this means that a key characteristic of recursion is that it allows the infinite to be created with finite means. Language is infinite in the sense that there are an infinity of things that can be said/heard but that infinity is built from the finite means of words, grammar and syntax (Smith 2004: 54–5; Hauser et al. 2002).

Several aspects of recursion are suggested even within this very brief recounting of a component of Chomsky's theory of language. The operating form is that recursion allows a particular process to use either itself or products or elements of itself back within that same process. We can take any sentence and use it within another sentence or we can add sentences to the sentence (or clauses to clauses) we already have. Recursion in operation can be initially understood abstractly as a kind of process which can be utilised within itself. The consequence of this is that recursion allows infinite results from finite means; here is where Chomsky explicitly refers to mathematics, in the form of recursive function theory, stating: 'There is a perfectly coherent sense to the notion of infinite use of finite means. This is what ended up being the theory of computability, recursive function theory and so on' (Chomsky 2000: 62; see also Smith 2004: 224, n. 17).

This introduces a second sense of recursion that is mathematical instead of linguistic and that is highly relevant to information politics because it leads directly to the general problem of computation. It is, fortunately, not necessary to fully enter the logical waters of recursive function theory

---

1. Chomsky is known as well for making recursion part of human evolution and a universal of human languages, and further well known is that this is contested by Everett's findings that claim to have examined a human language that does not include recursion. Neither of these arguments affect my own appropriation of recursion which I am not arguing is universal but am arguing is operating in particular information-rich political contexts (Everett 2009: 224–43; Hauser et al. 2002).

to understand recursion in this context. The essential point drawn on here is the ability to use mathematical or logical arguments nested inside one another such that the original argument can be called from within itself. Most interesting for a general understanding of recursion is how this connects to Gödel, Church and Turing's views and the meaning of computation. We can see this by looking in two directions from Turing's famous paper of 1936 that first introduced the idea of the Turing machine (Petzold 2008; Leavitt 2007: 30–67; Turing 2004; Dyson 2012).

Turing's paper is now often taken to be a foundation for computation and was written in response to a problem that both Gödel and Church separately worked on in relation to a logical foundation for mathematics. This particular context is not relevant here except that it set up certain problems in logic that were attacked by Gödel, Turing and Church, during which Turing's method of solving part of the problem (the famed to mathematicians and logicians *Entscheidungsproblem*) led to a definition of computation and to postulating a machine that could undertake computations. All three created quite similar logical solutions but Turing's method produced the clearest feed into the birth of computers as we know them by offering practical reflections. For present arguments it is important that within all three was embedded an idea of recursion first articulated by Gödel (Leavitt 2007: 30–40; Copeland 2004: 40–54; Casti and DePauli 2000: 80–1). Recursion occurs within the definition of computation because that definition involves the use within various computing devices (some of them human) of the results of those devices. This reaches its clearest articulation in Turing's definition of the Universal Turing Machine. I will briefly recount the Universal Turing Machine to show the connection to computation, and hence how deeply recursion is buried within environments dependent on computers, such as the digital and the internet. Then it will be important to look more closely at Gödel's understanding of recursion to conceptualise it further than Chomsky's sense of something that can be used within itself.

Turing was exploring a problem in the foundations of mathematics that required an understanding of what computation or computing meant. At the time he wrote the paper, 1936, a computer generally meant a human being who conducted whatever computation was put in front of them. Turing explored the then rather startling idea that a machine might be built to conduct a computation, though he can now be seen to have followed some lonely pioneers in this idea in Leibniz, Lovelace and Babbage. Turing offered practical reflections on how this might be done. Through his practical discussion Turing was able to define computation as a set of instructions that a machine can carry out to produce a result. A Turing Machine is then anything that can carry out a set of instructions (or an algorithm as it will become known) to produce a result (Copeland 2004: 15, Leavitt 2007: 59–60). The next move was to point to the possibility of a Universal Turing Machine that could include and undertake all the computations that individual Turing Machines might be undertaking. 'It is possible to invent a single machine which can be used to compute any computable sequence' (Turing 2004: 68). In the early twenty-first century, when many people are using devices, and often more than one, with similar properties to a Universal Turing Machine, this might not seem such a startling idea, but in a period when a computer meant another person, this was innovative. It is also an idea involving recursion in that the functions of each Turing Machine are replicated within the Universal Turing Machine. This is rather like the 'Russian doll' idea of recursion in which something is able to keep a copy of itself within itself and to use that copy (Davis 2000: 139–45; Leavitt 2007: 82–3; Turing 2004: 68–9).

Recursion as a process is not new; as Chomsky's arguments make clear languages of many types have been using recursive processes for a long time. The form of recursion that is embedded in Universal Turing Machines underpins not just the theory of computation but has also been embedded within computers as we use and know them. So far I have touched on quite simple forms of recursion like the Russian doll, which is similar to the kind of recursion that occurs when a picture is placed inside a picture of itself (leading to an infinite repetition of the same picture). To develop a theory of recursion relevant to information politics it is worth looking at the foundation of recursion as articulated by Gödel and embedded within computations and computerisation (Watson 2012; Davis 2000; Aspray 1990).

Discussions of recursion in relation to Gödel often focus on the mathematical technicalities of recursive functions, but instead of such a technical discussion recursion in Gödel can be approached by noting that his famous disproof of the logical foundations of mathematics, as then theorised by Russell and Whitehead, stemmed from an intuition into what can be seen as a form of recursion. Russell and Whitehead's work sought a rigorous, consistent and complete logical foundation for mathematics, but Gödel proved this was impossible (Nagel and Newman 2001: 45–56; Leavitt 2007: 30–4). He did this in two stages. First, he argued that he could invent a language in which he could express in numerals the logical structures proposed as the foundations of mathematics. Once he had expressed logical statements in numerals he could then mathematically test logical statements about the foundations of mathematics. Turing's Universal Machine embodied a form of recursion that includes one system within another, but Gödel's recursion here goes further in applying the analysis of the included system to itself in order to reach important conclusions about mathematics. Gödel's second step was to use this system to analyse the claim 'This statement is not provable.' Once he had translated this claim into his number system he could test it within that system and it led to him finding that 'For every consistent formalization of arithmetic, there exist arithmetical truths that are not provable within that formal system' (Casti and DePauli 2000: 50; Gleick 2012: 180–5). This led to the failure of the attempt to set mathematics on a certain and consistent foundation.

The issues of logic and the foundation of mathematics that follow from Gödel's analysis can be left here, as these are often commented on and many discussions can be found elsewhere (Davis 2000; Nagel and Newman 2001: 109–113; Casti and DePauli 2000). The more directly relevant consequence was that Gödel had developed certain ideas that would lead to the definition of algorithms in the context of computation and would connect to the work of Turing and Church, both of whose work fed directly into the work of those like Von Neumann and many others who built the first electronic and digital computers and established the computer architecture that underpins computation in the twenty-first century (Watson 2012; Dyson 2012; Asprey 1990). This work involves a second sense of recursion that appears in the definition of elements of algorithms. The latter can be understood as coded steps that allow a particular argument to be run. For example, somewhere in Google's software are algorithms that decide which advertisement will appear on a page, and if someone suddenly examines a few different sites (for example, various National Football League sites while setting up a fantasy football league team) then Google will start to deliver a whole range of advertisements that the algorithm has decided are relevant (for example, opportunities to buy online coverage of games or football kit). At this point algorithms need to be understood as arguments embedded in software that make a range of decisions to produce output based on the particular formation they have been given. Gillespie argues that 'algorithmic logic ... depends on the proceduralized choices of a machine designed by human operators to automate some proxy of human judgement or unearth patterns across collected social traces'. As Gillespie suggests, algorithms are a 'new knowledge logic' whose computational nature obscures their workings (Gillespie 2014: 192). It is within such logics that we find recursion is a, if not the, key technique.

Casti and DePauli argue that Gödel created the first precise definition of an algorithm because he offered an analysis of recursive functions, which are in their view 'essentially, a function for which there is a mechanical rule for computing the values of the function from previous values, one after the other, starting from some initial value' (Casti and DePauli 2000: 81). It is striking that there is often little discussion of the meaning of recursion when outlining such theories and their importance to founding computers, as opposed to the rules for making recursion work within algorithms that are meaningful in a rather limited and often instrumental way. A place to start is to note what is missing or is at best implicit in Casti and DePauli's definition of Gödelian recursion. They do not clearly note that whatever is being used inside the computation is, in part at least, already generated by the same system, but this needs to be articulated as otherwise there is no recursion only a linear computation. Casti and DePauli's definition has here an ambiguity in what they mean by 'previous values' and to see the power of recursion in its politico-technological form it is important to focus on the loops that recursions form. During the development of his Analytic Engine, Charles Babbage referred to Ada Lovelace's algorithm, which might have instructed the Engine's gears, as 'the Engine eating its own tail' (cited in Gleick 2012: 118). Similarly, 'previous value' needs to be understood in the sense of 'previous values, at least some of which were generated by the mechanical rules'. If this interpretation is added then we have a definition on which to base a theory of recursion.

Recursion means that there is an overall computation, function, argument or some such that consists of a series of moves or instructions that takes input and produces output. This implies a distinction between the programme and its components, as these components are steps in pre-set arguments, for which I will use the computer term 'sub-routines'. A programme may have one sub-routine, in which case it is identified with its sub-routine, or it may have several. What an input and an output are can only be defined by the programme. Second, some outputs of the programme must be able to become inputs to the programme, in the sense that they must be able to be utilised by the sub-routines. Third, inputs may be used by a sub-routine without altering that sub-routine or they may alter the sub-routine. That is, an input that was an output may be static in the sense that it is simply processed through an existing sub-routine or it may be dynamic in affecting part of one or several sub-routines and thus altering to an extent the nature of the programme. It may be particularly appropriate for sub-routines to be altered to ensure that new types of inputs will be properly formed for sub-routine use. A theory of recursion can now be offered.

Recursive programmes involve some kind of process having sub-routines that its own products can become input to, as well as possibly applying input from elsewhere to its processes. Recursion specifically involves the products of a routine applied to its own sub-routines and new input of the same kind as its own products applied to its sub-routines. 'Eating' its own products allows a recursive programme to both absorb its own information and to alter its own functioning. This does not exclude input that comes from outside the programme as long as this outside input is of the same nature as products from the routine. Information is not the only substance to which recursive programmes may be applied but it is in a sense a privileged substance because it is already concerned with difference or change.

One consequence of this understanding of recursion that is worth noting is that recursions must in some way create or modulate information so that information can be applied to itself. This means any recursive process must in some sense make the information it is using self-consistent in some way or other. This is a standardisation or homogenisation that will be specific to particular recursions but each recursion must include some process by which it takes the information entered or produced within its processes and ensures the input-information is formed in ways that allow enough consistency that information can be applied to information either nesting inside or by being transformed in active algorithmic processes. Recursions mean information has to be formed by the recursive process and in this sense information is always transformed by a recursion.

A further consequence is that recursive programmes have an inherent tendency to developments whose outputs are not linear. Rather, the more products that can be returned as inputs in a recursive programme the more information will be produced in that recursion. This will have a tendency to develop exponential growth in outputs, because what has already been produced is returned and used again, and if sub-routines are also recursively altered it is possible that several tendencies to exponential growth may exist within the one recursion. Exponentiality is important because of the extraordinary and rapid growth it describes.

A sense of recursion can now be taken forward. While any individual recursive programme will be spatio-temporally specific it will also have the general characteristics I have outlined. Further, I have argued that recursive processes are foundational to modern computing and are embedded deeply within definitions of algorithms, computer architecture and even computation itself. It is now time to make the shift that has been foreshadowed in which these abstract and somewhat technical issues are related to political and cultural ones, indeed they turn *into* politics almost directly in what may seem a sudden shift. However, this merely reflects the way ideas that were once technical have moved to the centre of key struggles over exploitation and liberation in the twenty-first century because information has become the site of one such struggle. To bring this abstract discussion back to the issue of forces and touches I will now connect this idea of recursion, the way information can eat itself, to information politics.

The Theory of Information Recursion as Exploitation

With a theory of how recursion operates in hand and noting that recursion is embedded deeply within computation, the question then becomes, how does this connect to the forces of information politics and exploitation?

First, recursion is not repetition, it is not the return of the same but the return of something that is transformed so that it can be used as if it were the same. Recursion is not iteration, it is not a building or altering such that each return produces some small addition such that each return contributes to an iteratively constructed different activity. Recursive activities define parts of themselves in such a way as to transform them so that they can return to be absorbed and put to work within the same activity, making it faster and more complex but neither repeating it as it was nor iterating it toward some goal. Recursion is not the return of the same nor is it teleological.

The consequences of the algorithms underlying so much online activity are clear to many of us through experience. At the start of a UK school year I have searched for various text books and now, amid all the usual clutter of post-Autonomist theory books, journalistic accounts of online life and surf videos, I find on my Amazon account a whole range of high school history textbooks being suggested to me. This experience in all kinds of digital environments is utterly familiar and it is produced through recursion. The information entered must be sensible to the algorithms that Amazon, or other similar sites, use to then suggest that my account should be fed back history textbooks in the hope of further sales.

The moment of transformation is key because at that point the information, the difference, that someone has entered into a recursive programme is re-ordered by that programme to ensure its compatibility and is then taken control of by that programme to be used. The recursive programme will often be controlled by someone or an agency different to the person inputting information, but the input becomes part of the recursive programme. The information that said something about me, that I had a child going to school doing history, becomes controlled by whoever controls the programme I have entered that information into. This is also then used to identify me according to various factors, such as age, sex, etc., that the system has collected (perhaps because without that information I would not be allowed to use the programme), and to start feeding my information into correlations with people similar to me. Accordingly, someone who had never entered any information about history textbooks but who was similar enough in profile to enough others who had entered such information, might suddenly find themselves with suggestions for such textbooks appearing.

This might well be thought of as a moment in which something the user 'has', in the information they enter, is 'taken' by the recursive programme and served up to the controller of that programme. This transfer benefits the ongoing work of the programme, thereby also benefiting the controller of the programme. Access to the programme may also be used to extort from the user other details, such as age, location and so on, that will enhance the value of the information by cross-referencing it, or such details may be mined or inferred from the use made of the programme. These ideas of transfers involve some notion of information ownership in which the controller appropriates information as a property even though that information was the property of the user. The idea of information as property will be discussed extensively in later chapters when considering whether the notion of private property is appropriate to the understanding of such relations. However, even putting a full conceptualisation of property aside for now, it is already clear that a key issue in any recursive programme will be what kinds of property relations are set up by each recursive programme. It is also important not to immediately pre-judge all such relations as exploitation or some kind of information theft, because the digital world has developed some interesting notions of what property means. For the moment and in the abstract, it is important to point to this juncture at which exploitation might be seen to be offered a natural place in recursive programmes because of the way they re-define and re-use the information entered into them. Further, as Gillespie notes, because such algorithmic processes are obfuscated, the moment at which a user enters information that is taken over by the algorithm in a programme and put to new uses will nearly always be obscured (Gillespie 2014: 191–2).

It is important not to jump too quickly to the conclusion that recursion necessarily involves exploitation because information is farmed and made private when it is controlled by the users of the programme. This is because each implementation of a recursive programme will itself define the meanings of property, ownership, user and controller that give specificity and empirical content to each system. This power of recursion is then not automatically a power of profit-seeking corporations like Google or Amazon but is made so by their particular implementations. Other kinds of controllers of programmes may well be imagined than companies, particularly drawing on the traditions of free software's redefinition of property licenses in such things as the Gnu Public License (Coleman 2012c; Berry 2008). Within this alternative tradition of property it is possible to imagine collective bodies holding a recursive programme and using it to define property that delivers the benefits of recursion back to a collective body, rather than to a private body.

For example, we should remember that Larry Page and Sergey Brin invented the form of search that underpins Google (in the use of backlinks to rate the importance of a website using the PageRank algorithm) while they were students at Stanford University and that it was not a necessary move for them to then embed PageRank in a corporation whose success would make them rich. The patent for PageRank is held not by its inventors but by Stanford University. Indeed, for some time Page and Brin tried to license their search engine to others as they were intending to return to university study (Levy 2011: 21–31). What might Google look like now if Page and Brin had chosen to make their search engine technique open source and had sought collective effort and funding in the same way free software projects such as Linux have progressed? Or if they had released their invention as an open standard in the way that Tim Berners-Lee released the standards that underpin the World Wide Web and then implemented a consortium to oversee those standards? The software that constitutes Linux and the World Wide Web are quite different entities to Google's search engine, and no doubt Google's development would have been different (Berners-Lee 2000: 91–102). For example, who would have funded the many computers Google needed to build to be able to create its superior search engine through processing its recursions? Perhaps Google would have developed more slowly and may not have become as competent a search engine as quickly as it did if it had been open. However, the point of this counter-factual is not whether the right choice was made in defining Google's use of its patented algorithm but that it was possible an alternative path could have been followed and that the controller of Google's recursions need not then have been a corporation seeking profit.

A further complication, and reason for caution, is that new information is produced within such algorithms and programmes through recursions, information that would not have existed without all these processes. Even if I were to narrowly define the information that I input to a search engine as my property, it is not clear who would then own the new information that recursion produces by using my information. The power of such systems lies not in my one input but in the application of many inputs to each other, and the result of such recursions is information that could only exist because such recursions were put in place. Yet this new information produced through recursion owes its existence not just to the programmes that produce it but also to the input that many users supply. If we need to be careful with simple ideas of 'ownership' of information, and I am only using such a crude version of personal ownership to make a point here, then it is also not clear who should be able to take the new recursed information. It is clear that only the recursion controllers will be able to recognise and define this new information and be able to take it for themselves, it is not clear whose property information is (and in later chapters it will be important to question the very idea of property in relation to information). What is clear in this complex is that recursion controllers have a considerable advantage over those who provide the necessary information to start the process and keep it going, because the controllers can form a stream of new information from recursions.

A point of potential exploitation emerges at the moment that a recursive programme re-purposes information and subjects it to its own control, removing it from the control of the user of the programme. Here within the heart of a key information technology process, recursion, lies a dark potential. It means that we must not forget to examine recursion as it functions. We must trace the transformation that allows recursion: How is an activity reconceived and what activity does this help? Who benefits from a particular recursion? The material conditions surrounding the implementation of a recursive programme alone may offer an understanding of whether exploitation is occurring or not. It is then important to note the power of recursion once such relations of force are understood because recursions can produce highly productive, at times exponential, increases in information. Who controls these heaps of new information that also feed back into creating further information? What is done with this information?

Conclusion

The forces that engage within recursion have been explored and their differential combinations understood in the way that information absorbed by a recursive system may fuel that system and drive information production and use. This is a deep lying system – though some of its effects may be obvious to us it is usually not obvious how productive such systems can be and how they work. It is also now clear that exploitation, in the farming and controlling of others' information, can be embedded deeply within the information systems the world is so reliant on. Such embedding is not necessary or inevitable but carries an obvious potential.

Recursion means that within programmes, primarily through algorithms, information can be fed to itself to produce new information. The feed can be either information coming from outside the programme or it can be produced by the programme itself. This feed of information is then integrated with other forms of information that are of the same quality and so can be recursed together; recursion occurs when differences of similar kinds move together to create more differences. Such recursions can then either simply be processed or might alter the algorithms and programmes they are part of.

Moreover, because we know that there are such recursions in the algorithms of the information world, we also know that they will be obscured from us, and that because of that obscurity it will not always be clear whose information is being used and who is gaining a benefit from it. Possibilities for exploitation and for communality open up here because it is not yet clear in these moments whose information is whose. A user might enter some information but if that is then recursed in relation to many other forms of information then it is unclear who those new differences should belong to. What is clear is the dark potential of privatising such recursed information because only the controller of the recursion process will be able to provoke and to harvest such new differences. What is also clear is that more is needed to understand information exploitations and information politics than just recursion.

There is another consequence of recursion that I have mentioned a number of times and which opens up the second major dynamic of exploitation and liberation in the information politics of the twenty-first century. Recursion produces information from information and then reuses and continues this process. Recursion is one of the key, if not the key, processes underlying the inversion at the end of the twentieth century from information scarcity to information abundance. The now widely recognised flood of information pouring through the world is driven in large part by recursion. This flood produces its own effects, which the next chapter will trace in analysing the second major configuration of forces in the information world – devices.

2

Technologies' Embrace

Information Technology Determines

Can you make ice cream with your mobile phone? If you have a smartphone and a decent connection, you could in many parts of the world now buy some ice cream and have it delivered. But the question was 'make' not 'make ice cream appear'. Thinking again you could probably look up a recipe online and order the ingredients to be delivered to your kitchen. If you were ahead of the 2014 state of everyday kitchen technology, you might even be able to set the week's recipe list and have your refrigerator sense what is missing from it. You might even be able to turn appliances on and off remotely, while a robot vacuum cleaner keeps the dust down for your return. But you could not make ice cream, you could not break the eggs, heat the cream (or soy perhaps), mix them in the right amounts with other ingredients, dark chocolate maybe, and then turn your mobile phone into an ice cream maker that freezes the mixture in that special way, ready for the freezer and later for eating. Even if a 3D food printer were available it would still be using the mobile phone to turn on a device, it would not be making the ice cream with the phone itself. Asked to make ice cream with your phone, you would most likely feel that you were determined by the technology of your mobile phone to be unable to do so.

Yet, the struggle just outlined to find a way of making ice cream with a mobile phone also showed that a great deal could be done. Look at the flows of information, the access to recipes and to shopping and automating your refrigerator to order goods. It is not so fanciful to start thinking that the boundaries between whatever it is that 'makes' some ice cream and the phone are melting. The question I asked becomes more complex as the connections between technologies, environment, animals (who after all make many of the ingredients of ice cream), humans, and their inter-mingled actions are examined.

The case of the smartphone being unable to make ice cream points to a stumbling block in front of everyone who wants to examine politics in which technologies play prominent roles, and this is true of information politics. The idea will arise that the technologies themselves decide what can and cannot occur, and that these determining technologies are separate from human, animal and other kinds of actors. This sense of being technologically determined separates technological factors from other social and cultural factors conferring on some the power to determine others. In what follows it will be argued on the contrary that any sense of there being a division in which technologies can play an active role that is distinct from human, animal or other actors is itself the result of certain dynamics of forces that create such divisions. This does not mean that technologies do not 'act' but that they always act with and are acted on by other actors in whose inter-relations the separation of factors is itself made. The issue then is what forces or touches create a separation of technology and sociality that makes us feel determined by a technology as if it were an 'outside' factor.

There can be no doubt that the question of information technologies is important for information politics, but the question will be answered poorly if such technologies are assumed to be in some sense separate from other social and cultural factors and able to affect those factors without being affected themselves. Instead, the issue is to see how any such separations are created and maintained. I will argue in addition that information politics has a core dynamic, a core relation of forces, in which particular divisions of technology and politics develop and in doing so structure the politics of information. The starting point is, then, not technology and politics but information and its flows. And the starting point in understanding this is the end point of the previous chapter: the role of recursion in creating the flood of information and the overwhelming number of differences powering their way around the world carrying an information techno-politics. Because recursions can create exponential increases in information, the era of digitisation and the internet involves a reversal of information scarcity and a new dynamic based on information excess. The flood of information sets a problem that produces forms of technological determinism, embedding particular politics in hardware and software. This, in turn, identifies those able to conduct this embedding as particularly privileged actors, both human and non-human.

This chapter will explore technologies and devices as a dynamic of power in information politics in three parts. First, it will examine the flood of information in the phenomenon of information overload. The link here is to recursion that underpins a large part of the increase in information in the twenty-first century by enabling exponential increases in information production. Second, it will examine how this flood of information is often ameliorated by interposing a technological device between the users of information and the flood of information. It will be seen that each such device is partial and culturally formed and so embeds within our information lives particular values that are formed into technologies. This section of the chapter will also examine the paradox that these devices also produce new information and so can repeat the problem of information overload by contributing to the information flood instead of ameliorating it. Finally, the chapter will examine how this dynamic of information and technological devices attributes a particular importance to expertise in information environments, particularly in the manipulation of software. This expertise may be disciplined in corporate and government settings or utilised in populist ways, but underpinning both uses of expertise is the importance of manipulating information in software forms.

Information overload answered by techno-political configurations that create particular forms of technological determinism that are then implemented and managed by a specific set of actors summarises the way technologies are embraced by information politics. Each of these three elements – information overload, repeated techno-political configurations, implementers and managers of configurations – will now be examined in turn.

The Disorganisation of Too Much Information

It is never just the amount of information that causes problems, it is also its organisational form that makes the twenty-first century a time of information overload. As Andrejevic points out:

> Surely during the 17th century people were absorbing all kinds of information directly from the world around them, as we do today through the course of our daily lives. There is little indication that our sensory apparatus has become more finely tuned or capacious. However, the amount of mediated information – that which we self-consciously reflect upon as information presented to us in constructed and contrived formats (TV shows, movies, newspapers, Tweets, status updates, blogs,

text messages, and so on) via various devices including televisions, radios, computers and so on – has surely increased dramatically, thanks in no small part to the proliferation of portable, networked, interactive devices ... Glut is no longer a 'pull' phenomenon but a 'push' one. We don't go to it, it comes to us. It is the mediated atmosphere in which we are immersed. (Andrejevic 2013: 2–3)

The infoglut that Andrejevic catalogues is driven, in large part, by recursions that push this complexity ever further, at times producing bursts of exponential growth that are likely to see the amounts of information created and made available continuing to double, triple and possibly more year on year. Many figures could be used to show this, but here one will be taken as emblematic: between 1966 and 2007 analog information grew from 2.62 billion gigabytes to 18.86 billion gigabytes while in the same time period digital information grew from .02 billion gigabytes to 276.12 billion gigabytes (Hilbert and Lopez 2011). Such figures showing massive information growth and their implied issues of information organisation confirm the period of digitisation and the internet as a period of information flood (Jordan 1999a: 117–27; Andrejevic 2013; Shenk 1997).

The immediate problem of information flood is twofold. First there is the obvious concern of simply finding the information that is needed amid all the many different possibilities. For example, finding information on the World Wide Web is usually a matter of learning to use a search engine. But search tools are also multiplying and becoming embedded in mobile devices, and are now also often available within applications or specialist sites, such as an internal search on a shopping site or a search tool within an app. It is not just a matter of learning to type www.google.somewhere into a browser but also of finding what is wanted in many different virtual places. At each turn, there are not only plug-ins and add-ons that may or may not help marshal information, there is also the information gained that itself seems to extend on. The sheer amount of information demands management and organisation. Management is also necessary because of the second problem of information flood which is the implication that with so much of it available, the required information 'must be' out there, if only one could find it. There is rarely an information need that seems like it obviously cannot be met and this leads to a near-metaphysical struggle to access the desired information. If the first problem of too much information leads to a scrambling then this second problem may lead to a failure to stop searching and accept that the information is not available and, instead, lead to an almost pathological quest to continue seeking out some kind of information which may or may not be already articulated. The recursions of information overload exist in the context of the digital – which combines both more types of media-objects (text, then pictures, then audio, then films, then live video, etc.) and radical reductions in the costs of producing and altering many media-objects – combined with the internet, with its restructuring of the distribution of media-objects and its innovations in communication. One example would be music.

If we take the point reached in 2014 then it is possible to access virtually limitless amounts of music, much of it for free (if one is willing to ignore legalities). First, all kinds of music can now be converted into the same digital substance or may be immediately digital, which is itself able to be compressed into a much smaller space than previously possible. As storage capacities simultaneously become smaller in physical size, larger in data capacity and cheaper to produce, so music can not only be reduced to the one format but can also occupy far smaller physical spaces (Wikstrom 2010; Kot 2009). This has become so accentuated that what were only recently almost unimaginable amounts of music can now be placed in a pocket.

This poses problems of course, in particular, how does someone find the music they want? This has two aspects: first, how does someone find something that they have already identified? Second, how do they find things they would like but do not yet know about? Being a digital question various tags and labels are searchable so this is really an interface problem in the sense of producing something that can allow searching, which repeats the general information overload problem of needing specialist searches embedded in particular kinds of devices. Finding out about music you do not already know is of course not an entirely new problem. In the same way as before digitisation, reviews, recommendations from friends, following new releases from old favourites, and so on will continue to be important when it comes to discovering new music. In addition, researching different genres becomes possible and even more viable when music is being downloaded for free as there is little cost. Pay-services also often offer ways of sampling, for example by making short snippets of songs available. A further means is that many streaming services offer the chance of hearing music in full even if they do not allow recording. And so on.

The effect of the digital on music is to create a huge sea of music, often seeming like all the music that has ever been recorded, and the only way to manage access to this is through a range of interfaces that organise searching in various ways. The same story could be multiplied across any media-object, from film and texts to radio and recorded speech, to photographs and so on. Moreover, each such sea of media-objects constantly poses the problem that the sheer amount of information overwhelms the search for the right media-object. Many of us will have experienced searching for a particular piece of music (or other media-object) and becoming lost in the multiple possibilities for finding it, while all the time managing the ethical and legal issues of whether to use free and/or pirate sites (Andrejevic 2013: 1–18).

The sea is enticing and threatening. At any time, drowning in the sheer amount of data is a possibility. If someone wants a specific song by a specific musician or a book by a particular author then it may well appear to many that our search devices allow us to navigate the data oceans. However, as soon as the search begins to shift into something a bit vaguer, like wanting a genre of music or looking for a book on a topic, then the search is likely to become less smooth and overload to become threatening.

A founding condition of information life is then the threat of information overload, the fear of being drowned in data. This threat is a constant presence, built on the vast amounts of data that are available and the fantasy that any desired information is really out there. Between the sea of information and the desire for information lies the experience of information overload.

Managing Overload with Devices

It was impossible to describe information overload in the previous section without mentioning the technological devices that we place between ourselves and the sea of information. For example, I often mentioned interfaces. Here is where technology embraces us in ways that become constituent and often hidden aspects of our politics. It is a moment so common and so embedded in our information lives that it takes a little excavating to see its significance.

In the previous section this significance was marked by 'search', and what was meant by this was an interface that allows a review to be done of a field of data-objects. This means that someone programmed an interface that was able to read various data-markers from the media-objects it surveyed, to order what it read according to some input from the user of the interface, and then to represent a subset of the data surveyed ranked according to assumptions made about the meaning of the input. This might seem to over-complicate an obvious process but there are parts of it that need attention because they are so often buried within the searches we use. The two key moments are the pulling out and re-presenting of a subset from the sea of data and that the mechanisms for doing this are based on an interpretation of what a user has entered into an interface that is itself offering only certain possibilities.

The technological devices we interpose, necessarily, between ourselves and information overload embed within themselves assumptions about the nature of what we want to find and return to us results based on interpretations of choices we make when we are only able to make certain choices. This embedding occurs repeatedly and sets an underlying dynamic that separates out those able to design and implement such information-management devices from those who can only use them. There are so many examples of this, from great to small, and they all conform to this general pattern of managing information through a technological device that re-presents subsets of data according to interpretations. Moreover, since such devices themselves produce information that needs to be managed, the whole process can be repeated with the device that was meant to manage information overload beginning to contribute further to overload.

Let me offer an example. Search, as has already been argued, is essential in an internet-connected world. Imagine, just for a moment, trying to find something you want by simply knowing its address or being able to intuitively navigate there. If you could find a starting point, for example if you were searching for anarcho-gardening composting advice (not a personal choice I admit) and knew the address for the site 'Gardening as an Anarchist Plot' then you might start there and hope for a link, but if, sadly, there were no links or advice specifically for anarcho-composting then you would be stuck again. Trying to find something on the World Wide Web when you have no starting point, or when your starting point runs dry, is a very difficult process both because of the sheer amount of information and because once a starting point runs dry the web is not organised to help find things but is grown according to whatever website producers choose to build. For these reasons, the vast majority of us need and use search and the majority of searches in the early twenty-first century go through Google. For example, in December 2012, Google had 65.2 per cent of all search engine searches worldwide with a total of 114.7 billion searches in that month; Baidu was second with 8.2 per cent and 14.5 billion searches (Sullivan 2013).

A Google search is a specific thing structured according to a number of pre-set variables of which three can be mentioned to make the point. First, Google uses a patented system called PageRank. This searches backlinks, that is links others have made to a website and not the links a site makes to targeted sites, and treats them as 'votes' on the importance of a site. The more people who link to a site the more important that site is held to be on its particular topic. Sites are also ranked in this way and a high-ranking site's links are worth more than a low-ranking one, so ten low-ranking links may be worth less in defining the importance of a site than one or two high-ranking links (Levy 2011: 21–5; Halavais 2008: 65–8). Second, Google personalises search by tracking where users go and what they do, and is able to tailor searches to the user. Perhaps a user can be identified as reading in a particular language, or a searcher's previous requests might allow Google to distinguish whether 'football' is really an interest in soccer, the US National Football League or Australian Rules Football (Feuz et al. 2011). Finally, Google sometimes shifts results if they believe, for example, someone has worked out a way to 'game' their system and gain a higher rating than their site deserved. There are also concerns that Google has altered search results to favour its own products – which it was rumoured in 2012 would lead to a government monopoly investigation – or for social reasons, such as to prevent information on how to commit suicide being easily shared (Halavais 2008: 71–6).

None of this is startling except it makes the point that the majority of searches conducted over the internet are structured by the technologies, the software code and server farms that Google has so successfully created (Hillis et al. 2013). This is not necessarily to attack Google's search engine – those who can remember searching prior to its rise may forever retain a soft spot in their hearts for Google. It is rather to point out that search is structured by a technological device that is used by searchers but is created and maintained elsewhere and whose workings are opaque. Moreover, the point is that search must be like this and will always have to be structured in some way, leading to the question: What can be known about how the searches that return information are made and operate?

Another example is BitTorrent. Within this particular highly popular peer-to-peer technology finding a starting point is often achieved by finding (perhaps with the help of a Google search) a BitTorrent site that holds an index of torrents that users have uploaded. The specific form of search on such a site then allows a user to examine databases of torrents according to names of artists, movies, audio, genres, etc. Most famously one might go to Pirate Bay and search for a piece of music. Again a particular piece of software interposes itself to manage information access. In this case, the choices become extensive enough that a further stage has created a site like Torrentz which does not itself hold a torrent database but searches a number of other torrent sites returning a wider range of results. This overcomes a potential balkanisation when someone searching, perhaps for an obscure piece of music, also has to search across a range of torrent sites if their choice is not found at the first, or second, or third, and so on, site. Again the particular nature of search on each site structures the kinds of information a user can gain.

Recursion is relevant here because many of these kinds of search sites then apply their own searches to themselves to help generate more accurate searches. We then sail the information seas by using and assuming various technological devices, just as we would use and assume that a sail will work if we really were on the ocean. However, something further happens here because we are dealing with information. As already noted, the device may well include forms of recursive information production, which can cause it to produce a new form of the very problem it was meant to solve. Technologies' embrace means not just that we have to rely on a technology, as we often do when driving a car or riding a bike, but involves the characteristic that is specific to information environments that the device may produce the very problem of too much information that it was introduced to solve.

This is a key feature of overload and its management through devices that distinguishes information contexts from many other contexts where technological devices are used to manage situations. It is not unusual to interpose some technology which manages a particular situation, after all knives, forks and chopsticks help to manage the task of eating. However, with information the problem requiring management can be exacerbated by the management that is put in place. Again this might seem like something that happens in many contexts, as someone learning to eat using unfamiliar cutlery can attest. However, cutlery or other technologies performing management roles fail when they contribute further problems and do not succeed by producing more of the same problem they were intended to solve, but this can be the case with information devices. Information devices differ in that their production of new differences to manage old differences can lead, and often by its nature must lead, to the production of new information overload.

Everything that we do to manage our information returns as further information; if this is a recursive process then it may produce exponentially increasing information flows. Torrentz was mentioned above as a solution to the problem of searching for torrent files that were separated across different individualised data-bases, and it did this by constructing a meta-database. In October 2012, Torrentz was cross-referencing 35 different torrent sites, indexing 21,567,904 active torrents from 84,171,744 pages. However, while such a strategy reduces information overload, stopping a searcher from having to repeat a search across 35 different sites, it also begins the process of reproducing the original problem. The intervention of a meta-search engine here produces a reduction in information overload, 35 searches reduced to one search, but at the same time it produces some new information. For example, how to effectively use Torrentz itself becomes some of the new information needed by a searcher. Moreover, Torrentz does not cover all torrent sites; for example, Sumotorrent was not covered by Torrentz at the time of writing. While there is no doubt an advantage for the searcher in using Torrentz against having to search 35 separate databases, when the searcher realises that there is a torrent site worth looking at that Torrentz does not cover, then the same information problem that Torrentz addressed reappears. One can imagine the point at which there are a number of meta-torrent sites that themselves could be gathered together by a meta-meta-site. At each such junction, new information is produced and recursed.

Nor does any device, meta or not, satisfy the abstract sense that something is out there. A search on Torrentz for the classic jazz album Blues and the Abstract Truth yields only a couple of torrents, only one of which might be worth pursuing with five individuals providing or 'seeding' it. Five seeding a torrent is small enough that it may not be possible to download from this information, leading to a search for other torrent sites – perhaps there is a jazz-themed torrent site somewhere? – or perhaps a switch to a pay site. The point here is not an issue of piracy or legality but an issue of information overload, management through device, and then further overload.

A second story similar to that of meta-torrent sites could be told about the rise of 'social media management' devices. There are many different kinds of social media, with some offering different functions to others and some offering more targeted audiences. While we might think that Twitter and Facebook, circa 2014, dominate social media and micro-blogging, there is LinkedIn for a more vocational and employment focused social media, Foursquare to locate oneself in space, and a range of other social media it is conceivable people would use, from old ones such as Myspace to Google+. This potentially creates another version of the balkanised torrent databases, with the added complication that whereas torrent sites all involved fairly similar kinds of searches that produced similar information, different social media sites may produce different kinds of information and require quite different kinds of management.

As a consequence, some meta-social-media devices have emerged in response to the potential overload of trying to see what appears on all the different social media sites. These devices offer such abilities as simplified ways of posting so that, wherever possible, one need only post something once to see it appear in different social media. The device Tweetdeck attempts to perform precisely this function, beginning with Twitter and then integrating Facebook statuses. Myspace was soon added, and in 2009 LinkedIn, followed in 2010 by Google Buzz and Foursquare, only for Tweetdeck to reverse and limit itself to Twitter and Facebook in 2012. Originally focused on managing Twitter, Tweetdeck was particularly liked, many claimed, for its ability to manage large numbers of micro-blog tweets ensuring that what a user thought of as important tweets were made visible. Tweetdeck then first expanded into and subsequently contracted from other social media. Anyone disappointed to have lost access to a range of social media sites once Tweetdeck reverted to a focus on Twitter and Facebook could instead install Hootsuite and begin learning how to manage Twitter, Facebook, LinkedIn, Google+, Foursquare, Mixi, Wordpress and several other social media sites all through Hootsuite. The creation of such devices leads to ever changing features so that simply managing is no longer enough and more sophisticated means of finding the most important information across social media have to be created.

A further complication is language issues, which mean there are a range of other sites which a multi-lingual actor might need. For example, Orkut was launched as a social media site by Google but largely failed in Europe and the USA, while creating a large constituency in Brazil and India. Any bilingual actor needing to project their social media presence may well then have both Orkut and Facebook and may start to ponder that information overload and how to manage it. Many Chinese internet users who are outside China have micro-blogging accounts to use within and without China, for example using both Twitter and Sina Weibo or Facebook and Renren.

Finally, we might remember that Facebook, like other social media, is itself a meta-device that links together and integrates a range of types of communication. Chatting, posting pictures, putting up short updates of one's status and so on were all possible prior to Facebook and the invention of social media, they were just often located in separate applications. For example, one might be running a blog through a website that included short updates but then using Internet Relay Chat to talk to friends online. Facebook introduced no new capabilities to the internet but put a range of existing services in one place and then used this power to make connections easier and more intuitive for many.

The cycle of information overload, driven as it is by recursion and oceans of data, is one in which each form of overload a particular actor faces is often managed by interposing a technological device that itself must in some way be a partial or biased device, in the sense that it must make choices about how information is conceived and managed. These devices themselves produce information and often, though not necessarily, lead to further forms of information overload, precipitating more technological devices. At each turn, as each set of information technologies becomes embedded into our lives and actions, the nature of the choices made to form each device tend to disappear into those devices. We are embraced by information technology (Jordan 1999a: 115–34).

For information politics this is an important process because we know that this embrace is constituted by many devices each of which is in some way formed and is never neutral. We need to think through this general politics, not because it is inherently oppressive to be embraced by such technologies but because we need to understand the particular forces that are created and sustained by the technological embrace that is driven relentlessly on by information overload. One angle on this is already clear, that in an information context we are drawn further and further into this embrace. A second angle is to consider the issue of bias or selectivity that goes into these devices, because this points to the actors who form the technologies. It is important next to identify a key basis for active forces in devices and then, in conclusion, to draw these threads together to see the second major dynamic of information politics.

The Expertise Basis for Information Power

Dependence on information cultures and politics that are embedded within information technologies is an ever spiralling process; as we manage information in new ways information itself mutates into new forms that often require new types of management. This connects to a hyper-consumerism that sees devices that perform largely the same functions with largely the same interfaces being differentiated through style and size – for example, the differences between an iPhone, iPod, iPad Mini and iPad, with someone somewhere no doubt finding different functions for all these and possibly a Macbook Air and/or Macbook Pro laptop as well (not to mention their Apple TV). This kind of commodification and (non)differentiation is typical of most aspects of modern branding and marketing; what is at stake for information politics when connecting to such processes is different. What is at stake in information terms is the control of these different devices and the ability to create and alter them, suggesting the role of expertise in forming digital environments. To see the way technologies' embrace produces an issue of expertise, it will be useful to first outline an example.

iPhones are, like most Apple products, as closed a technology as their company can make them. You can only find apps to add to an iPhone on iTunes and these only appear when approved by Apple; you can only get updates to your software through iTunes and you can only buy and download music through iTunes to your iPhone. This design (a topic to be returned to later when analysing the iPad) is made possible by the thousands of programmers, designers and other Apple employees who contribute to designing the iPhone. Such employees vary from the world famous designer Sir Jonathan Ives, credited with leading design of the iMac and then iPod, iPhone and others, to the 'top 100' employees who are invited to the annual meeting with company leaders (Steve Jobs when alive instituted and ran the meeting), to the thousands of programmers working to implement the visions those such as Jobs, Ives and the top 100 articulate (Kahney 2013). Jobs' vision was famously one of selling a closed system in which every aspect is determined by Apple and which then gives to the user an experience they never knew they wanted but, as has sometimes proven to be true, can now often hardly live without. This covers not only Apple design but also Apple censorship, thanks to its control over the approval of apps. Famously, Apple initially refused cartoonist Mark Fiore's app because it 'ridiculed public figures', and also banned an app that aggregated existing news feeds to show where US drone strikes had occurred (Bonnington and Aackerman 2012; Singel 2010). Apple's control of iPhones becomes absolutely clear in its delivery not just of a design vision but also of a political and artistic vision, both of which users did not necessarily know was better for them.

From this we can see that the closed design ethos of Apple, combining software and hardware, is just that – an ethos that could be quite different and which implements a very particular version of how information products should be made and sold. All this is made possible by the work of thousands of designers and programmers and those who make the physical objects or sell them in the temple of the Apple Store. The expertise required to design and implement the vision of an integrated device cannot be supplied by just one person, however big a say Ives or Jobs may have had on various products. Many skilled bodies are needed to help in the completion of the object and Apple manages these skilled bodies with the usual techniques of employment in capitalist companies in relation to hackers and creative labour. Importing a neutered version of hacker culture into companies, as do Apple and Microsoft, is a specific version of the general strategy in relation to creative or cultural labour of extracting high workloads and levels of commitment to the profits of a company by offering a pay off in creativity and contribution to projects (Banks 2007; Gill and Pratt 2008). The iPhone designed and maintained through all too familiar methods of using creativity and some ill-defined sense of participating in 'the cool' to extract high levels of labour, indeed high levels of creative surplus value, from programmers, designers and other information creative workers. Through all this in Apple is threaded the overall design ethos of the closure of technologies and the superiority of the designers' vision over the user. As a result, an iPhone gives the user what they did not know they needed and delivers this by denying the user control over their data and the device they have purchased (Jordan 2008: 112–7).

This closed nature can, however, be transgressed, and there may be many different reasons for conducting such a transgression: abstract principles based on the desire for free technologies; consumer rights reasons based on the desire to control the objects someone has bought; opposition to censorship based on disgust at the banning of some apps; or some other form of opposition to Apple's control of their software and hardware. Within Marxist theory this could also be understood as a more general reaction to the subsumption of labour that has become more intellectual and abstract at the beginning of the twenty-first century, in a sense fulfilling Marx's argument about the general intellect being subsumed as a form of alienated labour (Vercellone 2007; Dean 2012: 129). This Marxian view is useful in understanding the 'programming proletariat' who have been alienated from their intellectual labour of software coding, but it is not the only such process behind the ways some have pursued breaking open iPhones. While undoubtedly an important way of understanding the role of information in capitalism, to understand information politics it is also important to recognise that resistance comes from those who might be informationally alienated, rather than just alienated from their labour. Such information actors may therefore take up specific information issues, such as those just mentioned to do with censorship or control of technology, that are a politics in-itself rather than being a reflection of another important politics of resistance to capitalism.

Whatever the motivations, the term for taking control over Apple devices is 'jailbreaking', derived from a term used in Unix-like computer systems. Essentially, the design of the iPhone (and other Apple devices like iPods, iPads and so on) has been researched by volunteers who share information. Some techniques explore any available technical specifications, and often there are also attempts to reverse engineer the devices. These and other techniques are shared among developers who then produce software programmes, such as Redsnow, Ultrasnow, PwnagTool, that can free the iPhone. As is common on the internet, a great deal of advice is also available from 'how-to' guides that offer step-by-step methods of jailbreaking, or on forums dedicated to jailbreaking on which queries or problems can be posted and often answered. Once jailbroken an iPhone can connect to different sources of apps and updates than iTunes and offers opportunities for customisation that iTunes would block.

Against the corporate structure of Apple experts there are volunteer hackers creating alternative tools for an alternative Apple. For example, in November 2012 the key jailbreaking development team, iPhone Dev Team, listed just 28 members of their team on the 'who we are' section of their online portal. This, then, is not even a 'top 100', let alone comparable to the thousands that Apple can employ, but is instead a handful of hackers who can marshal expertise to reverse the closed ethos of Apple and allow users access to a range of different capabilities. Jailbreaking also allows a reversal of the key corporate strategy by which Apple sells exclusive access to their iPhone to a particular mobile phone operator, thereby ensuring that anyone who wants an iPhone may be driven to buy their mobile phone connection from particular operators. Jailbreaking allows users to simply insert their sim card and the iPhone will pick up whichever mobile phone company the sim card is connected to. The expertise of a hacking team here reverses what might seem to be an overwhelming corporate authority.

Moreover, these techniques mean that anyone who has an internet connection and is persistent enough can also draw on this rebel expertise to alter Apple's corporate control. Faced with an old iPhone of my own that was of more use as paper-weight than anything else, I was able with an afternoon's work based on no prior expertise to confirm that jailbreaking works. This was done at little more cost to me than my time and a few moments of frustration and cursing which eventually led to the success of a functioning jailbroken iPhone put back into use. In my case, the key actions were generally not taken by me but rather by the software I downloaded and used. Once passed on from the iPhone Dev Team, a programme like Redsnow became an actor that I was used by as it demanded I employ it properly or be reduced to failure and cursing, which usually led to seeking more advice and altering my actions till the software was able to work. Because of such inter-minglings of human and non-human actors it is important in information environments, and in many other political environments, to focus on what actions are possible and who or what is acting without presuming that it must be a human taking the action. Instead, the importance of technological devices and their embedding, often very deeply, in our lives means we have to analyse them as actors when and where that is appropriate.

In this story of the iPhone as closed corporate device or jailbroken open device, we see the two sides of an expertise-fuelled elite who derive much of their ability to take actions in the world that others cannot from their place as the producers and managers of all the various devices we insert into our lives to control information overload (Jordan 1999a: 135–41). On the one hand, this expertise can be employed and owned by institutions. The case I have followed is that of a large US corporation but it could also have been other types of institutions, with governments particularly important in this regard, as Snowden's revelations about surveillance have made clear (Harding 2014). Here many highly trained individuals are alienated from the control of their expertise as it is put to use for profit or for national goals. One characteristic already noted is the way these institutions often attempt to give a 'hacker' culture to their software programmers and designers thereby investing the actions these individuals can take with the appearance of a creative and countercultural activity that in many cases has no more substance than that of being a worker in a software factory and, moreover, a worker often exploited by short-term contracts, a lack of rights and expectations of long and intense hours of work. As already noted, this has a strong connection to Marxist discourse around the subsumption of labour, though it does not mean that information politics thus defaults to being entirely understood in this way. Rather, we see here an example of the use of multi-polar politics as a framing device because it is consistent to claim that such information workers and their alienation can be understood through Marx but needs to be articulated differently depending on whether one is focused on the critique of capitalism or on the nature of information as a politics. In the former case, subsumption of the general intellect is a viable articulation of the core issue of expertise in relation to capitalism's pursuit of surplus value and labour exploitation, but in the latter case it remains only a partial element of an account that needs to be articulated equally in relation to issues of recursion and devices that offer up expertise as a core source of the ability to act within and to effect information politics (Jordan 2008: 112–7; Neff 2012; Vercellone 2007). The connections between such poles of politics, or between political antagonisms, is an issue that will be taken up more fully later, particularly on the basis of concrete examples discussed in Part 3 of this book.

On the other hand, active actions can be created by people whose expertise is not alienated in large institutions because in information environments such actions do not need access to tools requiring huge resources to operate. Jailbreaking shows how a small team of creative programmers can fundamentally alter the control Apple seeks over its products. Jailbreaking also demonstrates that this expertise can be distributed and supported in such a way that even a cultural analyst like myself can learn to take the programming actions necessary to counteract the corporate control of devices. It is tempting then to see hackers as a new revolutionary class, and Wark certainly makes a passionate case for this:

> There is a third politics which stands outside the alliances and compromises of the post-89 world. Where both envelope and vectoral politics are representative politics, which deal with aggregate party alliances and interests, this third politics is a stateless politics, which seeks escape from politics as such. The third politics is a politics of the hack, inventing relations outside representation ... Rather than a representative politics, representing advocacy of movement or

opposition to movement, there is an expressive politics that escapes representation. (Wark 2004: 251)

Wark's assessment of the potential for hackers to reorder technologies' embrace identifies their ability to utilise expertise as a different kind of politics. However, this non-representative politics can already be seen to be subject to attempts to control and marshal it by institutions. The cynicism of such institutions means that they may employ methods to ensure their workers retain their culture as hackers while simultaneously converting them into members of the proletariat alienated from their very source of power (Jordan 2008: 6–7; Postigo 2012). For every programmer whose use of their expertise marks them as a producer of jailbreaking or of Wikipedia or Wikileaks, there are also far more programmers who operate within government and corporate controls that convert them into the equivalent of the car mechanics of the information age, able to alter and affect but with no say in the fact that cars are made and run in certain ways.

A further point is that because it is expertise that fuels the ability to intervene into devices this marks out even Wark's kinds of revolutionary hackers as different, even at times as an elite. When jailbreaking an iPhone I had to be used by certain programmes and had no ability to check those programmes because I lacked the expertise, which would have taken me years of training to attain. The sense in which these programmes ran me by demanding I used them properly to achieve my aims is also a sense in which the expertise of iPhone Dev Team hackers was embodied in those programmes and so it was their expertise that was using me to jailbreak. It is sometimes remarked that free software is more secure because what it does can be checked since the source code is available, which is true; but being able to read the source code requires a hard won expertise in software programming that is not available to the majority of users of source code and of information devices. If free software is to be checked then it will be checked by individuals from an expertise-based information elite. Even if Wark's expressive and non-representational politics is realised in such groups as the iPhone Dev Team, there is a further question to be asked about who is really able to be active and create differences. Did I jailbreak the iPhone? Or did I make myself the reactive tool of those who gave me advice, the programmes I ran, and those who wrote and distributed the programmes?

Fundamentally, it is the fact that it is information that is at stake, all those myriad differences being moved, that offers expertise in devices a key role in taking actions in information politics. Software is fundamentally malleable in a way that few things are because it is information at play, not because it is immaterial. We need to remember that information is always material or we are likely to ascribe its flexibility to magical processes rather than identifying the source of the ability to act in the management and control of the movement of differences. This expertise is then fuelled, intensified and embedded by the spiralling use of devices to manage information flows when there are always more and other flows being produced that need similar management.

The Necessity of Hidden Actors

Information technologies deeply and powerfully embrace us in the information age through these specific processes of managing information overload with embedded technological devices. The recurrence of information overload often follows in new forms channelled by devices and the further embedding of devices and abilities to take action in these processes that are based primarily on expertise. Many hidden actors are now whirring away managing and producing information and it will become an essential political task to identify and produce the actors who open up control of information actions, particularly the actions taken over and 'for' us. The Free Software movement and hackers emerge as key here, but we need to continue to explore to find out what their desires are likely to be within the political contradiction of information (Coleman 2012c; Kelty 2008).

To begin to see this we will need to add to the dynamic of recursion and of devices driven by overload a third fundamental dynamic of information politics inherent in the contradictory necessity that networks and protocols have for each other. Even so, at this stage it seems clear that the future will need to be jailbroken.

3

Network and Protocol Theory: Dis/Organising Information Power

Networks

Two dynamics of information politics and power have been outlined, recursion and devices. With recursion we see massive flows of information that both are differences and return as differences, and hence as more information, which means that anyone who can create a recursion can control the information that comes from that recursion; that is, information squatters are defined by the recursions they control. The possibility of exploitation is here opened up depending on what the squattocracy do with the information that is gifted to them through their control of a particular recursive form. Do they take as their own what is after all collectively produced but channelled through their recursions? Or do they try to promote collectivity by opening up their recursions to those who use them? We should be careful of implying an instant morality here because though the information flows are collectively produced they are only exploitable because of the implementation of some kind of recursion, and that recursion only exists because of the labour of recursion creators as well as of users.

The second dynamic of information power builds on this potential for information commons production and privatisation because recursions produce exponentially increasing amounts of information – more and more differences move. These information flows are increasingly dealt with by the introduction of devices that manage such flows: the spam filter, the friends list, the auto-distribution of email, the 'meta-app' that manages several apps and/or several app accounts, and so on. The exploitations and liberations that may come with recursive flows are embedded in technologies and this begins to submerge and obscure such collective relations within technological infrastructures that are then simply 'used'. Yet each such device must produce its own kinds of information, often also creating new recursions and so producing further information flows. Sometimes a device will help manage the information flow and sometimes it will begin to produce new gluts of information. As each device is introduced and then trained for its task of management, it embeds within infrastructures its own specific form of forces.

The final dynamic of information politics and power is the organisation of such recursions and devices into coherent and repeatable patterns of interaction between many kinds of actors – human, technological and other. Here one of the most commonly used words in the twenty-first century becomes important, for this organisation of information power is done through networks. Without networks all the recursions and devices that manage information flows add up to little more than individualised instances; with networks, particular types of organisation of information powers emerge. This chapter traces this network effect, understanding networks in the context of differential relations of forces that flow through information.

This dynamic of networks has been noted by many in many contexts and has produced extensive debate. Some aspects of these debates will be reviewed in the next section, but at this point it is worth noting that while the debates cover a wide range of theories and contexts they often do not address the issue focused on here, that of identifying information as a political antagonism. The discussion of networks is accordingly problematic because there is so much written about networks across many different kinds of conceptual and empirical terrain. That is why the brief reminder given above of the first two dynamics of information politics is important because networks have to operate at their conceptual level. Because of this the next section will review some existing network theories but is in no way comprehensive. My analysis focuses particularly on the most widely influential conceptualisation of networks, that of Castells, and on what should be just as influential a theory, namely Galloway's analysis of protocols (which is closest conceptually to my arguments), though several other network theories will also be touched on.

Following this examination of some relevant existing theories of networks resulting in the linking of networks and protocols as one form of organisation, I will extend these concepts by putting them into conversation with an example of networks. If the network is the organising principle of information power then it is worth seeing it in action. Accordingly, a key empirical example of network theory will be explored in the internet's architecture. Following this it will be possible to complete the abstract theory of the dynamics of information politics by outlining together the three inter-related dynamics.

Theories of Networks and of Protocols

The transformation of all aspects of society in the late twentieth and ongoing into the early twenty-first century has a symbol: the network. There is an extreme, almost hallucinogenic vision of networks in which every aspect of society was once organised according to hierarchies that were pyramid like and in which authority was centralised to always be exercised from the top down – or as Tony Soprano succinctly put it, 'shit flows down and money flows up'. The vision then argues that the pyramidal structures were transformed into a 'dis-organisation' in which all are peers connected equally to each other with authority distributed across nodes of a web-like network. Though this is an acutely stereotyped version of what the rise of the network has been taken to mean, it dramatises the opposition many felt was being played out across such different realms as business – where it was thought team-working and globalised networking was overtaking centralised production lines – through to populist political activism, where the centralised political party and organised unions were often held to be giving way to decentred, dispersed social movements struggling over a multiplicity of issues.

The straightforward transformation of society from pyramidal centralised authority to networked distributed relations is clearly a myth, if for a moment we think that it accurately and completely describes the transformation of society at the end of the twentieth century. However, it does reflect the evidence that some significant aspects of society have been transformed through the rise of networking and that this has led to social change. The clearest articulation of this is in the work of Castells, defining what he names 'the Information Age'. In this work Castells argues that many aspects of society are being transformed according to network logics (Castells 2000b). While it is not necessary in this conceptually driven context to give a full account of what Castells believes has happened to society, it is worth asking what he means by 'network'. A critique of Castells' theory of the network both addresses key aspects of networks that are being discussed and will be a basis to introduce Galloway's articulation of protocol as a concept both as important as that of the network and as inescapably linked to networks. From these two sources a theory of inextricably linked networks and protocols as the organising principle of information environments will be formed.

Castells argues that networks have become the dominant form of social organisation and source of power (Castells 2009: 10; Castells 2000a: 6–10). He goes to great lengths to empirically describe this network society, but repeating this is unnecessary here. The key issue is to examine what he means by a network. Unfortunately, despite his extensive description of twenty-first-century society as a network society, Castells offers little definition of a network apart from claiming, 500 pages into his analysis, that 'A network is a set of interconnected nodes. A node is the point at which a curve intersects itself. What a node is, concretely speaking, depends on the kind of concrete networks of which we speak' (Castells 2000b: 501; cf. Castells 2000a: 15). In his later theorisation of power in communication Castells argues in a bit more detail when he reasserts the conception of a network as a series of nodes and a node as a curve that intersects itself, while adding that the importance of nodes lies in the processing of information. He then develops his theory by arguing that networks tend to reduce the distance between nodes to zero, that is, a network tends toward the connection of every node to every other node. For Castells, this means that networks are the unit, not the nodes, as the nodes only make sense (including their relative importance) depending on the nature of the network. Further, networks are constructed and directed by human agents toward certain purposes. The result of seeing networks as directed toward a certain activity, in which all nodes gravitate to connecting to all other nodes, is that networks have a binary logic of either inclusion or exclusion. This extends to connections between networks, called protocols, which mean that networks once connected tend to absorb or reject each other as nodes connect or fail to connect (Castells 2009: 19–22).

Here we have in a condensed fashion a theory that articulates the idea of the network in the twenty-first century. Networks are anti-hierarchical connections of nodes that are peers to each other, that is, nodes can connect to all other nodes directly, creating a flat, horizontal form of coordination. I will borrow the term 'dis-organisation' from participants in the alter-globalisation movement to refer to this kind of organisation. The term was (and is) used among activists who sought such networked forms of connection to ensure that they were not only protesting against exploitations but were also, at the same time, constructing or 'pre-figuring' a more just society by creating direct democracy within their own groups. This articulates the moral claim often made about networks that they are a more democratic and equal form of group cohesion than hierarchies (McKay 1998; Jordan 2002).

This is a vision of a flattened hierarchy in which each particular node connects to each other node, creating an opposite vision of authority and organisation to the idea of pyramidal organisation in which authority flows up to fewer and fewer nodes who each have authority to direct each node below them. Such a vision of networks is not unique to Castells, and can be found in the work of many others who examine society after the rise of digitisation and the internet. As Mueller comments:

> We are said to live in a networked society or, even more grandly, the networked society. Instead of the wealth of nations, we read about the wealth of networks. Political scientists searching for new labels to describe the ferment in global governance have joined this parade. We hear of global policy networks, transgovernmental networks, transnational advocacy networks, and networked governance. (Mueller 2010: 17)

Mueller might also have mentioned the idea of 'networked individualism' as the 'new social operating system' (Rainie and Wellman 2013). At the same time there has been a more general rise in social network theory that often addresses different kinds of networks than those Mueller describes (Kadushin 2012).

With this initial understanding of networks, I can turn to what is the most important criticism and development of such network theories, by paying attention to the dimension that Castells mentions only at the end of this theory of networks, namely the idea of protocols. Even if we accept the vision of networks just given and can make sense of the idea of a node being the point where a curve intersects itself, we are still left with a question about what constitutes a node and the ability of a node to connect to another node in any network. At a general level, Castells misconstrues this question as being about the connection of nodes to each other, whereas it is an issue of the rules by which nodes are constituted in such a way as they are able to connect. Castells mentions protocols but tends to underplay their importance because he confuses the rules by which connections may or may not be made and maintained with the actual connections that are made (Castells 2009: 20). This might seem too subtle a distinction to make a difference, but without it the importance of protocols is missed because once we focus on connections in action then our attention is already back on the network and the consequences of connected nodes, thereby limiting the role of protocols in favour of the anti-hierarchical nature of networks. Galloway's work makes it clear that the concept of protocols as rules for connecting nodes is at least as important in understanding the (dis)organisation of information power as the idea of the network as a flattened hierarchy of peered nodes.

What keeps a network together? The focus with networks is often on their dispersed, decentred, peer and directly connected nature, but we can ask what brings a network into existence and keeps it in existence? What is missing from much network theory is a sense of what kinds of nodes can connect to each other, what they can send and receive and how they maintain connection. While flattened hierarchies have received much attention, the forms of control that establish a network's boundaries and connect it internally is a form of control that draws less attention. This is where Galloway's work has been important in recognising the role of protocols and the mechanisms of control in networks.

If we consider any network then we have to solve the problem of what makes a node in a network and what enables it to connect. In any network connection is not automatic but must be made. Galloway argues that 'in order to initiate communication, the two nodes must speak the same language. This is why protocol is important. Shared protocols are what defines the landscape of the network – who is connected to whom' (Galloway 2004: 12). Nodes in a network must in some sense 'speak' the same language and be able to recognise this in each other, and it is the protocol that defines what this language consists of and what this language will allow to happen in the network – whether it is a computer network operating according to certain software codes or a train network operating according to switches and rails.

Galloway's view of the internal mechanism of a protocol can be connected to the earlier discussion of algorithms and recursion because he argues 'that the protocol is not by its nature horizontal or vertical, but that protocol is an algorithm, *a proscription for structure* whose form of appearance may be any number of different diagrams or shapes' (Galloway 2004: 30). If a network has often been characterised through such terms as horizontal and vertical, particularly in their opposition, then the protocol operates differently with the step-wise argument of the algorithm. The 'new knowledge logic' that Gillespie identifies as key to algorithms is at work here, with protocols being defined by the particular 'proceduralized choices' the relevant algorithm consists of (Gillespie 2014: 192). These are specific algorithms that are focused on the nature of connection and the maintenance of connection, which means that through these choices being made within a protocol's algorithm a node may come into existence because it is able to connect; that is, connection is defined by the protocol and to be a node in a particular network is to be able to connect. This ability to connect must also deal with the definition of what can be done, because to be able to connect is to be able to transfer whatever it is that travels within the network.

> Protocol is a universal description language for objects ... Protocol ... is a structuring agent that appears as the result of a set of object dispositions. Protocol is the reason that the Internet works and performs work. In the same way that computer fonts regulate the representation of text, protocol may be defined as a set of instructions for the compilation and interaction of objects. Protocol is always a second-order process; it governs the architecture of the architecture of objects. Protocol is how control exists after distribution achieves hegemony. (Galloway 2004: 74–5)

For these reasons, protocols tend toward an absolute logic of connection or no connection. Meeting the requirements of a protocol means not only that a node on the network comes into existence but also that that node gains all the possibilities of that network. Only if another protocol intervenes does each node find itself restricted or restructured in some way, but meeting the requirements of a protocol means that, in a flash, a node appears and gains the status of other nodes that meet the same requirements. 'To follow a protocol means that everything possible within that protocol is already at one's fingertips. Not to follow means no possibility' (Galloway 2004: 53, 167). For this same reason, protocols are often invisible because once their requirement is met and a connection is made then it is the network's possibilities that become the focus of any node or user of a node. Once one connects a broadband router and one's computer negotiates the internet protocol with that router, then connection is made and all the variety of the internet becomes the focus of attention. The protocol makes this possible, but the strong tendency toward an 'all or nothing' logic of a protocol means that once connection is achieved the manner of connection is no longer of concern, having been superseded by what using that connection can bring to a node.

My understanding of Galloway is then that protocols are formalised and proceduralised logics that define the language of a network. Meeting the requirements of the protocol means both becoming a node and being able to connect to the network, gaining all the capabilities of that network as defined by the protocol. Such a logic tends strongly toward an all or nothing in which connection is either possible or is not possible; one can either be a node or not, the protocol offers no middle way. Such is the logic of control in decentred networks and without protocols no network could exist. Forgetting the protocol is also therefore often the forgetting of control in distributed networks and leads to an idealisation of the nature of networks and what they offer.

From this understanding further complications may be explored. A key one is that protocols can be nested inside protocols, meaning that whereas protocols often have an absolute logic this may at times be obscured because in fact a node is negotiating several protocols at once and is involved in a complex of networks being controlled through a number of protocols. Using the internet means negotiating one protocol, while connecting to a social media network means negotiating a different protocol which works 'on top' of the internet protocol and relies on it. Negotiating, for example, the privacy settings within a social media network then means engaging with a third set of protocols that define what a node is and what it can do on an internet-dependent social media network. Protocols are often nested inside each other or are built on top of each other (Galloway 2004: 50–3).

The idea of protocol is as important as that of the network because neither can exist without the other. The key point is that networks and protocols *together* constitute the organisation/dis-organisation of information power. The forms of organisation of information in the political antagonism of information are fundamentally the joining of what appear to be opposite logics: the network of peer-to-peer, many-to-many connections and the protocol of total control with its logic of complete obedience or disconnection:

> *Networked power is based on a dialectic between two opposing tendencies:*
> *one radically distributes control into autonomous locales; the other focuses*
> *control into rigidly defined hierarchies.* (Galloway and Thacker 2007: 19)

If networks destroy hierarchies then protocols maintain them, even if the latter might be the simple hierarchy of 'yes or no'; and the two opposed logics are essential to each other: no networks means no protocols and no protocols means no networks. Protocols function in complex pyramidal hierarchies with formal and absolute logics and forms of control because they are often constituted by algorithms and may be nested inside each other. Before completing this understanding of networks and protocols as the organisational logics of information power, it will be worth outlining an example which, though discussed in many places, remains the clearest example of this network and protocol organisation of information, namely, that of the architecture of the internet itself.

Internet Network and Internet Protocol

The internet has been seen as both one of the most powerful existing networks and as a model of networks. Many have focused on particular aspects of the internet to exemplify how they think networks operate and what changes they bring. One recurrent and key example is the often repeated claim that the internet was designed to withstand nuclear war because it had ways of routing traffic using multiple different routes, meaning the elimination of even a significant number of nodes could leave the network still operating successfully. The moral lessons drawn from this claim have been various. Two key ones are that the internet is uncensorable, it will route around damage as John Gilmore said, and that since it was built by the military it should be treated with some suspicion as another example of the militarisation of society (Jordan 1999a: 35–6). Neither of these morals are strictly speaking true, if only because the original story itself is not true.

The internet was not built to withstand nuclear war and has always had key centralised features whose destruction would have led rapidly to a serious degradation of traffic across the internet, and quite probably to its failure. The key predecessor to the internet, Arpanet, was built with money from USA defence research budgets, but it was not built, strictly speaking, as a military communication network but rather as a way of linking computers to allow remote access. This in turn led to the internet as a network joining together different networks based on the kind of design Arpanet pioneered involving decentralised packet-switching and centralised addressing (Abbate 1999; Mueller 2002; Jordan 1999a; Brand

2003). But the myths of the internet being uncensorable or being a tool of the military are important, even if inaccurate, as they provided ideas that have shaped the future design of networks and conceptions of their use. In understanding networks and protocols the internet provides not only a now well-researched and clear history but also an exemplary network around which various hopes and fears helped to conceptualise networks. I will explore the internet as an example of a network by focusing on its key organising principles in distributed packet-switching, the domain name system and the internet address space. As will be seen, networks and protocols form contradictory organisational approaches to information and yet they are needed by each other for each to function and for the internet to exist.

Packet-switching is one of the most often discussed features of the internet. This refers to the way that once a media-object of some sort is digitised it can then be turned into a series of 'packets' that are sent out onto the network. Once on the network each media-object's packets can travel via whichever nodes seem best, with nodes updating each other on their connection speeds and availability. Here lies much of the anti-censorship potential of the network technology of the internet, because if one node is down or even goes down while a media-object is in transition then the packets can just reroute and be resent to travel successfully.

Such a clearly network-like technology – in which all nodes are potentially roughly equal, only distinguished by rapidly updated information about speeds of transmission and availability, and nodes are often peered to several other nodes – is constituted by a protocol. For example, each packet has to be formed correctly according to the Internet Protocol (IP)[1] to be able to travel over the internet. This means that each packet (called a datagram) has to be constructed in the same way with meta-data that includes the addresses that send and receive and other relevant information, including the information needed to reconstruct whatever the media-object is once all the packets have arrived and the information that is the 'payload' of the media-object. Again, protocol logic is that each networked event of a packet must be formed correctly in an absolute sense or it will simply be dropped and disappear.

---

1. Technically, as many will want to point out at this stage, the Internet Protocol is the Transmission Control Protocol/Internet Protocol (TCP/IP). For convenience I will follow the growing tendency (admittedly that seems to have been growing for a long time) to refer to TCP/IP as the one protocol for governing the internet, or IP (Mueller 2002: 74–7).

The second often discussed organising feature of the internet, usually mentioned when analysing centralisation, is the domain name system. The functionality here is fairly straightforward. Each computer attached to the internet has a number assigned to it that identifies it as a location. As numbers are easy for computers to use but not so easy for humans, the numbers are registered in the domain name system as a particular set of words, hierarchically organised under different names and levels of names. Each address, such as google.co.uk or whitehouse.gov or thing.net, can then be used in a web browser or as part of an email address (obama@ whitehouse.gov for example), and so on. Each time such an address is used the domain name system translates the words back into numbers. The domain name system is itself hierarchically organised with portions of it delegated; this is not peer-to-peer delegation but hierarchical, meaning that a registrar in the UK would deal with domain names ending in .uk but would ensure their list was registered upward to create one unified domain name space with the same paired numbers and words available to any node on the internet (Mueller 2002: 77–82; Abbate 1999: 204–12). The distributed nature of the World Wide Web, with different websites able to spontaneously develop a peered network wherever they wish and to share their sites via distributed packets of data, is thus also bounded and organised by a form of strict hierarchical control.

The unique number that identifies each computer is known as its IP number. This is a second form of hierarchy that is sometimes less commented on, given that the domain name system illustrates a similar point, but the Internet Protocol address space is an even clearer example of the way protocols are necessarily connected to networks. Internet numbering connected to packet-switching creates the internet not as a single network but as a bounded set of networks and protocols.

To see this we can return to the datagram or the packet that is so emblematic of the vision of the internet as a horizontal and flexible network. Each packet is able to travel across the nodes of the internet, and we should remember that the internet is really a set of connected networks all of which implement the Internet Protocol (IP) to allow the routing of packets across them. There is then a complex, flexible and flattened network in operation over which packets may flow. Each such packet is made up of a header and a payload, with the latter being a portion of the information being sent and the former essential meta-data that directs the packet, ensures it can be connected once it arrives, and ensures that failed packets are replaced by being resent. For a packet to travel across the internet, and in a sense for the internet to be constructed, the packet's header must include at least two IP numbers for the sending and receiving computers. Each number must be formed exactly according to IP, and though usually stored in a binary format that can be quickly computer-read they may be familiar in the following example of number notation: 172.34.221.2.[2] Each such number is mapped to a particular computer located somewhere on a network that has also implemented IP. Given the nature of computers as versions of a Universal Turing Machine, 'a computer' may here refer to one physical machine or to a series of such machines that are themselves linked in a local network or even to one physical computer that can present itself as several machines. However, whatever the complexity of resolving the end point, it remains the case that the IP address must map to some form of computer (Mueller 2002: 32–7).

Like domain names, IP addresses are issued by a descending order of registrars who are allocated blocks of numbers. Each registrar assigns a particular IP number to a resource that is identified in some way, perhaps by its MAC address (a serial number that is stored in the hardware of a network interface device most usually in some implementation of an ethernet port). These numbers identify a physically located connection to a computer resource which identifies that resource absolutely on the internet. The numbers are then communicated between databases, again held hierarchically and rigidly so that there is no chance of confusion (Mueller 2002: 35–9).

IP addresses and domain names were only distributed because both quickly became so large that keeping them in one file communicated from one central database to each connected routing computer became unfeasible. The databases were then hierarchically distributed so that there was no duplication and so registrars and naming authorities each had control over a portion of each name space. These databases are then communicated upward and downward in a hierarchical fashion to ensure one consistent and uniform name space, as required by their protocols. This, in the end, leads to the key point that there is a root server for the internet, which is the top level address space from which other address spaces branch off. While the issues of the governance of the internet are beyond the scope of the present argument, it is useful to note that governance of the root and of the name space lies at the core of arguments

---

2. This is a randomly made up IP number according to IP Version 4, a number according to IP Version 6 would be more complex but the same underlying arguments about hierarchy and authority hold.

about who should control this key centralisation point of the internet (Mueller 2010; Collins 2010).

The addressing protocol is fundamental to the operation of the internet because it identifies where information can come from and be sent to; it defines what an address can be and what is needed to create a well-formed packet that can travel on the internet; and it defines an address space that bounds and organises nodes. It also identifies a physical computer that is the node for information for a specific IP number. This is the fundamental architecture of the internet, which is thus not simply a network but a combination of a flattened, distributed network with a pyramidal hierarchy defined by protocols.

Not all networks and protocols combine rigid hierarchy with distribution as clearly as the internet does. For example, music sites vary. Napster as one of the first peer-to-peer music distribution sites combined distribution of music – stored on individuals' computers that then shared music directly to other computers – with a hierarchical central point consisting of a database of information about who had what music. With the failure of Napster attempts were made in such networks as Kazaa or with protocols such as BitTorrent to create fully peer-to-peer networks to share data with no central point – 'maps' of who holds which information were distributed so that once connected that information needed to create connections, the protocological information, could be shared peer to peer as well. The same combination of protocol and network is required in such networks, it is just that the database that organises nodes is itself broken down and distributed. However, even in such networks, there is a tendency for indexes to develop as a more efficient way of being able to find information (such as Pirate Bay and so on). In fully peer-to-peer networks protocols remain the means by which nodes are defined and how information may be shared; being part of the network means implementing the protocol, but the protocol itself may then be flattened as much as possible. This also means that the more distributed the sharing of information about information on the network is, the slower the network may be in sharing, while it may be more robust in keeping that information distributed. For example, if I query a peer-to-peer network for a particular song, if the song is not popular it may take considerable time to find a node that has a record of it or it may not be found at all if the relevant nodes are not online at the time, whereas a central database of all songs could serve the information back quickly. The search for information about which song I will then request and start downloading may be affected by delays or even failure within a radical distribution of protocological information (David 2010: 29–37; Wikstrom 2010: 65–6; Kot 2009: 52–66).

As the great exemplar of networks and as a key innovation in information flow and management, the internet's basic architecture teaches something different to a vision of a dis/organised world in which peers relate directly to each other by connecting horizontally and eliminating hierarchies. What the architecture of the internet shows is that something like distributed networks are possible but only if they are also governed by a protocol that strictly defines the information space, bounds it by defining who can join and how, and exactly specifies what has to be done to successfully transfer information. Networks without protocols are impossible and protocols have little meaning if they are not creating a space in which a network can proliferate. As noted earlier in the quotation from Galloway and Thacker, it is the interplay of radical distribution of control with a rigid hierarchy that defines how information is organised in the twenty-first century.

Network-Protocols

All the information flowing through devices and being multiplied and reapplied through recursions is bounded and organised in combinations of networks and protocols. These set the kinds of information that nodes can constitute and determine how nodes on networks can communicate. They tend to operate with a combination of radically different forms of authority that manifest in different parts of information processes: sometimes a combination of a network and protocol may appear to be primarily about the network side with distribution and peering of nodes, but sometimes it can be the opposite, for example when someone's IP number is banned from an online resource blocking their entry because the protocol identifies them. What is clear about the nature of networks and protocols is that networks tend toward distribution and direct connections while protocols tend toward hierarchical authority and clear definitions of boundaries, and that each requires the other.

The key point here is that the combination of networks and protocols produces an organisational and dis/organisational form for information. Sets of recursions and devices will be linked and formed into recurring patterns by networks and protocols. It is tempting to start referring to networks now, instead of the unwieldy term 'networks and protocols'. However, this would be a mistake because of the emphasis that already exists in analysis of the digital and the internet in which networks are believed to be about distribution and peering and in which the role of protocols is minimised and often lost altogether. An alternative that will be used in the following will be to refer to networks and protocols with the one word 'network-protocols', though still somewhat ungainly it is useful for naming the one logic of dis/organisation that is formed by the necessary connection of networks and protocols. The two should not be separated and neither can stand in for the other. The third dynamic of information power flowing through information as a political antagonism in the twenty-first century is then the network-protocol.

Amid the many different political antagonisms of twenty-first-century society, there is one that flows around information – understood as a difference that moves – in the complex cultural and technological context that arises after the popularisation of the digital and the internet and their complex inter-relation. As has now been argued, this form of information politics can be understood through three inter-locking dynamics in which different forces inter-weave: recursions, devices and network-protocols.

Each of these three dynamics gives rise to characteristic ways in which access to or benefits from information may begin to benefit one group over another group. Recursion offers the possibility of information that can only be collectively produced being taken by whoever controls specific recursions. Moreover, the nature of recursions entails that this privatisation of collective production will be somewhat hidden, as only the recursion controller can easily see the collective of information as a collective. However, this is not straightforward as collective recursions are only produced because whoever controls the recursive process creates this process even though the information supplied comes from users of that recursion.

Devices embed particular information processes within what appear to be black boxed technologies available for use. Devices are structured by a broad information process of responding to information overload by, in part, interposing devices between the user and the flood of information. Such devices, however, embed a particular structure to information flows within themselves, creating a settlement in which the device both hides and ensures a particular relation between users, their information and information flows. Clearly here there is another point at which exploitative relations may be embedded. It is also clear that the nature of information means that certain forms of expertise will become important in relation to devices, both in terms of opening up their workings to scrutiny and in intervening to change devices or create different devices. A basis for intervening in exploitation and liberation, including ways of structuring recursions, opens up with devices.

Network-protocols offer up a way of theorising the organisation of recursions and devices into recurring systems or structures of information. Protocols open up the possibilities of defining nodes of particular networks in absolute ways that may deny entry into certain networks. Similarly, the tendency toward distribution and peering in networks opens up flatter sets of connections. Network-protocols offer up many handles and points of purchase for struggles over processes of information exploitation and liberation.

To take this theory forward I will examine two different kinds of points at which the dynamics of information power engage with more specific and material instances of information politics. I will use the terms 'platforms' and 'battlegrounds' for these different cases. By following the theory into such engagements it will be possible to develop the theory and so return to offer a fuller conceptualisation. I am calling the first of these engagements 'platforms' following the increasingly common use of the term that extends the technical idea of a computer platform to wider architectures. Platforms in this case refer to material configurations of information politics. Platforms offer prototypes, plans or architectures from which specific materialised forms of exploitation and liberation can be created. Platforms are still generalisations but are materially directed generalisations in the sense that they are meant to give birth to or to summarise already existing socio-technological forms.

In the next part of the book, I will examine the three platforms of clouds, securitisation and social media networks. At this point, a decade and a half into the twenty-first century, all three appear to be long lasting and significant examples of platforms. It is, however, important to emphasise that these are only three of a range of possible platforms. For example, I might have considered the platform of the 'portal', which is a particular design of websites that seeks to aggregate users by continually offering new services from one online presence rather than focusing on one service. Yahoo is an example of this with its homepage in 2013 listing 17 different services, from dating, horoscopes and weather to 'omg'. Prior to the early 2000s portals were a popular business strategy in the West, the idea being that users would stay on the portal-site and hence revenues would follow. This strategy fell to pieces in the West after the dot.com bust but it has proven more successful elsewhere, and particularly so in

China's dot.com boom that has seen the growth of a significant number of portals (So and Westland 2010). Another example that might have been considered is the idea of 'big data', which in 2013 broke through to public and governmental consciousness in the West. Whether this will prove to be a passing information fad or one that grows into a long-lived platform cannot be known as I write, but it is worth mentioning if only to emphasise there are many platforms (Mayer-Schoneberger and Cukier 2013) apart from the three that will be considered here.

Platforms are also not mutually exclusive but inter-penetrate and interpolate each other. A theory of platforms as information power must involve not only the analysis of particular platforms but must also recognise the way platforms as abstract architectures are able to borrow from each other and at times to contradict elements of each other. This is not the world as a jigsaw, with each part slotting into its allotted place in a zero-sum game to make a coherent whole, but is a multiple world with multiple perspectives, multiple uses and re-conceptions of what seem to be similar phenomena. What is important across platforms is to see how information exploitation is or is not embedded into the abstract architectures that lead from platforms like search, social media, portals or clouds to specific socio-technological relations embodied in sites such as Google, Twitter, Sina Weibo or Amazon.

Part 2

Platforms

4

Clouds

Cloud Computing

Clouds sound so ethereal and so distant, it is unsurprising that much iconography of heaven and the gods places both in fluffy white clouds looking down. The migration of computing to such welcoming clouds has become a social, political and business strategy that embeds this iconography into the heart of an important platform of information politics in the early twenty-first century.

The cloud is a platform in the sense used here because it is an abstract architecture that has a range of specific applications. This architecture also creates a type of information power, putting into play the politics of information as theorised in the preceding chapters. Exploring this will be done in a number of steps. First, I will look at how clouds are defined within the cloud computing literature, where we will find a great deal of discussion of flexibility, mobility and scalability. Second, I will examine two essential components, legality and trust, that are often missing from definitions of clouds. Third, these five aspects of clouds – flexibility, mobility, scalability, legality and trust – and how they generate a form of exploitation, including possibilities for contesting exploitation, will be examined using the example of Megaupload. Following these steps it will be possible to draw conclusions about how computer clouds effect information exploitation.

Technology and Architecture of Clouds

The vision of cloud computing is so dominated by the ethereal that, paradoxically, what many who define clouds feel compelled to say first and most emphatically is that cloud computing is not about fluffy immateriality but consists of particular arrangements of wires, radio-waves, computers, buildings and software. There is very little so often asserted in relation to clouds yet so persistently mistaken as that the cloud is material, because, as we shall see, immateriality also plays a key role in clouds. I will argue that it is a particular kind of relationship between materiality and immateriality that defines clouds. Even if every cloud requires a material basis, this material basis is always somehow associated with a sense of immateriality. The architecture of cloud computing is largely formed around the fact that its materiality is essential if often obscured, while its immateriality is dominant in its public and self presentation, and that both are essential in defining user and controller roles in managing and using clouds. Pitting materiality against immateriality obscures the cloud's dynamics of power because clouds as a platform are both earthly and magical.

As noted earlier, depending on which claims are believed Google is either the largest or one of the largest manufacturers of computers in the world (Levy 2011: 181; McMillan 2012) and is the largest or fifth largest manufacturer of computers as servers (Steinert-Threlkeld 2011; Hachman 2012). However, while you can buy a tablet, mini-tablet, smartphone or Chrome notebook from Google, you cannot buy a server or a desktop computer from them, and you will not find Google included in the lists of personal computer manufacturers such as Dell, Lenovo and so on. What the figures for computer manufacturing dramatise is Google's production of and appetite for data. As already discussed, there is all the data Google gains through the searches people do (over a billion a day [Google 2013a]) and there is the need to both mine this data and make it available for recursions, but there is also all the resources that Google makes available to users over the internet (from which data can again be harvested). As an example, we can consider Google's service called 'Drive' (sometimes called Gdrive and which now integrates Googledocs). You can use this to store files on Google's computers and use their applications to word process documents or work with spreadsheets and keep all the results not on any local computer but on Google's servers accessed over the internet. Google claims that you can access these files from any computer that has internet access, that you can share them with anyone who can also access the internet, and that Google will keep them safe for you. Here is the 'cloud' in action, requiring no local drives but with the assumption of internet-connectivity and both applications and storage all held remotely, somewhere in the 'cloud' of Google servers.

Amazon also offers cloud services both directly to consumers and in the background to anyone who wishes to run a cloud of their own. In the former case, Amazon is trying to compete with Apple's success with iTunes by running its own cloud music service, by which music can be bought through Amazon and then listened to anywhere that is connected to the internet by connecting to the Amazon cloud service. Providing clouds that others can rent is exemplified by the fact Wikileaks ran, at least in part, on Amazon's cloud servers until the release of US State Department cables led to pressure from US Senator Lieberman's office, among others, and to Wikileaks being kicked off Amazon and having suddenly to relocate its services (Sifry 2011: 176–7). Apple similarly tries to serve and keep its consumers by offering the iCloud, in which music, photos, communications and so on are all able to be moved across different devices because the relevant files are kept on Apple's servers (deAgonia et al. 2013).

From these examples, clouds seem, in a sense, to be simple, they consist of 'clients' that are some kind of computerised device – smartphone, tablet, laptop, desktop – that connects to a networked series of servers (also computers) configured to provide various services – such as storage or an application like a spreadsheet editor, music player or a database. Cloud computing reverses the move from the 1960s onwards when computers shifted from being huge, expensive and centralised to become local with each individual having their 'personal computer'. With clouds the computer again becomes a client to the network with a potentially minimal computerised service provided by the local machine that is dependent on a massive remote system (Watson 2012: 89–160).

Before turning from examples to the architecture of cloud computing, it is worth noting that the dynamics of information power are already appearing. Information is still generated by users of clouds, all the individuals adding and listening to music, sharing spreadsheets, making family movies and so on are producing information that could be recursed. Differences that move are being produced but when they are in the cloud they are enclosed by those cloud technologies and so become part of specific clouds, part of Google's cloud, or Amazon's or the iCloud. As one Google employee has argued, the move to cloud computing is important for Google because:

Google makes money with advertising online, that's about 20 percent of total advertising spent. Eighty percent of the time, people's attention is offline. To the extent that we can make computers better, everything will go online, and Google can participate in that advertising space. (Linus Upson, VP Engineering Google, Cited in Levy 2011: 211)

Upson makes clear that recursions that use the information flowing through a cloud offer up insights that fall into the lap of whoever controls that cloud, in Google's case as part of their advertising product but other collective uses are possible. The recursions that produce information come from the input of many but are harvested and used by the controller of the cloud, without whom the ability to correlate inputs would not exist. To create this cloud not only are devices required, from individual technological artefacts like a Chromebook or Amazon's cloud music player to the server farms housing thousands of computers and linking globally to other server farms that all take the form of networks. The particular engineering of such a network of computers will also require the various protocols, including legal and cultural as well as technological requirements, that define who can or cannot connect and what the boundary of a particular network is.

To grasp more fully the architecture involved it is useful to move to the general ideas of cloud computing that present the cloud more formally and abstractly. Here the tone is different to the rhetoric of the iCloud – 'access your music, photos, calendars, contacts, documents and more, from whatever device you're on' – or Google's Drive – 'access everywhere' – that dissolves the racks of computers in server farms into the immateriality of the cloud; instead, technical specifications and definitions of different computer architectures emerge. There is also necessarily a shift toward computing science, and as such the discussion could easily become mired in the technicalities of terminology and differences of technical infrastructure between perspectives that are essentially engineering and functional and which now can be found across an extensive literature (Armbrust et al. 2010; Vaquero et al. 2008, Wang et al. 2010). To avoid this, and to ensure the present discussion remains focused on the politics of information, we will look at just one high level attempt to define cloud computing drawing on technical discussions, which can be taken as representative of definitions of the architectures of cloud computing. This is the definition created by the US Department of Commerce's National Institute of Standards and Technology (NIST). According to NIST, the essential characteristics of cloud computing are:

On-demand self-service. A consumer can unilaterally provision computing capabilities, such as server time and network storage, as needed automatically without requiring human interaction with each service provider.

Broad network access. Capabilities are available over the network and accessed through standard mechanisms that promote use by heterogeneous thin or thick client platforms (e.g., mobile phones, tablets, laptops, and workstations).

Resource pooling. The provider's computing resources are pooled to serve multiple consumers using a multi-tenant model, with different physical and virtual resources dynamically assigned and reassigned according to consumer demand. There is a sense of location independence in that the customer generally has no control or knowledge over the exact location of the provided resources but may be able to specify location at a higher level of abstraction (e.g., country, state, or datacenter). Examples of resources include storage, processing, memory, and network bandwidth.

Rapid elasticity. Capabilities can be elastically provisioned and released, in some cases automatically, to scale rapidly outward and inward commensurate with demand. To the consumer, the capabilities available for provisioning often appear to be unlimited and can be appropriated in any quantity at any time.

Measured service. Cloud systems automatically control and optimize resource use by leveraging a metering capability at some level of abstraction appropriate to the type of service (e.g., storage, processing, bandwidth, and active user accounts). Resource usage can be monitored, controlled, and reported, providing transparency for both the provider and consumer of the utilized service.[1] (Mell and Grance 2011: 6)

The rhetoric of this abstract architecture is instructive, with absence as powerful as presence. The internet is nowhere mentioned, perhaps this is meant to disentangle the abstract definition of cloud computing from the specific network form of the internet, but given the near ubiquity of

---

1. The paper also defines software models and deployment models but as these are primarily related to implementation they will not be discussed here since it is the essential characteristics of the abstract architecture that are key for the present discussion.

the internet as the form of access and that the definition is not so coy when mentioning client platforms (tablet, laptop) it seems an interesting omission at least. The dematerialisation of a key network in this way links to a further absence in the removal of human actors for software and other technological agents, both in user choice of computing services and, though less absolutely, when providing rapid changes in the amount of service. This, as the definition notes, allows the system to appear to the user as infinite, and we may observe in such a system's infinity and automatic availability something close to magic. A further point is the equation of 'countries, states and datacenters' on one level of abstraction. It would appear that incommensurate categories are being joined here, but this is only to define the way the user will by design have no sense of location within a cloud. The controller and creator of the cloud is going to have to deal not only with unruly computers in data centres but with potentially unruly governments.

This definition codifies an architecture of provisional magic. The magical qualities are all provided to the user-experience; mobile, endless, multiple. To the user the cloud should provide ways of doing things that ignore spatial, data and creative limits. Anything should be doable anywhere, at any size and any time. On the other side, however, the architecture cannot escape the material: it relates to states and it must plug seemingly endless wires into seemingly endless computers that must be complexly configured to allow instant changes in the amount of resources being used by any user, must deal with different forms of user behaviour – listening to music, working collaboratively on a spreadsheet, creating pictures, sharing statuses, revealing secrets – and must keep this all going twenty-four hours a day every day. The creation of such a division of magic and materiality needs some explanation: Why would this rhetoric work out in this way? Why foreground some things but leave in the background things that seem just as important (like the internet)? Further, this division obscures two crucial elements of clouds in the law, which forms a connection and hinge between materiality and magic, and in trust, which structures the interests of users and controllers of clouds. These two extra elements each need some consideration.

Every user of a cloud is necessarily embroiled in a set of intellectual property relations between their use of their own information and whoever runs or owns the cloud in which it is stored, yet this is elided in the NIST definition. Each cloud will implement some form of legality for each and every instantiation of the abstract cloud and these legalities will vary from those that claim ownership of anything and everything that someone transmits to systems that build on free-software-like licences to try and assert an openness. No matter where on the spectrum of closure and openness a cloud lies, some kind of legal moment will occur. This is of course true of many online situations, whether cloud-like or not, as has been discussed by others in relation to the debate around 'terms and conditions' and 'end user license agreements' (Halbert 2009). Despite this moment not being exclusive to clouds, it is an essential moment in them and one that fundamentally structures them by defining who has rights over the collective products of the cloud. This also suggests that the utility of offering 'magic' as the user's primary experience may be that they no longer concern themselves with what happens when their information is recursed. Instead the user focuses on the magical experience their information undergoes in the cloud.

For example, the iCloud terms of service include many of the usual claims, such as Apple's right to terminate the service at any point with no responsibility for returning to users anything stored on the iCloud. In 2013, the terms also included the following: 'You understand that by using the Service, you consent and agree to the collection and use of certain information about you and your use of the Service in accordance with Apple's Privacy Policy' (Apple Corporation 2013). Immediately after this the terms state that any content added by the user is their responsibility. Taken together we see Apple claiming as its own any aggregations, any of the information that is 'extra' and is generated from the interactions of users, while also ensuring they disclaim responsibility if users add something illegal or in 'bad taste', and reassuring users that their individual bits of data are their own. If that is not clear enough, there is also: 'You further consent and agree that Apple may collect, use, transmit, process and maintain information related to your Account, and any devices or computers registered thereunder, for purposes of providing the Service, and any features therein, to you' (Apple Corporation 2013). Google's terms of service similarly locate intellectual property rights over content that is uploaded to whoever uploads it, while also stating:

> When you upload or otherwise submit content to our Services, you give Google (and those we work with) a worldwide license to use, host, store, reproduce, modify, create derivative works (such as those resulting from translations, adaptations or other changes we make so that your content works better with our Services), communicate, publish,

publicly perform, publicly display and distribute such content. The
rights you grant in this license are for the limited purpose of operating,
promoting, and improving our Services, and to develop new ones. This
license continues even if you stop using our Service. (Google 2013b)

Again we see embedded in the legal terms of use of a cloud that ownership
of collectively produced information is conferred on the maintainer of the
cloud. Many have tried to make this seem a natural or normal situation,
after all these companies create and pay for the clouds. Why should they
not take what would not have existed without their cloud? The point
here is that such legalities are an inherent part of the architecture of the
cloud and they define the nature of a specific cloud. There must be a legal
moment in which any cloud maintainer enters into a relationship with the
users; even community social network initiatives have to develop some
kind of terms of service.

Such legal moments could be a point at which ownership of the
resources of the cloud and the information produced there could be
analysed or discussed. It is entirely possible that recognition could be
given to the joint production of extra information through the cloud
between the cloud maintainer and users. However, if terms of service in
clouds conform to the normal style of obfuscation and platform-owner
dominance found across the internet (Halbert 2009) then this feeds into
the further issue surrounding of clouds, namely trust, which, like legality,
is present only by implication within the NIST definition. When users
commit their information to the cloud some form of trust is required
because if users do not trust a cloud, their use of it becomes less likely if
not irrational. Here we run into the main function of magic in the cloud
metaphor, which is to misdirect attention to the servers, wires, software
and so on that make up the materiality of the cloud and generate instead
a sense of immateriality in which one's information is simply 'out there',
free, mobile and accessible in the trustworthy cloud! Instead, as is often
noted to little effect, all cloud users should be clear that information
sent to the cloud is always 'somewhere', on some server and therefore
under some jurisdiction, owned by somebody or some company or some
government who is being trusted with a user's information. The division
between magic and materiality here appears as a way of structuring the
benefits and interests of users and controllers in clouds.

Trust can be dramatised in a number of ways. For example, all information
held on computers controlled by companies with their headquarters in the

USA is subject to the Patriot Act, which means that no matter where the information is stored the US government can require those companies to turn it over. All the data collected by Google, Facebook, Tumblr and so on must be legally supplied when the US government formally requests it, no matter whether it is stored outside the USA or not (Deibert 2013: 14). This dramatises the trust required to place information, which may be personal or confidential, in the cloud. Magic clouds obscure these workings from users and in doing so obscure issues of trust.

By now it is also clear that magic comes in two forms: experience and ether. The experience is magical in providing instant, scalable, mobile and so on access to information and applications to manipulate information. The experience is also magical in presenting this mobile, remote and scalable experience through the reassuring iconography of the cloud. The ideology of the cloud is that of the ether and white fluffiness, like so many pleasant sheep gambolling in the heavens, which gives a visual and mythical dimension to the magical experience of using the cloud. The experience of the user and the ideology of the cloud are both forms of magic.

By offering users mobility, elasticity and all the other aspects that the NIST definition focuses on, the everyday experience of the cloud is one that obscures materiality, legality and trust. What this amounts to is that differential relations of power are obscured as if by magic. Hillis and colleagues notice this kind of 'aura', which has an air of both mystery and holiness about it, in relation to Google and search, not only quoting Google engineers who argue that search will become more 'magical' but noting the transition between magic and materiality that is hidden by the aura:

> For most searchers, the glowing white box into which we type our requests for enlightenment is also a black box, a kind of altar on which the ritual of search is enacted ... this is magical empiricism at work ... When we consecrate Google as equivalent to god, it is we who confer the blessing, yet Google remains the same – a corporation based in Mountain View, California. (Hillis, Petit and Jarrett 2013: 14–5)

While Hillis, Petit and Jarrett are focused on search and Google they identify the meaning of magic in search in a way that articulates what I am claiming here about clouds. The elision of materiality in clouds underpins a magical relationship to the mobility and elasticity of information in clouds, whereas in search it creates the consecration of answers to questions. This side of the cloud was brought into sharp relief when it was revealed that the IOS 4 operating system for the iPhone was automatically recording the location of the phone in real time in an unencrypted file. This is a problem Apple says was a bug that has been fixed. Even so, it highlights the fragile nature of trust in the cloud when the magic dissipates to reveal the materiality underpinning it. The file which identified an iPhone's real time and location migrated across applications so that if someone swapped their iPhone for a new one or an iPad then their history was maintained across the different devices. This meant that someone's location could be plotted against time. This was being done by triangulating against mobile phone towers so it was independent of GPS. The terms and conditions of iTunes at the time were over 15,000 words long and included the following 80 or so words:

> Apple and our partners and licensees may collect, use, and share precise location data, including the real-time geographic location of your Apple computer or device. This location data is collected anonymously in a form that does not personally identify you and is used by Apple and our partners and licensees to provide and improve location-based products and services. For example, we may share geographic location with application providers when you opt in to their location services. (Arthur 2011)

By anonymously, Apple mean that when they take the file from a specific iPhone then the information should be anonymised, but what was found in this case was that Apple's assurance was not true – anyone's iPhone or iPad could be mined for this data clearly identifying those devices' location over time. Nothing would prevent this data being requested legally or otherwise by the police or a court wanting to identify any IOS 4 iPhone user's location at particular times. The case here then is that even with the terms and conditions protecting anonymity, a bug, an imperfection in the materiality of the system, allowed a file that anyone could access on a device that identified someone's movement history. Most GPS-enabled devices may well be collecting such data, with Android and Microsoft powered phones also collecting such databases with similar guarantees of anonymity. In a response to questions from the US Congress, Apple had already stated that it was collecting this data, but had insisted that it was anonymised (which it appears to be when sent encrypted to Apple's database) and was used by them to build up its own location database, for example to track difficult reception areas. Despite these reassurances from Apple this failure of their stated system was only discovered when researchers external to Apple stumbled across it (Schonfeld 2011). The point of this example for our analysis of clouds is that the iCloud's offering of location identification is not so vague, not so fluffy, and clearly has legal and trust implications.

The cloud metaphor, the magic of sheep in the ether, primarily addresses issues of trust, rather than saying anything about how clouds function or the politics of legality, flexibility, mobility and so on that are the functions the cloud as a platform tries to deliver. But the cloud metaphor addresses trust by trying to deliver it *a priori, that is magically*, and to misdirect users away from the necessity of considering the nature of trust either legally or morally. The message is to trust the cloud because it is a cloud. When the cloud metaphor is used we can expect to see some attempt to gain our trust without dealing with the issues of trust that a cloud creates.

The emphasis here is on the way in which the architecture of the cloud necessarily obscures itself to the user, here again is the division of magic and materiality. This opens up a particular kind of information relationship in which the user experience, and particularly the more successful and routine that experience becomes, leads to the fading into the background of the cloud itself. This helps us to understand why the metaphor of the cloud has seemed so appropriate and been so easily accepted because it expresses how the cloud is experienced by most people (when it works!). Needless to say, those maintaining the cloud have a quite different experience in which keeping servers active, installing new computers and removing old ones, tracking use and monitoring links to datacentres and so on, all foreground the distinctly non-ether like nature of cloud computing.

Looking at these examples and following the abstract architecture they involve has allowed cloud computing as an information platform to be explored. But it is important by way of conclusion to connect this more thoroughly to the idea of a politics of information by extending the analysis. Clouds are networks that offer mobility, scalability and flexibility in the storage of data and the use of applications, which engages both users and cloud-maintainers in a necessary legal and trust relationship but in which the experience of users is that of a magical phenomenon which obscures the materiality of the cloud. How does this understanding play out as a form of recursion, devices and network-protocols?

The Architecture of Cloud Exploitation

Clouds are one kind of architecture that organises information; they enclose and pattern differences that move. Moreover, clouds are an architecture that we can already see implements the potential for a particular form of exploitation. They also have the characteristic of obscuring exploitation through the production of a magical experience for the user that deliberately, both symbolically and practically, disconnects the user from the materiality that is the primary focus of the producer and maintainer of the cloud. In this magic, a certain definition of property is imposed where the information provided is reconceived as a property the holder of the cloud can control.

Clouds are generally organised with one or two main functions. First, storage of information, and second offering applications to use on the information being stored. Clouds do not need to obscure these workings but they do obfuscate the necessary legal relations while offering flexibility, mobility and scalability of information storage and management. The storage and then manipulation of data allows recursions that the cloud maintainer can in turn manage. The cloud maintainer can think about what is being stored and how, they can make connections between regions and types of data, and they can follow groups of users related to all kinds of different objects, tastes and so on. All this new information is produced both because the cloud exists and because the cloud is used; it comes from collective user interaction with the kinds of resources the cloud produces. Such new information can then be applied back to itself, back to the same kinds of information from collective processes that is being produced, meaning that exponential information generation may result.

If we take the example of one famous cloud, Megaupload, that offered data storage as a basic service. With significant amounts of video being uploaded Megaupload both attracted new video uploads while also serving existing uploads by offering Megavideo, which allowed ad-supported video watching. The information drawn off was recursively placed back within Megaupload's functions to direct ads and to understand their own service. For similar reasons, picture, live streaming and audio support were added. This focus also added to the widespread perception that Megaupload was one of the main centres for the storage and viewing of pirated material on the internet. Recursions here involved, at least, pulling information about Megaupload from Megaupload and then using that information again within Megaupload to structurally alter its behaviour. The more information it recursed the more Megaupload managed to attract, hold and draw profit from its users, and the more collectively produced information was being gifted to it.

Devices are usually simultaneously implemented with recursions to produce and manage information. From this perspective, clouds are one response to the huge amounts of data being made available in twenty-first-century society and the need to somehow manage and access this data. Clouds are a powerful platform because the devices they implement in apps, servers, wireless and wired connections, websites, applications that word process or play cloud-located data, and so on, form an information world by allowing users to forget where their data is or how much storage they have, and allowing them to quickly change their requirements. These devices then also respond to the production of information within the cloud; each cloud becomes itself something that produces information which in turn needs to be managed and which requires its own devices. The spiral continues while there is information flooding into and through the cloud.

For example, Megaupload added devices as it progressed. An advertisement system was originally rented from Google through use of its AdSense system, utilised by many online companies, but in 2007 Google withdrew their system over concerns about pirated content on Megaupload. This led Megaupload to design and implement their own ad system that provided income alongside free services (charging was also introduced for premium or ad-free services) (Anderson 2012). This required Megaupload to implement a device, a complex one, within their cloud that could define and serve ads. This itself then produced information about which ads were being clicked on, which were making money and so on, ensuring that further collectively produced information was both enabled and fell to the cloud maintainer, producing further overload in the need to manage this new stream of information. The device of a programmed advertisement system was embedded into Megaupload.

The cloud requires network-protocols that create a boundary by defining certain protocols that allow access to its own network and through which information provided is conceived of as something that can then be 'held' and used by the platform controller. The cloud's use of magic also obscures the kinds of network-protocols forming each cloud. The production of magic in clouds here needs to be located within the network-protocols, as these need to be formed in a way that offers the user an experience that diminishes the network's material configuration. The protocol is important then in bounding the network and dividing experience of it between magic for the user and materiality for the cloud maintainer. The network-protocol will be implemented through the materials of wires, software and hardware and such things as passwords and usernames to be entered to gain access. These divide the experiences of user and owner/ maintainer and in doing so create a particular cloud from which the owner can draw information gifted by the collective as long as the owner creates devices to harvest the information. It is not that the cloud maintainer does nothing to exploit the collectively produced information, rather it will require examining each cloud to see what collectively produced information there is and how it is being created and used.

To return one last time to Megaupload: it consisted of a network of computers and a series of protocols, from logging on to using IP to identify itself, to the range of computers' that data was held on. This became more than obvious when Megaupload was raided at the instigation of the FBI for intellectual property piracy, with key employees and the owner arrested in New Zealand at the behest of US security agencies for offences caused by a company which was based legally in Hong Kong about data that was held in a number of places around the world. Using a redirect enforced through the domain name system by seizing the domain name ensured anyone seeking to access their data on Megaupload was suddenly confronted with a screen stating that several 'individuals and entities' associated with Megaupload were being pursued under US law. From this time on all the data in this cloud was inaccessible, and it was unclear if it would ever be made available to users or even be maintained by the hosting service that Megaupload had used. It was also revealed that Megaupload did not own or run its servers but had been buying storage from a different network altogether (Kravets 2012). The network-protocols governing the boundaries of Megaupload were suddenly made obvious when the internet protocol was used by the FBI to seize the domain name. The data held within Megaupload's bounded space was denied to users and the nature of protocols dramatised.

The case of Megaupload, like that of Google, Amazon and so on, are particular examples of the cloud platform creating a means for cloud maintainers to benefit from free data that is collectively produced but can only be harvested by the cloud maintainer because of the particular cloud they have put in place. If the recursions of a cloud produce extra information then it is in the nature of cloud network-protocols and cloud devices to ensure the cloud maintainer benefits from this extra information. The cloud further obscures this relationship by separating users from maintainers of clouds, the former being offered magic and the latter buried in materiality. As with all technologies, the nature of the cloud is dramatised and laid bare when it fails, as can be seen in the Megaupload case. Clouds, however, must also be understood in terms of their normal operation. In this respect, clouds are a platform that articulates the dynamics of information politics – recursions, devices, network-protocols – in such a way that storage of data and applications to manipulate that data are offered according to the five principles of flexibility, mobility, scalability, legality and trust. The dynamic of a cloud ordered according to these five principles produces a split between the magical experience that users undergo, which tends to radically dematerialise the cloud so that it hardly appears to exist, and the work and experience of cloud maintainers, who are up to their ears in the materiality of wires, computers, software and legalities.

5

Securitisation of the Internet

Excerpt: Proceedings of the Standing Senate Committee on National Security and Defence, Parliament of Canada, April 30, 2007.

Senator Day: You indicated, toward the conclusion of your remarks, that you have technological challenges, and that you complemented our partners with respect to some of the technology they have been able to share with you. In general terms, are you able to tell us what we are talking about? Is this a major change from analogue to digital – adjusting to that kind of activity?

Mr. Adams (Associate Deputy Minister National Defence and Chief of the Communication Security Establishment, Canada): ... The volume and type of communications is literally endless. That combination is the challenge for us. Our vision is security through information superiority. We want to master the Internet. That is a challenge that no one institution – be it ours or the National Security Agency, NSA, for that matter – can manage on their own. We try to do that in conjunction with our allies.

At the same time, we have a threat that is very diverse, very distributed around the world – similar to needles in haystacks. We have the combination of the technology and the threat that, together, make it virtually impossible for any one organization to manage it on its own. That is what we mean by working together. If we are to *master that Internet*, we will have to do it together; and we are focusing on that. (SSCNSD 2005)

Architectures of Exploitation and Architectures of Technology

The cloud is an example of a technologically centred platform that was able to be analysed beginning from a technical standard. Other computer platforms are similar, for example the computer itself may be considered a platform and particular standards are articulated for it (Gillespie 2010). A book series devoted to platforms similarly assumes that the technological architecture of a platform is a good way of framing its cultural analysis, with books focused on, for example, Atari and the Commodore Amiga (Montfort and Bogost 2009; Maher 2012). However, platforms as architectures of information politics cover several types of architectures. If clouds were a clear initial example of platforms partly because it was possible to build from an existing technical definition, then other platforms may not be framed so simply by beginning from their technology.

This chapter will deal with such an example of a platform, looking at the consequences for the internet of information subject to securitisation; that is, the ways states have reacted to information politics and in so doing have, in some cases, defined a particular architecture intended to 'secure' or 'master' the internet. Unlike clouds this is an architecture of relentless materiality in which there is no sense of users and maintainers of services as there is with clouds, only of state and corporate agencies building particular systems that seek to secure the internet in their interests. Deibert clearly outlines the opportunity such agencies see for themselves:

> Although cyberspace is often experienced as an ethereal world separate from physical reality, it is supported by a very real infrastructure, a tangible network of code, applications, wires, and radio waves ... In addition to being complex and fragile, this physical infrastructure contains a growing number of filters and chokepoints. Pulling back its layers is like pulling back curtains into dark hallways and hidden recesses, which, it turns out, are also objects of intense political contests ... also growing in leaps and bounds and becoming a critical part of the domain [is] data. Information related to each and everyone of us (and everything we do) is taking on a life of its own. It, too, has become an object of geo-political struggle. (Deibert 2013: 48–9)

Deibert points to the combination of physical infrastructure and information growth as an issue of geo-politics; as his work makes clear, it has become an opportunity for states to do more than offer services to their citizens or consumers and to extend into security issues. This chapter will trace securitisation as a platform, as a patterned and repeated way of inter-relating the dynamic forces of recursion, devices and network-protocols that some nation-states have created in order to master the internet in their own interests.

Making sense of this process of securitisation in and between nation-states means understanding how these processes have constructed a particular kind of platform that is implemented in various ways by different states. To do this an additional concept is required because although the meaning of platforms and the dynamics of information power have been discussed, securitisation has not. Further, securitisation references an extensive debate in international relations and international security that needs introduction. To understand the securitisation of the internet I will first briefly survey securitisation theory. It will then be possible to examine the specific nature of securitisation of the internet in the linked processes of collecting all information and then subjecting it to profiling techniques. 'Mastering the internet' has been attempted by nation-states by creating a platform that links three practices: securitisation, collecting all information and social profiling. I will examine these in turn.

Threats to the Existence of the People

The question of what governments of nation-states can do when they successfully claim that the citizens of their nation are under some kind of mortal threat is at the heart of the securitisation debate. This has been conceptualised in three broad ways. From what is now called the Copenhagen School of international relations has come the concept of securitisation, while in response to and criticism of that School has come critical security studies. There has also been a related dialogue, basing itself in critical legal studies, around Agamben's concept of 'states of exception' (Buzan et al. 1998; Browning and McDonald 2011; Agamben 2005). All three bodies of theory reflect on the ways that in positing some kind of a threat a state can divest itself of legal and democratic controls in order to take actions that the state itself would, under normal circumstances, consider illegitimate. Further, they all explore the way in which what is presented as an extraordinary situation may become normalised. In what follows I will touch on all three theories to draw out some common threads before applying that conceptualisation to information.

Securitisation as a term is most closely associated with what has become known as the Copenhagen School. The ideas here were developed as a contrast to previous studies of security that had focused on the military, violence and nation-states to try to come to assessments of security threats. These prior ideas were rooted in what was called a 'realist' belief that security threats were 'out there' needing to be accurately assessed. Instead of the description of 'really existing' threats, the Copenhagen School developed the idea that securitisation was a particular social process based on the insight that:

> The invocation of security has been the key to legitimizing the use of force, but more generally it has opened the way for the state to mobilize, or take special powers, to handle existential threats. Traditionally, by saying 'security,' a state representative declares an emergency condition, thus claiming a right to use whatever means are necessary to block a threatening development. (Buzan et al. 1998: 21)

Security is not then based on objective assessments of an external threat but is a claim for the political legitimacy of certain actions based on the exceptional urgency of the claim. What, in this account, gives securitisation its specificity is that it is the process of making a speech-act like claim that a community, usually represented by a state, is facing a threat to the existence of its people. If the process of securitisation is successful then an 'issue is presented as an existential threat, requiring emergency measures and justifying actions outside the normal bounds of political procedure' (Buzan et al. 1998: 23–4). Securitisation in this version includes the processes – legal, media, military, governmental, technological and so on – through which a social actor claims its constituents are facing a threat to their existence and therefore this social actor needs to be allowed to undertake extraordinary actions, even actions that contradict the nature of the social actor itself, such as a democratic government suspending democracy. A successful securitisation occurs when such a claim is accepted and acted upon.

Agamben's concept of the 'state of exception' is perhaps more spatially resonant than the Copenhagen School's notion of securitisation but it addresses a similar complex of various governmental, state or social actors suspending the very reason they exist in order to ensure the survival of those who are governed by or who make up that actor. 'The state of exception is not a special kind of law (like the law of war); rather, insofar as it is a suspension of the juridical order itself, it defines law's threshold or limit concept' (Agamben 2005: 4). Agamben notes the fate of detainees in Guantanamo Bay as being that of having entered a state of exception in which they have no rights, because the state holding them has denied them the rights of the Geneva Convention even though that state has signed and pledged to uphold that convention. Here the US government denies the law while claiming to uphold the law by declaring those in Guantanamo Bay to be beyond the law (Agamben 2005: 87). We might note further the USA's return to assassination as a legitimate political tactic, converting the state of exception over terrorism into a killing machine as Agamben defines it (Browning and McDonald 2011: 240). These are clearly implementations of the kind of state of exception and securitisation that former US Vice-President Dick Cheney claimed was required soon after 9/11:

> We'll have to work sort of the dark side, if you will ... We've got to spend time in the shadows in the intelligence world. A lot of what needs to be done here will have to be done quietly, without any discussion, using sources and methods that are available to our intelligence agencies – if we are going to be successful. That's the world these folks operate in. And, uh, so its going to be vital for us to use any means at our disposal basically, to achieve our objectives. (Cheney cited in Mayer 2009: 9–10)

Though coming from different intellectual frameworks Agamben and the Copenhagen School both articulate a similar idea and one that Cheney exemplifies. This idea articulates the paradox of state and government agencies that define a threat to be of such significance that to deal with it they suspend their own reason for existing. Agamben quotes the political scientist Rossiter's formulation that 'No sacrifice is too great for our democracy, least of all the temporary sacrifice of democracy itself' (cited in Agamben 2005: 9).

Critical security studies develops a third set of concepts in this area particularly through a dialogue with and criticism of the Copenhagen School, though it arguably also drives forward some key elements of the concept of securitisation (Peoples and Vaughan-Williams 2010). McDonald and Browning suggest three broad principles that form critical security studies: a critique of 'realist' security studies that privilege force and the state; a focus on what security does politically, particularly in defining actors and the legitimacy of actions; and, an examination of the ethics of security with an assessment of which interests different forms of security serve or which political agendas they progress (McDonald and Browning 2011: 236). This kind of approach radically opens up the nature of actors in securitisation, particularly pushing beyond the nation-state.

For example, critical security studies allows within securitisation the study of the ways all kinds of groups band together and take actions in reaction to existential threats, such as in protest groups like ecological activism. It also opens up the kinds of actions that are taken, moving beyond violence and the military and exploring why the claims to a particular existential threat – such as global warming or terrorism – resonate with particular communities. This move ensures a critical focus on how and why certain processes of securitisation are successful or not (McDonald and Browning 2011: 241). Importantly, critical security studies, by opening up both actors and actions in these ways, also opens up the meaning of securitisation for politics and focuses attention on the ethics of security. Critical security studies ensures questions are asked about who benefits from particular processes of securitisation.

Securitisation, critical security studies and the state of exception are concepts with extensive theoretical frameworks, each on their own unfortunately beyond the scope of present concerns, but for my limited purposes here they all present concepts that can frame a discussion of securitisation and the internet. Moreover, while I agree with Browning and McDonald that 'the suggestions that security has an inherent, universal logic (associated with urgency and exceptionalism, for example) is a claim that lacks attention to the multiple ways in which security is understood and practiced' (Browning and McDonald 2011: 241), this does not mean that securitisation as a concept needs to be thrown away. Instead of claiming all securitisation issues have one logic of exceptionality, it is possible to examine particular ways in which securitisation occurs. This also means it is important to be able to include actors other than nation-states in the dynamics of securitisation. In the context of information politics, this means looking at processes of security as they have been applied to the internet with attention centred on nation-state agencies but not exclusively focused on them. From this perspective, and taking into account both the differences between the three sets of concepts examined and the criticisms of those broadly within critical security studies, I will retain the term securitisation and frame it with three concepts so far discussed: security as a response to an existential threat; security as a legitimisation of extraordinary measures; and security as a political move that benefits a particular group or social actor. This may appear very close to the Copenhagen definition of securitisation but my use should be read as taking account of the criticisms and revisions of critical security studies and the related conceptualisation of Agamben.

In particular, I take forward the opening up of securitisation as a process available to multiple actors, not just state-actors. In the case of the internet, however, it is clear that the idea of exceptionality has played a key role, and while I would not assert the universality of exceptionality in securitisation I would assert the need to examine exceptionality as used by those seeking to master the internet.

The internet is also no stranger to processes of securitisation, which have been present almost from its beginning and even given birth to an internet meme in the 'four horsemen of the infocalypse' (Assange et al. 2012: 43). A good example of this occurred in 1999 when the then FBI Director Louis Freeh stated that 'Uncrackable encryption will allow drug lords, spies, terrorists, and even violent gangs to communicate about their crimes and their conspiracies with impunity' (cited in Greenberg 2012: 73). This statement is only remarkable for its failure to include paedophiles in the circle of evil that some kind of internet freedom will engender. In particular, early battles over cryptography, anonymity and free speech on the internet led to an ongoing popular recognition of processes of securitisation of the internet, codified in one way by cypherpunk Tim May in his Cyphernomicon (often also called the Cypherpunk FAQ): '8.3.4. "How will privacy and anonymity be attacked?" ... – like so many other "computer hacker" items, as a tool for the "Four Horsemen": drug-dealers, money-launderers, terrorists, and pedophiles' (May 1994; Greenberg 2012: 76–81). This ironic and often bitter understanding that securitisation is aimed at the internet remains current from these early times (Assange et al. 2012). For example, in the run up to a televised US Congressional hearing about Bitcoin in November 2013 a member of a Bitcoin forum suggested that forum members watch the hearing but respond with a drinking game:

> Every time someone mentions one of the Four Horsemen of the Infocalypse in the hearing, take a shot. (the four horsemen is a term referring to drug dealers, terrorists, money launderers, and child pornographers. i.e. the four most common bogeymen used as an excuse for things like the patriot act, the NDAA, CISPA, SOPA, the constant and unrelenting murder of innocent civilians in the middle east, etc.) (Anon 2013)

Securitisation is a process many feel they have faced as the internet moved from a minority to a mass phenomenon and many 'early adopters' have sought to defend what they take to be some of the internet's most important characteristics, such as freedom of speech. That many US-based internet early users were also partial to libertarian ideas, including some key influential groups such as the cypherpunks, further reinforced the suspicion on the part of these users that false or minor threats would be blown out of proportion to try to bring the internet under some central or direct government control (Greenberg 2012; Turner 2006; Levy 2001).

The four horsemen of the infocalpyse references a securitisation debate around the internet that is roughly contemporary with the rise of the internet to mass use. This is a debate that stretches from early freedom of speech and cryptography arguments all the way through to fears about child pornography, trolling and criminality online that have dominated headlines invoking fear of the internet in the first decades of the twenty-first century. What the internet folklore of the four horsemen of the infocalypse does not tell us is how securitisation has been implemented, beyond articulating a fear of the censorship and control of the internet. What kind of a platform, that is what abstract machine of information power, can be identified as having developed as part of the securitisation debate by those who invoke the four horsemen of the infocalypse for support? When drug dealers, terrorists, paedophiles and money-launderers (and their adjuncts or alternatives such as trolls, hackers, hacktivists, crackers, phreakers, cyber-criminals, dark web forum admins, bot and zombie-net controllers, and more) are invoked, what kind of repetitive circuits of information power are created?

Openness, Echelon, Prism

The internet was designed as an open platform almost accidentally, with early infrastructures far more concerned about connecting nodes of its network than securing identities or communication. This has left the internet open to intervention because so much of its traffic is available to those who can dip into the flow of data. This openness relates both to the origin and the destination of every set of data packets and to the contents of each data package that will only be closed if the sender does something extra to secure the contents. In early 2014 one of the designers of the internet protocol, Vint Cerf, said he wished that IP had been designed in the early 1970s with a security layer, making it clear that security was not built into the fundamental design of the internet (cited in Roberts

2014). This openness combines with the nature of the internet's address space so that the default state of the internet has been total identification of the origin computer and the receiving computer (as well as hops in between) and openness of the contents of data packets. This has changed fundamentally only since the 2010s as version six of the internet protocol includes some security and has begun to replace version four, while other security mechanisms such as secure connections to websites have been laid on top of IP. While the restriction and control of the freedom of the internet has often been a legitimate fear, it is this openness that has been of most interest to those seeking to securitise digitised information. What was developed was a securitisation of openness, not necessarily to close the open – though this may happen – but more usually to infiltrate the open. Further, all this data is more easily handled by computers than by humans, meaning that the ability to sift the data for surveillance is determined by the same computerisation capabilities that produce the data and that correlate with dramatically decreasing costs of storage and exponentially increasing computer power. The creation and transfer of data has grown in lockstep with the ability to collect, analyse and store the data. The power of information is to recurse and multiply, implementing devices in ways that continue to feed recursion and that are organised through protocols and networks. It is clear that limiting such flows is possible, and censorship through such things as filters is a recurrent feature of internet public policy, but this is to limit information instead of attempting control through the propagation of information.

The revelations from Edward Snowden about massive US state intervention seeking ubiquitous surveillance on the internet may seem an obvious place to start analysing securitisation, and they will be important to discuss because Snowden revealed a remarkable flowering of a platform to securitise the internet. However, it is also important to recognise that though Snowden revealed that the war on terror drove this securitisation home, this is a direction that has been travelled for some time, and that a reason for securitisation – or which of the four horsemen is invoked – is less important than the ongoing nature of the securitisation platform that seeks to use flows of information power and the openness of internet architectures. This has a longer history than such programmes as Prism, Tempora, and more can be seen by remembering their previous highpoint and its connection to pre-internet surveillance in the Echelon programme. Looking at earlier internet securitisation allows us to see the basis for such programmes in the fundamental architecture of the internet and not just focus on the revelations of Snowden.

The Echelon programme offered an implementation which both recognised and relied on the architecture of openness and identification that is embedded in the internet's architecture, with the specific task of intercepting worldwide satellite communication. It was formed in the 1990s and its existence was confirmed by a European Union report in 2001 that revealed the nature of this securitisation of the internet (Schmid 2001). Echelon was a worldwide system for intercepting all satellite communication and subjecting it to both targeted searches and to generalised keyword searches. It was formed and run through the UKUSA agreement (often called the 'Five Eyes') that was developed during and after the Second World War between the intelligence agencies of the USA, UK, Australia, New Zealand and Canada and that grew in strength throughout the Cold War (Walton 2013: 141–55). It has been argued that in addition to its Cold War purpose this agreement allowed intelligence exchanges ensuring that countries could spy on their own populations, where that was prohibited, by asking an allied agency to carry out the spying. What seems beyond doubt is that this inter-agency group ran Echelon to intercept all satellite communication, allowing access to communication worldwide, and that it intercepted an unknown amount of radio communication and messages travelling over cable (Greenberg 2012: 235–6; Schmid 2001; Harding 2014: 86–7). The limitations of this network were its restriction to satellite communication, the unknown amount of cable and radio communications intercepted, and limitations of staff being able to examine and interpret the flood of communications it received, which during its later period began to include rapidly increasing internet traffic.

Despite the obvious securitisation justification for such a network, its role in defending capitalism in the 'life or death' fight against communism for example, Echelon was confirmed (if not revealed) by the European Union Committee report because there was strong suspicion it was used for industrial espionage. Prior to the European Union report there was considerable suspicion about the existence of Echelon, including particularly journalist Duncan Campbell's work that subsequently helped trigger the EU investigation. In relation to industrial espionage in particular, France believed that communications affecting Air France and deals involving selling Airbus aircraft had been intercepted and passed to US plane manufacturing companies – in one case it was claimed a $6 billion deal was affected (Schmid 2001, see sections 1.2 and 10.7). The EU report recommended that all companies using satellite communication begin to use encryption, that private citizens rights be protected because 'An intelligence system which intercepted communications permanently and at random would ... not be compatible with the ECHR [European Convention on Human Rights]' (Schmid 2001, see section 13.1), and that in particular the UK, as a member of both the EU and the UKUSA security alliance, and Germany, which contained bases used for UKUSA interception stations, should answer a large number of questions (Schmid 2001).

Despite this report and the subsequent widespread recognition of the existence of Echelon, little change seemed to follow. Protests did result, including 'Jam Echelon Day' in which activists asked people to send multiple emails on a single day including 50 keywords designed to trigger Echelon searches, both in the hope of jamming the system with too much information and in the expectation of alerting those who ran it that many citizens worldwide knew of their activities and disapproved (Anon 2011; Oakes 1999). What we have in Echelon is a confirmed, as much as it is possible to confirm such things, system which included the automated collection of all communication and its subjection to searches that identify patterns.

If Echelon was part of an attempt to gather all communication and interpret it that was limited by the forms of communication available at the time, then the series of programmes revealed by the leaks from Edward Snowden form a fully fledged implementation of the platform that securitises the internet through information power (Harding 2014). This platform does not seek to degrade or limit access, it is not a nation-state firewall that censors content, but rather seeks to collect and correlate all communication ensuring the information it collects is recursed, implementing various devices that ensure ongoing collection, and redefining ideas of privacy or integrity of communication by implementing new protocols which connect, sometimes unwilling, networks together. This implementation of a platform does not consist of one socio-technical device but knits together a range of different devices all of which use information power to collect and profile communication. The extent and complexity of these revelations, and the fact that at the time of writing they are ongoing with more being made public and more analysis likely to help clarify their meaning and significance, means a comprehensive analysis of them is not possible; but, as will be shown, it is fortunately also not necessary for understanding the securitisation of the internet. Outlining several of the programmes within the overall platform the US and allied secret agencies have constructed will be enough to understand what is at stake and how this implements a securitised internet.

As is now well known, in 2013 there were a series of major leaks that detailed surveillance carried out primarily by the US National Security Agency (NSA) and the UK Government Communications Headquarters (GCHQ), but also with other 'Five Eyes' secret services. Not long after the leaks began appearing in newspapers worldwide Snowden revealed he had been the source of the leaks (Harding 2014). The best way of understanding the significance of what was revealed is to outline a number of the programmes that Snowden's leaked documents revealed. These accounts are taken from the *Guardian* newspaper's website dedicated to the leaks on which, at the time of writing, many of the leaked documents can be examined (Guardian 2014).

Prism was one of the first programmes to gain attention and also demonstrates some of the questions posed both by the evidence for the leaks and the nature of the securitisation platform. Prism is a programme which claims to allow the NSA access to information kept by major US-based technology companies including Google, Facebook, Apple, Microsoft, Yahoo and others. The kind of information taken by the security forces from these companies includes both the metadata[1] and the content of messages, including email, search history, file transfers, live chats and more. The companies listed as participating are claimed in the NSA leak to be assisting the programme, but all companies asked about the story denied their involvement, and some of them have records of only agreeing to legally valid demands and of running transparency sites which list such requests (Harding 2014: 206–8). Prism was set out in a powerpoint presentation that was leaked, and later leaks suggested that data from these companies was being collected without their knowledge by accessing the fibre optic cables along which their data ran, effectively sitting within their networks and siphoning data away (Harding 2014: 155–69; Rushe et al. 2013; Guardian 2014). Prism ensures the totality of data about users of any of the services of these companies is obtained by

---

1. Metadata can mean a number of things but in this case the definition 'information about the message' generally describes what is being discussed. This can include what system sends the information, who sends it, what path the information takes, who the information goes to and so on.

the security agencies. In terms of information power, all the differences that users produce, from a search on Google to a like on Facebook, are moved from one enclosure to a nation-state security forces' enclosure. Devices are interpolated at each stage of such a process to automate it, from the taps on fibre optic networks that siphon data from companies without their knowledge to the databanks that hold information and the computerised systems for analysis. Finally, various kinds of protocols set up a network of information that makes up the Prism programme, from the legal protocols followed to obtain data to the illicit protocols required to drag data from companies whether they know and approve of it or not.

Another information collection programme is the GCHQ-run data-hoovering programme called Tempora. GCHQ tap into undersea fibre optic cables that carry most of the data moving between continents. Tempora simply copies all this data, holding, it is believed, all the data for three days and the metadata for 30 days (Guardian 2014; Harding 2014: 155–69). This is very similar to the Prism programme in that it opens up opportunities for recursing through various devices and network-protocols but in itself the aim is simply to collect huge amounts of data by indiscriminately copying as much as possible.

A useful additional point that demonstrates information power in relation to such collection programmes as Prism is the NSA programme called Boundless Informant. This programme collates the amount and type of metadata being collected across different collection and analysis programmes within the NSA to keep track of what kind of information it collects, how much of it there is, and where it is coming from. Boundless Informant was controversial when it was revealed as it suggested NSA claims that they could not keep track of the data they collected were not accurate. In terms of information power, this programme represents part of the information spiral where particular devices, such as those in Prism, themselves produce information that contributes to information overload. Boundless Informant attempts to place itself into the information flood and offer NSA operatives some control over it by recursing all the data through a new device, in this case a GUI interface that visualises data (Harding 2014: 140–1).

There are several other programmes that also seek to add data to the system. For example, it is clear from the documents provided by Snowden that the NSA/GCHQ between them attempt to crack open encryption and privacy programmes that they encounter. They have capabilities to remove encryption from widely used security programmes on the web, such as the https protocol which is supposed to provide secure exchanges when providing credit card details or online banking. It is also clear that privacy networks, such as the TOR network, are targeted to try to obtain secured information. Any environment in which information exists is a target, as was made clear when it was revealed that online games such as World of Warcraft or the Xbox Live Network had been examined with both automated collection mechanisms, agents placed in games and the recruitment of informants (Ball 2013; Guardian 2014). A pillar of information securitisation becomes apparent here in the attempt to collect every available bit of data. One aim of the securitisation of information platform is to collect all available information and enclose it in ways that ensure only security agencies know the enclosure exists. This creates a second issue of what to do with the data. Boundless Informant already demonstrates that the data is mined, though it is more of a 'meta' programme that produces information about the surveillance. If universal information collection is one element of the securitised internet, how is the information then handled within its securitised enclosure?

One example is the programme XKeyscore, detailed in a presentation from 2008 that is among the leaked documents (XKeyscore 2008). The presentation details a cluster of Linux servers that can be scaled up to meet demands and which performs analysis of phone numbers, email content, web traffic (including usernames, buddylists, cookies), log ins, user activity and more, based on a rolling three-day buffer of unfiltered data. Clearly this is a system that sits on top of the kind of data Prism, Tempora and other information collection programmes record. XKeyscore's presentation discusses how to use this data by developing a 'strong selector' for targets that can be used to sift the data, pointing out that anomalous events should be looked for and giving examples such as someone using encryption, a language out of place for a region or 'someone searching the web for suspicious stuff' (XKeyscore 2008). In each case, the meaning of 'strong selector' is to form a view of activity that might be considered suspicious and using that to sift out anyone engaging in that activity. This is equivalent to what is called profiling in criminological and advertising research (Elmer 2004; Harcourt 2007). A more complex meaning of this will be discussed in the next section, but at this point it simply needs noting that having built an enclosure that has all the data, it is then possible to use that information to identify types of individuals by defining certain characteristics they may have and then crunching all the data, examining everyone's records, to try and find such people. Once located, the internet's combination of openness and identification means that not only can data like this be collected but once someone is identified by their location in the information sphere, often through their IP number as well as other characteristics, it will also often mean they can be found in offline life.

This massive effort – and I have only mentioned a number of the relevant programmes while there are others such as Bullrun, or the effort to build a quantum computer to help crack cryptography – is clearly funded as part of the massive securitisation that followed the 9/11 terrorist attack in New York City (Rich and Gellman 2014; Harding 2014). In response to 9/11 the US government both increased funding enormously and demonstrated an increased willingness to break or change rules it had previously lived by because the survival of the nation and its citizens was perceived to be threatened (Woodward 2003; Mayer 2009; Bamford 2009). This led to such developments as the legitimisation of torture and assassination, rendition policies, Guantanamo Bay, use of drones and so on, as well as to the suite of programmes (and the funding and will to create such programmes) exemplified by Prism, Tempora and Xkeyscore. Echelon and the four horsemen of the infocalypse remind us that instances of securitisation are not restricted to terrorism, though it seems clear that the post-9/11 securitisation programme known as the 'war on terror' has been a particularly intense period of securitisation.

In relation to the internet, and the part Prism plays alongside the orange jumpsuits of Guantanamo detainees and the Cold War of Echelon, securitisation creates a platform out of two components built directly from the nature of the internet and which flow decisively with the powers information offers through recursion, devices and network-protocols. These two components are the collection of all available information and the identification of individuals through profiling. These connections have been argued to be characteristic of some modern states, most influentially perhaps in Balkin's definition of the 'national surveillance state'. Securitisation of the internet is particularly powerful because these techniques are 'at home' in the information world.

This combination of collection and profiling to construct a securitised platform is not the only thing that the internet and digitised information are used for by nation-states, there is also espionage, censorship and viruses. However, the two components of information collection and profiling form the platform that securitises the internet; they are the ways in which nation-states grasp information power for their benefit rather than, through such things as censorship, trying to run against the flow of information power.

The Securitised Internet

The meaning of searching a set of information for 'triggers' has been analysed in a number of contexts. Elmer's examination of the personal information economy connects the collection of data and profiling to the debates around dataveillance, that is, surveillance by database, and to its commercial use as an element of communicative capitalism (Elmer 2004). Balkin's definition of the national surveillance state has been influential in arguing that total data collection and profiling are now integrated into nation-states' strategies for population control. Balkin emphasises both the overwhelming collections of data and the fact that 'Government's most important technique of control is no longer watching or threatening to watch. It is analyzing and drawing connections between data. Much public and private surveillance occurs without any knowledge that one is watched' (Balkin 2008: 12). Criminology has also picked up profiling as a key issue, particularly in relation to racial profiling. Harcourt's work offers one example that both draws together this extensive research and critically engages with the meaning of a justice system that is becoming based on correlations and probabilities used to define those most likely to conduct criminal acts whether any such acts have been carried out or not (Harcourt 2007). Since the early days of cultural and social analysis of the internet the possibilities for total surveillance have been discussed (Jordan 1999a: 201–4). The following analysis of the abstract platform that securitises the internet relies on all this, and other prior work, while taking it forward in relation to information politics to argue for two components to the fundamental functioning of internet securitisation as a platform: total information collection and profiling.

It is the combination of access to all data and the means by which the data is interrogated which form the two pillars of securitisation of the internet as a platform. By this I mean that we can identify an abstract architecture formed by the two principles of total data collection and profiling to interrogate that data which has been implemented by nation-states through securitisation in various specific programmes, such as those mentioned above like Echelon and Prism. The two pillars of universality of data and profiling, which are dependent on the openness of the internet, flow with information power, offering opportunities to recurse information, to insert various devices so that more information is constantly produced and captured, and connecting these recursions and devices through networks whose protocols are justified by securitisation strategies, the third pillar of internet securitisation.

Universality of data here means that the aim is to collect all the information being produced. It is a desire for total collection which drives the platform of securitisation. The possibility of collecting all data seems tantalisingly close, driven by the capabilities of information power. Echelon simply scooped up all satellite traffic. Prism grabs everything that major technology companies collect by simply copying it from the cables that create these companies networks. Tempora grabs all the data from undersea cables. Such extensive copying of all kinds of information including the content and the metadata is an ongoing and never-ending project, as can be seen in the transition from Echelon to the suite of Prism, Tempora and so on. Not all such implementations of information collection are successful nor are they necessarily purely focused on collection. For example, the Chinese government announced that from 2009 all computers sold in China would have the programme known as Green Dam Youth Escort installed, which would both block and automatically update lists of blocked sites, limit access to parts of the internet, and record and report each computer's use. Green Dam's installation was then downgraded to being optional and removing it or disabling it was allowed, leading to government funding of the company maintaining and producing the software drying up and the company moving close to collapse (MacKinnon 2012: 31–40; Deibert 2013: 74–5). Here is an example of a failed attempt to master the internet and a reminder that such processes are material and uncertain. Here also censorship and collection went hand in hand, yet it is collection that is able to mould information power to produce more information and correlations, whereas censorship works to limit and restrict information powers and limit recursions.

The collection of all available data is the first pillar of securitisation of the internet as a platform, built on the internet's openness and capacity for precise identification. It is this combination of an open interconnected network with a protocol that requires precise identification on pain of not being able to connect to the network that underpins the possibility of total collection. Nation-states realising this possibility and then implementing particular programmes to collect all such data creates a connection between nation-states and the core principles of information power and politics by building on the fundamental internet network-protocol. Nation-states and their security and police agencies may do many things in relation to the internet, but when they implement things like China's Great Firewall or the UK government's policy that internet service providers must automatically block lists of sites, they then struggle to hold back and restrict information. When government agencies instead identify and grab all the information they can, then they move with information power and in doing so produce a core problem of information overload. Since the analysts faced with these massive amounts of data are not going to be able to examine them directly, techniques of automation are required.

Automation is done through profiling, which means stereotypes of behaviour that are considered suspicious are put together and then automatically used as a trigger across all the available data. As established in relation both to commercial and criminal profiling, this means that everyone whose data is caught by the initial collection is then treated as if they are guilty; their records are examined, and are only released as innocent when the sifting produces no similarity to the profile being used. Elmer argues that this gives profiling a particular logic.

> I believe that a relatively simple logic is behind the need to construct a picture out of the seemingly infinite qualities of everyday life. To profile is to attempt to account for the unknown – our inability to adequately capture, contain, or regulate and govern behavior, thought, language, and action. (Elmer 2004: 134)

Elmer here draws on Bogard's work that defines this kind of profiling as 'observation before the fact' (cited in Elmer 2004: 73). Whole populations, in the case of Tempora this means pretty much all users of the internet, are treated as guilty until it is clear they fail to meet the requirements of a profile constructed to catch a terrorist, paedophile or other horseman of the infocalypse (Harcourt 2007: 173–86).

Profiling builds on recursions by taking information about behaviour, which must be made consistent enough with other taken information, to be applied to itself. This recursion seeks 'triggers' by applying data to itself to identify suspects. However, because it is built on recursions, which thrive on more information, such profiling takes as much data as possible and so ensures that all are made into suspects until they are cleared after investigation. It also means subjects are likely to be profiled again when further information emerges, often as a result of recursions deriving new information from the first examination of data. Moreover, the desire for better recursions incites a desire for more information reinforcing the ongoing desire for total collection of information.

In a context of securitisation where existential fears often drive a 'do what it takes' mentality among government agencies, information power underpins a way of incriminating everyone and creating the desire for more information so that incrimination can proceed more accurately. Preventing the next bombing or finding a paedophile ring become powerful incentives to gather data and subject it to what are expected to be ever more exacting profile searches. But by indicting everyone who is caught in the data dragnet and by seeking to be preventative, everyone is then necessarily judged by their similarity to some stereotype or summary of what a criminal is supposed to be like, prior to their having conducted a criminal action. Recursions require some consistency in information to be able to apply that information to itself; in this way everyone's information that has been collected is made comparable within the specific programmes of securitisation of the internet; we are all guilty until proven innocent.

This drive that securitisation produces also differentiates securitisation of the internet from clouds, where they might seem to have some similarities. Indeed, it is not hard to imagine securitisation as the construction of a cloud for a nation-state's security forces, but there are significant differences particularly around law and trust. The reason why securitisation has no need of magic and instead, as noted already, is a platform of relentless materiality is that it has no need to create or maintain trust. Securitisation means already being within the nation-state's security apparatus and assuming that the activities undertaken are trustworthy. It is in this light that we can understand how objections to surveillance can be met, sincerely, with the claim that 'what is the problem if you are doing nothing wrong?' This also explains the lack of legal concern in the foregoing, as when the issue of trust is considered resolved a priori by the official status of those conducting securitisation, the legal framework bends to securitisation when it is successfully implemented. For example, even when the UK government's legal justification for surveillance was thrown into doubt by a European court of justice ruling, the response was immediately to pass new legislation (the so-called DRIP legislation), supported by all three main political parties, to re-implement surveillance (Travis 2014). As Agamben notes, in a state of exception legality may be contradicted from within, such that the US government both signs international conventions on human rights while also suspending them in Guantanamo Bay (Agamben 2005: 87).

Where trust is not an issue no magic is needed; only the materiality of pursuing total surveillance and profiling is required. Legal systems are then freed from the requirement to trust the state, as the state assumes this trust because it makes the law, and legal requirements follow the successful securitisation of the internet and are contested where the securitisation is itself contested. This also explains the bafflement within security agencies about why the citizens they believe they are protecting object to their surveillance practices; by assuming trust the material work of securitisation is how the process appears within security agencies. Finally, mistrust of governments and securitisation, the cynicism of so many who felt 'we knew they were doing this anyway', appears here as the flip side of an assumption of trust. No one outside of security-cleared employees, except for a limited number of elected officials, is told about or enrolled into or given a chance to approve or disapprove of the way the internet is securitised, and when this securitisation, particularly the sensational extent of it revealed by Snowden, is revealed the platform may be mistrusted but is largely immune because it runs not on popular approval but on a successful securitisation.

Neither does anything in this identification of this information platform suggest that these methods may or may not be successful. A terrorist plot in the making may be found through such methods and, at the same time, these methods also ensure everyone with data in the system is guilty until proven innocent, a guilt that does not relate to things they have done but to their similarity with some conception of a person who takes criminal actions. Given the drive to collect more and more data and subject it to profiling, the population of the guilty is swiftly becoming co-extensive with everyone.

Conclusion

The platform that results from the nation-state's securitisation of the internet has three components. Just as with clouds this is an abstract architecture that is implemented in specific programmes with variable success. Further, it is a platform of information power that defines particular relations of recursion (applying information about populations to itself), devices (embedding automated collection and profiling machines), and network-protocols (defining the means of information connection). The three components of this platform are profiling, collection of data and securitisation.

Profiling defines populations as guilty and embeds prediction through stereotypes. Analysing sets of data looking for 'strong selectors' allows targets to be identified who can be followed, whether they have committed a crime or not. As the then UK Foreign Secretary William Hague said when responding to some of Snowden's leaks: 'If you are a law-abiding citizen of this country going about your business and your personal life, you have nothing to fear' (cited in Baraniuk 2013); nothing to fear even though you will be identified by profiling is what is meant here. There is no freedom from being profiled and what being 'law abiding' means here is not being identified by whatever characteristics it has been decided make a trigger to identify a criminal, terrorist, paedophile and so on.

Collection of data drives toward totality. Nation-states, we now know, will drive for this data in whatever way they can; voluntary agreements to share data will be sought with companies; data will simply be taken whether users, companies or any other agency realises this is occurring; automated data collection will be inserted into the devices people use; attempts to restrict access to data will be attacked and broken and so on. The common denominator here is the drive to collect more information that is linked to making recursions. This information is then added to an enclosure that states both attempt to hide and allow only their agencies to access.

Finally, all this coalesces into an information platform, with this architecture of recursion, devices and network-protocols, under the dramatic impetus of securitisation. This is truly the mastering of the internet and of digital cultures in which the collection and profiling of digital information is driven by fears for the existential survival of populations. There seems no doubt that the post-9/11 war on terror provided a huge impetus to funding for securitisation, but it is also clear that such processes have been applied to the internet and digitised information from the time they became popular. The meme of the four horsemen of the infocalypse indexes the ongoing use of securitisation by nation-state agencies to construct platforms of identification and control that flow with information.

Securitisation, collection and profiling constitute the nation-state's platform that takes advantage of information power. The platform for securitising the internet is not the only action taken in relation to the internet by nation-states, but it is the abstract architecture of what they can do when they wish to flow with and take advantage of information power. This is the platform that seeks to 'master the internet' for nation-states.

6

Social Media Networks

Introduction

Social media has become an integral platform not just of twenty-first-century information life but, for billions, of life itself. There are generic sites for networked sociality that cover nearly all human activities, such as Facebook, Renren or Google+. There are also more specialist sites that have a particular focus within social activities, such as LinkedIn for work and career or A Small World for travel and elitism. There are also elements of social media embedded in many online sites and services, for example with comments pages that now sometimes become gatherings of their own on YouTube channels. Social media or social media networks are a key component of virtual life, having provided a new form for what for a long time were called 'virtual communities' (Papacharissi 2009; Baym 2010: 72–91). Social media networks also have aspects that are similar to both clouds, in their articulation of an enclosure, and securitisation, in their surveillance and profiling of users. The third example of an abstract architecture understood in terms of information power, following clouds and securitisation, will accordingly also allow the portability of elements of such architectures to be seen.

Social media networks continue and also change the mediation of community through online socio-technologies. Here we return to some of the issues already aired surrounding the exploitation of collective information resources through control of the enclosure in which these resources occur. The picture can now be developed and significantly complicated by examining the architecture of recursion, devices and network-protocols that characterise such communities in the twenty-first century. In doing so, it will be important to see this architecture not only as something that a massively popular implementation such as Facebook or Renren has altered and reformed, but also as a platform that was forming before and carries on after particular implementations: finding and adding a friend may exist on Facebook, but it also existed on Friendster, exists on Myspace and Snapchat, and no doubt will exist on yet to be launched networks (boyd 2006).

As will be clear from the previous chapters, identifying abstract information architectures made out of recursions, devices and network-protocols is the process of identifying platforms of information power. In relation to social media networks there are two intersecting processes which form their information dynamic in, first, the rise of networked privacy and publics and, second, the use of devices to enclose social relations. In the former, a particular dynamic of being private and public in relation to definitions of individuality and collectivity define the kinds of communities and social relations that social media networks produce. These kinds of relations are channelled through devices that then produce enclosures that ensure that the social relations at stake can only be conducted within each enclosure. Here network-protocols and devices intersect decisively to form the walled gardens of internet sociality. In this chapter, these two dynamics will be outlined and examined in turn. Following analysis of these two linked dynamics it will be possible to identify the exploitations of communal relations that social media networks are prone to, as well as the ways in which communities might control their enclosures rather than relying on their privatisation.

Public-Private or Networked Publics and Networked Privates

The issue of privacy in social media networks is a useful way of opening up the capabilities that attract users to these networks. Privacy is always a division of public and private; neither term makes sense without the other. I will argue that the key attraction to users of social media networks is the intersection of two different ways of creating public-private divisions. One way of dividing public and private is based on the idea of the individual as owner of their identity; the other is based on networked forms of the public that then offer understandings of privacy. It is these underlying ways of dividing public and private that found all the different actions users take on social media networks, such as posting, liking, friending and so on. These two dynamics will be examined in turn, beginning with Rainie and Wellman's understanding of the individual, connection and privacy in social media networks:

One potent imperative of social networking is for actively sharing information and creations. People cannot build networks without describing who they are, what talents or skills they posses, what they know, and what their needs are. There are also some pressures toward deliberate, considered disclosure in social media when people cannot fall back on close, long-term friends who perpetually stand ready to help them.

Besides the imperative to share, there is a push to be connected. People cannot easily ask for help from their networks without using digital tools and they cannot be available to help others if they are off the grid. The social requirement of the age of networked individuals is to be connected and findable. It is a precondition to successful networking and network building. It is also a reality that is anathema to privacy and solitude. (Rainie and Wellman 2012: 289–90)

Rainie and Wellman see a 'triple revolution' made up of social media, the personalised internet and mobile connectivity which results in an era of what they call 'networked individualism'. They see a new society as having emerged that shifts from smaller, more densely knit groups such as families or small locality based communities to more diverse and overlapping groups in which individuals have 'more room to manoeuvre and more capacity to act on their own' (Rainie and Wellman 2012: 9). This is an environment, they argue, with more possibilities for individual freedom but which requires greater effort on the part of individuals to set up and maintain networks.

Networked individualism is an understanding of social media, in relation to the internet and mobile media, that retains the human individual as the locus of networking. This individual uses all kinds of technological affordances to create and maintain looser but also more extended and more complex webs of social interaction. Rainie and Wellman are not proposing a naive, solipsistic individualism; they fully recognise that as much as people think they act alone they are always already part of social groups and are influenced by such groups (Rainie and Wellman 2012: 38–9). However, while the conception of the individual they reject is of someone who is not influenced at all by others, the conception of the individual they keep is that of someone who is knowingly part of social connections and who acts from their own motives. Within this idea of the individual they conceive of privacy along the lines of it being something that the individual holds which is or should be shown only to those to whom the individual chooses to show it (Rainie and Wellman 2012: 238–43).

This is, at root, a similar concept of privacy to that which Neill argues underpins many divisions of public and private that require 'a particular stance regarding human moral personhood, notably with respect to whether and for what reasons it requires or does not require the protection for and control over its innermost "sacred" self' (Neill 2001: 5). Within networked individualism there remains a conception of the individual as a subject with an 'inner' core that is theirs to own and dispose of, which Rainie and Wellman note is subject to the demand to connect, to be visible and to be transparent (Neill 2001). That core of a person is something that may be inconsistent, changeable and negotiated, it may be part of a decentred subject, but it is still the complex inner core of a subject. Privacy in this conception is not the presumption of a self-consistent inner identity but of a complex inner identity that yet still remains each individual's to dispose of.

The division of public and private that is at stake here remains essentially the same as that generally accepted in the West for some time because, though networked, the individual remains a citizen of modernity with inner being that is theirs to distribute. Such conceptions have been explored widely, for example in Foucault's analysis of the basis for a desiring subject, that conceives of desire as a kind of inner truth, and of governmentality theory, that traced the creation and management in the West of a private self (Foucault 1985: 26–31; Rose 1999: 217–32; Neill 2001). What we have in networked individualism is a conception of the self as holding information about the inner self that is a twenty-first-century and information version of a longer process that Rose identifies.

> The self is not merely enabled to choose, but obliged to construe a life in terms of its choices, its powers, and its values. Individuals are expected to construe the course of their life as the outcome of such choices, and to account for their lives in terms of the reasons for those choices. (Rose 1999: 231)

Given such a conception of the self, networking may become a challenge to privacy and be seen as a necessary diminution of privacy in favour of the public. A related view, based on the same conception of the self, is to understand networking as a bargain with the devil, where one's inner self is displayed to others in return for access to services that connect individuals. In either case, the underlying understanding of privacy is that of individuals with an 'inner' essence, access to which defines the division of public and private. However, boyd derives a different, perhaps inverted, view of changes in public and private brought about by social media networks, by focusing first on the public:

> Networked publics are publics that are restructured by networked technologies. As such, they are simultaneously (1) the space constructed through networked technologies and (2) the imagined collective that emerges as a result of the intersection of people, technology and practice. (boyd 2011: 39)

By starting with networked publics boyd immediately brings into play not just individuals but technologies, cultures and practices. This focus on the possibilities for practices that technologies create, such as profiles, friends lists, liking and so on, and on the collectives that are produced in and through such practices, has significant effects on private-public divides, which she lists as one of three central dynamics of network publics (with the other two being invisible audiences and collapsed contexts) (boyd 2011: 49). By starting with publics and paying attention to potential actors other than individuals, here generally meaning technologies, boyd begins to push beyond issues of individual control of inner meanings by noting how social media networks 'alter practices that are meant for broad visibility and they complicate – and often make public – interactions that were never intended to be truly public' (boyd 2011: 52). Here boyd seems to be pointing to something that is beyond a public-private divide because she points to practices that may be seen under some definitions of public and private as being simultaneously public and private and intended to be both.

From this point, boyd both takes forward a sense of something different about the public-private divide and slips back to something more like an inverted version of Rainie and Wellman's inter-relation of individual and network. She argues that her point is about control and by focusing on a networked public she is not subscribing to the fear of the end of individual's privacy some have claimed social media lead to, which she calls a naive stance. Instead she argues that: 'I believe that we need to examine people's strategies for negotiating control in the face of structural conditions that complicate privacy and rethink our binary conceptions of public and private' (boyd 2011: 52). This asserts both that privacy in the sense of inner property remains, underpinning boyd's concept of control, and that a new version of public-private division is underway, which however needs to be understood in part in relation to how individuals will regain control of their inner property to determine their public-private boundaries. She asserts both the individual who has inner property and that social media may have led to public-private divides in networks which no longer derive from versions of privacy and publicness that previously existed.

It will always be tempting to locate individuals as the nodes in networks, and often useful when doing empirical work to do so (Barabási 2011: 1). It might therefore be tempting to try to reconcile boyd and Rainie and Wellman's approaches as two sides of the same coin by converting the networked individuals of Rainie and Wellman into nodes of the networked publics of boyd and, vice versa, connecting the networked publics to the actions of networked individuals. It is not that either of these two ways is being held up as being fundamentally incorrect, rather that their different approaches to seemingly similar phenomena suggest bringing them together. If boyd's work is taken further, it is possible to see how what might be interpreted as two different versions of dividing public and private suggested in her work reflect a more complex and paradoxical situation which suggests the possibility of the co-existence of two different kinds of public-private divides.

> The public/private distinction, in short, is not unitary, but protean. It comprises, not a single paired opposition, but a complex family of them, neither mutually reducible nor wholly unrelated. These different usages do not simply point to different phenomena; often they rest on different underlying images of the social world, are driven by different concerns, generate different problematics, and raise very different issues. (Weintraub 1997: 2)

Following Weintraub, I think it is important to examine the intersection of different dynamics for creating distinctions between public and private in social media and it is the simultaneous management of two divisions that define one side of the flows of information power in social media networks. One division of public and private is that already discussed based on a conception of the individual having an inner self that is in some sense theirs, implying it is the individual's right to determine what to do with their inner property. The second division is one boyd begins to articulate in which a network makes demands of what is placed on it, meaning that the network as a community of some sort has some kind of right to define where public and private divide.

The first of these dynamics sees a shifting and contested relationship between a privatised individual, conceived of as having an 'inner' core which is their property to dispose of and a public that is not simply a collection of such individuals but also involves the right of the collective to ask of its individuals (citizens) certain things. The public-private divide then involves a struggle over what it is right for the private to keep private and so any collective demands have to be justified against the pre-existing right of the individual over their inner self. As already noted when discussing Neill, Foucault and Rose's views, this is both a Western and a modernist conception of the self and privacy.

Here the right to the property of one's self is understood to be the dividing line in what should or should not be public or private. Privacy may be violated or respected but the central dynamic remains one of examining the extent to which the individual remains the author of what they reveal of their inner self. The key here is not how such dividing lines are created but the underlying presumption that there are inner selves, elements of which are inalienably an individual's. It would be a mistake to see this kind of understanding of privacy and identity as being eliminated by social media networks. A quick review of the privacy settings on Facebook (or indeed any social media network) will show up examples of privacy understood in this way. In early 2014, a whole category of Facebook privacy settings were grouped by Facebook under the heading 'Choose Who You Share With', and here is Facebook's answer to the question 'What does "Public" Mean?', remembering this is in the context of defining what audiences a Facebook user may show themselves to:

> If you're comfortable making something you share open to anyone, you can choose Public from the audience selector before you post. Something that is Public can be seen by people who are not your friends, people off of Facebook, and people who view content through different media (new and old alike) such as print, broadcast (television, etc.) and other sites on the Internet. When you comment on other people's Public posts, your comment is Public as well. (Facebook 2014)

Clearly, the understanding of public and private here is that the public is created from whatever the individual makes available from their store of inner being. The user of Facebook is the author of their public-private divide based on their ability to deliver up elements of their identity – photos, friends, likes, comments, and so on – to the publics Facebook suggests the user can choose. Yet, many do not experience privacy on social media networks as something entirely under their control. Again, Facebook is a useful example, as despite the control it suggests it offers for the private over the public, there is deep suspicion about the way Facebook changes privacy settings. For example, in 2013 a change in privacy settings was widely interpreted as ensuring that those with Facebook accounts could no longer hide themselves by making their names unsearchable (Constine 2013). There are other examples of a sense of Facebook, and other social media networks, fostering not individual user control but demanding connections that reflect a public. This is not so much a change within the public-private divide understood as a dynamic driven by individuals with inalienable inner property, but suggests a different dynamic altogether. We glimpsed this dynamic in boyd's sense of control being at stake, and can see it in the following interpretation of what Facebook does not offer:

> The social network could surely offer an option to lock down all your personal information the same way it does for your old posts, but it doesn't. It could offer a way to opt out of appearing in any type of search results, not just searches for your name, but it doesn't. It wants your friends to be able to find you. It wants Graph Search to be a comprehensive utility. It wants to foster the connection your friendship and News Feed posts generate, which also keep it in business. But it's protecting its access to these things by sacrificing your right to choose just how much your identity is indexed. (Constine 2013)

In the next section on enclosures it will become clear why creating such connections against the individual's right to control the revelation of their inner being is good for business on Facebook, but at this point it is important to see that there is also something here of a different relationship of public to private that contradicts the conceptualisation of privacy so far discussed. This division has fermented in information environments because the utility of recursions makes the removal of information something that diminishes the environment and any new connections between information will enhance an information environment. Here what we might begin to think of as the rights of the network to connect begin to assert a different meaning for a private-public dynamic.

How does one come into existence in a social media network? By being seen and read by a network of others. One cannot achieve existence on a social media network unless one is read. If an individual self has a complex private being that they own and parts of which they either reveal or are forced to reveal, then this places the self in the position of author, of having something that they produce to be read by others. However, this presupposes that a being exists prior to it being read. The construction of privacy based on private inner being asserts in this way a priority of author over reader and implicitly always focuses on the modality or nature of existence through private-public boundaries rather than examining how the individual with inner being comes into existence in the first place. But social media networks produce a different existence, one which does not pre-exist being read and in which authors can only come into being after their readers. This different sense of where existence and being lie then produces a different dynamic through which public and private are negotiated. On the internet you are read before you (can) write.

Consider joining a social media network. An individual exists already to be able to join and so joins taking forward a sense of what it is that they will open up to others on that social media network. The social network presents itself and is experienced as a series of practices through which the pre-existent self offers itself up, through posts, likes, comments and more. But the social network also operates differently, for if someone receives or makes no links then it is as if they have not joined the network at all and in this sense opening an account is not the same thing as joining a social media network. The network is only joined when readers start to pick up this new self that has appeared and that self only becomes solidified and part of the network if it is increasingly read and embedded in networks. That self will also only maintain itself and have its own characteristics if it can continue to be read and be associated with its own characteristic kinds of posts – photographs of sunsets are typical of one friend, while posting on which games they have played may be of another. We can see this in the phenomenon of people logging into someone else's social media network and posting in ways that they would not normally post, usually leading others to guess that it is a brother, friend, mother or someone who is not the normal identity posting. The marker of identity, the 'handle' or name a user has chosen to go under, will be trumped in these cases – as with spam emails that spoof email addresses – through a recognition that this is not this identity's 'style'; the audience will disbelieve the author is the author if an author cannot be read in their usual style. This phenomenon of coming into existence by being heard is one I analysed in relation to communication and the internet and it recurs here within social media (Jordan 2013a).

This understanding of how an individual who opens a social media network account then comes into existence can be applied to private-public dynamics to argue for both public and private being understood as produced in ways that do not rely on assuming there is a property to a private self that may be revealed. Instead, networked privacy relies on the ways in which networked publics demand participation for an identity to become a node in a social media network. What can be kept private can then be understood as that which does not appear on a social network when this lack is derived from the context of what is public. Here the inversion reveals that what is private becomes the negative of what is public; it may be that someone forms groups in a network and only shares some information with different groups and so can only make private what is made public to others. Where the private property of the self makes the public into something that contests the private, here in networked public and network privacy we see that the public is always present with the private only arising from within an already existing public.

We can see this in the example of Snapchat. This social media network might be thought of as a 'single issue' network as it does not, like Facebook, Renren or Google+, seek to provide multiple practices but relies on the one practice of taking a picture, allowing writing on the picture and then sending it to a network of other users who are only allowed to see the picture for 1–10 seconds. To exist on Snapchat one must produce something public by posting whatever picture one chooses, one must share something and in doing so produce identity by being seen. Once shared what lingers is not the photograph, which usually fades away, but the fact of connection and the style conveyed by the connection. A networked public has to exist for a user on Snapchat to exist as only then can they create public displays of identity through whichever connections a user receives and sends photos to. Someone's identity as a user of Snapchat can only come into existence through this sharing and in this identity their privacy is only created in the photos that are chosen for some and not for others. Networked privacy only comes by refusing to include a part of the networked public.

The networked public feeds on more connections. The more connections, the pieces of information that may connect up, then the more complex and substantial the networked public becomes. This is how information power drives a networked public and networked private divide, because the more connections the more recursions may be driven which create more connections. The practices of each social media network are themselves then embodied in devices, whether it is the concatenation of hardware, software and networking that allows photos to be transferred through Snapchat and then deleted or the ways in which 'liking' or 'friending' are embedded in particular social media networks (boyd 2006; Papacharissi 2009). Devices here channel and solidify practices within social media networks, managing the information in recursive processes and integrating the return of recursed information. We can see network-protocols at work setting up the boundaries not only of who can be on and who is off, but also in the more fine-grained network-protocols that allow networks to be made within each particular social media, such as in Google+'s technique of groups.

This new form of public-private divide does not supplant or remove the dynamic of dividing public and private based on the individual's inner self, instead utilisation of social media networks brings both dynamics for dividing public and private into play. Users must then navigate simultaneously two different ways for creating and managing their public and private divides. This connection is something Papacharissi recognises:

> Networked and remixed sociabilities emerge and are practiced in multiplied places and audiences, that do not necessarily collapse one's sense of place, but afford a sense of place reflexively. A sense of place is formed in response to the particular sense of self, or in response to the identity performance constructed upon that place. This presents the modus operandi for the networked self, and the context of newer patterns of sociability and routes to sociality that emerge. (Papacharissi 2011: 317)

Uneasily coincident here are the self as someone who comes to the network – in terms of private and public this is likely to be someone who comes with their identity as property – and the performances the identity puts on, which are required to exist on the network and so require publicness (Baym and boyd 2012). This will always be an uneasy relation because the two dynamics will tend to contradict each other and position each user and identity in a different kind of public-private divide. There will also, accordingly, always be evidence for those who like to see social media networks as introducing a complete change in privacy, in which case the networked public and its demands come to the fore, or anyone who wishes to defend privacy as a right of the individual based on their inner self, in which case the private self as property comes to the fore. It is, however, the intersection of these two dynamics for creating public-private divides that connects social media networks to information power by defining in part its abstract platform. To create an instantiation of a social media network, an actually existing network, means creating a way of users and individuals being engaged by and engaging with two ways of dividing public and private.

However, this is only part of the story. These public and private divides are what are most attractive to users and individuals. In these dynamics we find all the practices that seem to obviously make up social media networks such as photo sharing, liking, friends lists, circles, pokes, likes and de-friending. But earlier all this activity was also located in relation to the business of Facebook and its tendency to remove, as its history suggests it often has, the opportunities for its users to preserve the property of their inner self in favour of the creation of publics through connections. Facebook, having at January 2014 a market value of around $125 billion and 1.2 billion users, is a pre-eminent example of a social media network that creates riches both social and monetary. There are also many other social media with a similar issue of how to turn their users and the value of their social interaction into income. Here is the other side that defines the abstract platform of the social media network in enclosures within which these two kinds of public-private divides are created and intersect. Social media network practices revolve around creating, maintaining and re-ordering two different kinds of public and private divides, but these divides have to happen somewhere and here we find the enclosure that also opens up monetisation.

Devices and Enclosures

Issues of private and public underpin what seems obvious and primary in social media networks through the creation of identity and sociality in concert with digital and internet technologies. Much research on social media networks focuses on these significant changes, for example in much of the work of boyd (2011), Papacharissi (2011), Baym (2010) and others. However, social media networks as platforms involve a second set of issues that is indexed when Papacharissi discusses the different architectures that networks have or when boyd discusses the technological affordances of different social media networks (Papacharissi 2009; boyd 2011). This perspective opens up the issue of social media networks as platforms created by architectures and technologies that is most powerfully examined in the second main area of debate around social media networks found in the analysis of the way some social media draw financial profit from the opportunities they provide for online sociality. Here we find the abstract architecture of the social media network platform draws on the cloud platform; indeed it may even be understood as a specific form of the cloud platform, in which enclosing the dynamics of public and private create possibilities for the 'monetisation' of our identities and social relations.

Clouds offer the potential for a form of exploitation based on enclosure and mining of the data that is produced within the cloud. This is secured through various legal mechanisms, such as 'terms of service' and so on, and is obscured through the symbolic association with the cloud and the obfuscation of the materiality of the cloud, as previously explored. Social media networks take advantage of these aspects of clouds but articulate them into a particular architecture that focuses on identity and sociality resulting from the interaction of the two dynamics of dividing public and private. This revolves around the meaning of a platform that commodifies both the inner self and relations between selves. Stark argues that in what he calls 'hyperentrepreneurial' capitalism any practice can be the object of profit extraction and that, in line with capitalism's nature, ever more practices from which profit can be extracted will be pursued. For Stark the anti-hierarchies and networks of information societies assist these processes by unbounding creativity to propagate more practices that can be subject to profit taking (Stark 2009: 206). In this context, social media networks have a ready home.

As hyperentrepreneurial capitalism looks for new spaces to mobilize the creative energies of 'members', social networking represents an effort to capitalize not only user content but the users' personal contacts as well. Commercial social networking is an expression of the centuries-long dynamic of capitalism: the ever-greater socialization of production combined with the privatization of profits. Social networking sites then become sites of contention over this latest effort at commodification and the intensification of the search for value. (Stark 2009: 209)

In short, our intimate inter-relations are finally directly subject to capitalist processes that rely on social practices to produce private profit. Stark, in common with other authors, points to the importance of free labour in these information contexts as the socialisation of production, as can be seen in all the time put into social media practices like friending, liking and so on, and in the production of ourselves, our friends, our family and our society (Stark 2009: 209–10; Terranova 2004: 73–97). Dean has a similar reading of the reach of commodity value into our inner being:

> Communicative capitalism seizes, privatizes, and attempts to monetize the social substance. It doesn't depend on the commodity-thing. It directly exploits the social relation at the heart of value. Social relations don't have to take the fantastic form of the commodity to generate value for capitalism. Via networked, personalized communication and information technologies, capitalism has found a more straightforward way to appropriate value. (Dean 2012: 129)

Like Stark, Dean locates a particular relation between capitalist profit taking and social media networks in which the most intimate of our social relations are turned into commodity values that the owners of a specific platform can sell (Dean 2012: 119–55; Fuchs 2014: 169–70). Such analyses surely grasp a core dynamic in social media networks in that the use-value to the user of the network is their sociality and many controllers of social media networks attempt to turn that use-value into an exchange-value. Identifying each instance of a particular practice as a moment of commodification makes it clear that each photo or comment posted, each like and each friend request denied or accepted, is a moment in which social media networks may seek to transform a voluntary action that has the use of building sociality into a moment of exchange value beneficial to the controller of the platform. Here we find that a particular conception of information as property is embedded. In return for the services offered by a social media network, the user exchanges their information, and because of this the benefits of recursing become the property of the network controller. In this conception, information becomes a property that is transferred between users and networks even though information is able to be used fully by both. This particular way of conceiving of information as property will be returned to when summarising information exploitation, but for now the relevant issue is that this property relation can be embedded in social media networks.

It is also clear that to be able to create such a moment of commodification of the self, as part of an industry of likes and tweets and a socio-economy of public and private, many of the dynamics of the cloud must be in place to ensure that each social media network is able to recurse its data by creating an enclosure for the information created within it. Network-protocols create the absolute situation of being on or not on a particular social media, and the various devices that implement and oversee these network-protocols manage both the absolute of presence or not and the various forms of connection that are possible once presence in a social media is created. Once the network-protocols define access and devices codify this into a series of practices, then an enclosure is created which the controller of the platform can begin to draw information from and recurse. All this is cloud dynamics focused on creating an architecture that offers users multiple dynamics for dividing public and private of inner property and of networked community. Recursion also suggests a nuance in the versions given by analysts such as Dean and Stark, in which the social substance and personal identity is commodified.

Recursion is a second-stage process. By this I mean that it cannot operate on single instances of information but needs several bits of information to begin to feed on itself and it must take the information entered and ensure that it is consistent so that it can be applied to itself. It also means that the more data is available the more recursions are possible, so that the dynamics may become exponential. However, this means that there is a need to distinguish in social media networks between a user creating an account and entering their data, which they must do to fully come into existence in the sense of being able to be read by networked publics, and recursions coming into play creating whatever connections are made to be siphoned off, read by the databases and massaged by the algorithms to offer up that extra which only the owner of the architecture can access. My like of a page is of no consequence in terms of commodification unless my like can be correlated to other likes, and my like's value to commodification increases the more it can be correlated. In the direct commodification of social relations this aspect of recursion locates the issue, as it is relations between users not an individual user's information that allow recursion. Elmer has already defined this dynamic in relation to profiling, and his logic holds for social media networks if we interpret 'feedback' to be the same as practices in social media:

feedback does not simply inform the production of commodities, offering objective input on desired products for individual consumers. Rather, feedback techniques are often used to cluster like-minded consumers together so that their aggregate purchases – and hence psychogeographics – can be cross-referenced with production, distribution, and sales data. (Elmer 2004: 71)

Each instantiation of the platform architecture of social media, each 'really existing' social media network, is then also a form of rent in which users exchange access to practices, which give them a form of identity and sociality, for the controller of the architecture's ability to treat these social practices as free labour. In his analysis of search, Pasquinelli identifies this as rent, claiming that it is a different kind of relation to exploitation than exploitation understood as the extraction of a surplus. His claims also hold in relation to social media networks because enclosure is employed to ensure recursion, as outlined above. 'Rent is the other side of the commons – it was once cast over the common land, today over the network commons' (Pasquinelli 2008: 93). Social media networks are free to use but not free in consequence. Users rent their social relations and identity to access spaces in which their social relations are then commodified. This rental creates a space for the recursions which gift up information that is only available to the owner of the architecture. However, where Pasquinelli argues that this rent is a profit source in relation to search, the arguments here suggest that the role of rent in social media is as part of an environment in which the user can experience practices as entertainment and sociality while the owner of the platform can simultaneously and without notice or contradiction treat exactly the same practices as free labour. With this transition in place, the platform can transform our sociality into a value form, as Stark and Dean argue.

Unlike in the counselling or therapy industries, the inner psyche of the individual is not the source of value for social media networks, it is the raw stuff that is required for social media value but only generates value when psyches are connected and sociality is creamed off the top. In this moment, voluntary contributions that appear to each user as entertainment, emotional connection and personal creativity become free labour that is siphoned away unseen to be sold on to marketers or returned in voluble and vulgar form as advertising. Again, the idea of information as an exclusive kind of property is implicit here. Information must be conceived of as something a user can give in return for access to services, creating the right of the platform to then take and use that information as it sees fit. This conceptualisation of information as exclusive property is, as will be discussed in the final chapter, contrary to some of information's potential and has to be imposed through the various legalities embedded in devices and network-protocols. Rent is created through network-protocols that define access and that ensure the simultaneity of practices that in each action create the possibility of both emotional solidarity and sociality for users and of free labour that creates value for owners of a specific existing architecture.

It is key to note at this point that there is no necessity to privatise these recursions, taking them from the enclosure to be kept only by those who own the architecture. Recursions do not happen automatically, they must be implemented and formed in the architecture. Moreover, I will later argue this is a key point of exploitation, since information has a quite different potential in its ability to be held and used fully by many simultaneously rather than exclusively by one owner. There is then nothing that requires the recursing of practices conducted in a social media network; they could disappear into the information winds. Similarly, there is nothing preventing an architecture making recursions and then offering them to the users whose inter-relations create their possibility. My individual 'like' may be of little value in itself but joined with everyone else's likes it takes on a new value – a value that need not be privatised but could be collectivised. This is a point that will be returned to in the following section on battlegrounds of information politics, because here is one key, recurrent aspect of information politics that defines a potential for liberation and mutual benefit on information platforms. This concept of recursion providing collective benefits does not, however, change the fact that a social media network requires an enclosure of some sort through network-protocols, and that enclosures make exploitation possible through the sociality of users being turned into free labour. The products of that labour could be returned to the users but it remains the case that this transition must be implemented for the social media network to create itself with recursions that fuel it.

An example of such a different approach is the social media network Diaspora, which refuses unified ownership by distributing ownership of the network to all those who use it. The system operates by allowing anyone to set up a local 'pod' that can host a portion of the Diaspora network, also allowing the administrator to control access. The idea is to offer a network that refuses profit taking or commodification of social relations while still delivering the dual public/private distinctions that make a social media network. Fuchs argues that this at least partly creates a socialist version of a social media network (Fuchs 2014: 173–4). However, this does not mean that the process of recursion and of turning sociality into free labour does not occur on Diaspora, only that the benefits of such things are radically distributed to its users. For example, a pod administrator could use the log files to explore recursive relations to ensure that the pod, and its connections to other pods, function properly. There may be no advertising on Diaspora but analysis of interactions may still be needed to help with the labour of maintaining the network.

The abstract architecture of the social media network platform involves network-protocols that define the boundaries and rights of connection and disconnection that are created and managed by devices which implement access through device-defined practices to two dynamics of dividing public and private. This abstract architecture does not require that this channelling of information into an enclosure be mined for profit, but it creates that possibility.

Conclusion: Private, Public, Profit

The abstract architecture of social media network platforms consists of two intertwined dynamics. First, social media networks are marked out as social by their creation of a space in which two dynamics of public and private inter-mix, and, second, they are marked by their enclosures that produce recursions from all the practices of sociality and identity that are contained within them. It is only the connection of these two practices that makes social media networks what they have become. Putting these two together also joins the two main bodies of research on social media networks, in the analyses offered by those like boyd and Papacharissi on the nature of identity, sociality and architectures, and those like Stark, Dean and Fuchs on the socio-economic meaning of social media networks.

This abstract platform may be made into really existing social media networks in different ways. Facebook is not the same as Snapchat, Twitter, Renren or other such networks, however all of these implement some ways in which a duality of public/private divisions can be negotiated while at the same time enclosing those relations in ways that allow the sociality of users to become labour for the platform controllers. There are other implementations than seeking to profit from this enclosure; it is not profit seeking that is required for a social media network to exist but an enclosure that turns sociality into free labour for that particular social media network. What is done with that free labour is another issue, and one that identifies a point at which the politics of information will be articulated.

Three different platforms have now been analysed. All operate at a level of abstract generality that defines the possibilities that specific forms of each platform may create: iCloud, Tempora and Facebook are each a specific materialisation of the architecture of, respectively, clouds, securitisation and social media networks. Other platforms exist and may be created in the future. The point here has not been to offer a comprehensive analysis but to examine and apply the theory of information power that links the dynamics of recursion, devices and network-protocols. And in each platform we can see a distinct connection of these three that forms a platform. The enclosures of the cloud foreground devices and network-protocols because the enclosure within which recursions may take place has to first be created by devices that implement certain network-protocols. Securitisation, by contrast, pursues widespread ways of making recursions available to nation-state interests, and in the pursuit of total access to data that can be profiled a whole range of devices and network-protocols have been developed which do not have the goal of creating one enclosure that the subject-citizens of each nation-state have to enter but which automatically grab information about subject-citizens no matter where that information is. We are not required to log in to the surveillance state as we are required to log in to clouds and social media networks, because the securitisation platform does not call on us to use it but follows us whether we know it or not. Social media networks embed both the enclosure-like nature of clouds and the examination of information about its users familiar from securitisation; with these connected a particular kind of sociality can be created at the heart of which is a complex relationship between different ways of dividing public from private and living those divisions.

No doubt further analysis of platforms like search, big data or multiplayer online games would add more nuances. But the point is made that the three dynamics of information politics may be articulated in different ways and in doing so flows of information may be directed toward different ends and interests. Exploitations in surveillance and in turning social life into labour for profit have already been identified. In addition, the complexity of recursion as a second-order process has arisen, raising questions about who should control information if a cloud or a state recurses the information users provide. However, the general question of exploitation and of liberation in the information era is not answered by these examples of platforms, even if we have identified specific instances of exploitation. Before returning to the general theory of information as a political antagonism, it is important to pursue information politics one step further from the abstractions by turning to specific case studies. Even more so than platforms, these can only be partial and cannot empirically identify all moments of information political struggle, but they are also essential in seeing information politics in concrete action and in making sure that connections between different forms of struggle are explored: in theory, in platforms and next in the battlegrounds of information politics.

Part 3
Battlegrounds

7

Battlegrounds and the iPad

Introduction to Battlegrounds

Where does the political antagonism of information play out? Where can all these different dynamics and platforms be seen in their complexity and messiness? To see the political antagonism in action I will present case studies that offer individual and specific answers to such questions. These are the 'battlegrounds' of information. These are the places where conflicts occur and the political stakes of information address our lives directly in our moments of subjection and struggles for liberation. The three case studies will be of the iPad, the moment an avatar 'dies' in online games, and hacktivism. This will bring the argument closer to politics as experienced in the immediate and the everyday, and ensure that there will be points where the mess of the universe we have to meet halfway offers its own commentary on the theory so far proposed.

A second reason to consider battlegrounds is that the political antagonism of information will be shown to be inextricably embedded in other antagonisms and vice versa. It will not be possible to examine the iPad without also examining changes in working practices, the super-exploitation of global labour, gendered divisions in work, and environmental degradation. It is not possible to examine each antagonism of class, gender, environment and others with the same level of detail as that given to information, but there is also no need to do so given that each is already analysed by existing powerful literatures and is struggled over by multiple practices. These are connections made within particular contexts that will vary between those contexts; it may be that gender is key in one battleground with class also involved, while another battleground will foreground environmental struggles and their connection to information struggles. The nature of such connections is also the last theoretical issue that needs definition to complete this theory of information as a political antagonism. As connections between antagonisms is the theoretical issue closest to the mess of action and practice it will be reflected on after the case studies are explored and in the final chapter.

Forces and touches are information politics at their most abstract; here the dynamics and bodies were argued to be recursion, devices and network-protocols. Platforms are plans for the use of such dynamics that then take particular material forms in which information politics is configured; clouds, securitisation and social media networks were examined as examples of platforms. Battlegrounds are particular moments and concrete struggles in which information and other politics play out. Though information politics will obviously be a focus for discussion and the examples in the following case studies have been chosen partly because they are relevant to a politics of information, it will also be clear in each case how the dynamics of information power relate to other dynamics of exploitation and liberation.

The iPad

In January 2010 Steve Jobs – whose very looks, it has been suggested, offer a combination of seduction and cruelty that mirror his management style – stood on stage presenting the iPad as something in-between a mobile phone (iPhone, of course) and a laptop (Powerbook) that would, he claimed, create a whole new category of devices (Dormehl 2013: 100–1; Isaacson 2011: 526). This category, usually called tablet computers, had of course been 'invented' some time before, but the iPad would finally establish tablets as a widely used device and its product launch was (by some measures) the most successful ever (Kahney 2013: 237). The iPad was and is also a battleground over which flow clashes in many political antagonisms, and the harnessing of some of these – particularly environmental, class and information exploitations – underpin its massive success and contributed to Apple Corporation's enormous wealth.

At launch the iPad had caused some confusion over what it would be used for, but this very quickly changed in the face of huge sales and lavish praise for its intuitive interface based on a touchscreen that filled the tablet's face with as small edges as possible and did away with a pen or an inbuilt keyboard. The iPad has undoubtedly been successful both as a product – the then Apple CEO Tim Cook stated that 170 million iPads had been sold between the launch in April 2010 and October 2013 (Hughes 2013) – and in redefining the 'tablet computer' to make it a legitimate category of information device when at the time of its launch the idea of a tablet was widely perceived to be floundering (Arthur 2012: 222–5). Apple did not, then, invent the tablet, nor did the iPad appear out of nowhere within Apple, given the way it built on iPhone and iPod design. Tracing briefly the design history of the iPad will open up some of the intersecting forces criss-crossing it.

When considering the history of tablets most note the similarity between them and the 'Dynabook' hypothesised in 1972 by Alan Kay, who was then researching technology at Xerox Parc. Kay had designed a flatscreen hand-held computer with a keyboard attached at the bottom which was meant for use by children (Dormehl 2013: 443; Kahney 2013: 231; Manovich 2013: 53–106). Jobs was aware of the Dynabook though it is also clear that he and many others were widely aware of the idea of tablets, and that Kay thought of his own idea as being much more closely tied to education and different to the iPad, making this a case where Apple's innovations were neither stolen by them nor from them (Gruener 2010). As a number of tablets became available around the mid 2000s they were widely perceived to be underpowered, slow compared to laptops, and to have awkward interfaces requiring a stylus pen and various kinds of keyboards usually attached to screens. Initially Jobs, at least publicly, derided tablets, offering a common view about input methods combined with an ironic dismissal:

'You could never keep up with your e-mail if you had to write it all out. If you do e-mail of any volume you've gotta have a keyboard. We looked at the [Microsoft] tablet and we think it's gonna fail', he said in April 2003. It might work as a reading device, he allowed: 'If you've got a bunch of rich guys who can afford their third computer; they've got a desktop; they've got a portable; now they're going to have one of these to read with – that's your market. And people accuse *us* of niche marketing.' (Jobs cited in Arthur 2012: 224)

In fact, even as Jobs derided tablets Apple had started work on one, legend has it partly incited by a Microsoft employee badgering Jobs at dinner about the benefits of tablets and annoying him into a response within Apple that called for a tablet that did not use a keyboard or stylus. Simultaneously, breakthroughs in technology that allowed greater touch interactivity were coming from work on touchpads on Apple's MacBook. These changes produced a touch-sensitive screen that allowed movement and multi-touch (Isaacson 2011: 467–8; Arthur 2012: 224–5). However in 2004 issues with the screen and battery continued to make the tablet seem bulky and unwieldy (Kahney 2013: 233). At the same time, the innovations in touch were recognised as solving some of the issues with the then developing iPhone and iPod Touch, whose development had come after the internal call for an Apple tablet but which then took precedence over it.

This introduces two infrastructures within Apple that came to underpin the iPad with the iPhone and the iTunes/iPod infrastructure. Some commented that the iPad was a scaled up iPhone and jokes were made at the iPad launch about the 'giants' the new iPhone would be useful for. There is some truth in this as the operating system was a scaled-up iPod Touch and iPhone system. In addition, the implementation of an accelerometer and a gyroscope in the iPhone – which, among other things, allows the user to tilt the screen and have it follow their orientation – were developed for the iPhone and then implemented in the iPad (Dormehl 2013: 445–6). Similarly, the development of the iTunes software, the app store and cloud infrastructure behind it were originally built to provide a paid-for music service to go with the iPod – bringing Apple not only revenue from selling music but also from selling the devices to listen to it – but were also relevant to iPad design (Levy 2006; Dormehl 2013: 431–5; Isaacson 2011: 396–7; Arthur 2012: 96–107). However, pulling such existing design and technological infrastructures together involved further development, for example in the conductive and strong glass needed for a screen the size of a tablet, a problem that was eventually solved with Gorilla Glass. And the elegance of the design, including such attention to detail as the famous 'sloping' of the back of the iPad to make it inviting to pick up, also required new production techniques in use of the Unibody manufacturing process – in which aluminium is milled down to the required size and shape unlike in earlier systems of moulding plastics or building up metals – which had originally been developed for Apple laptops (Kahney 2013: 236–7, 240–50; Isaacson 2011: 470–2).

Encompassing these existing infrastructures and techniques is a third factor that characterises Apple as an information power: the belief in building the 'whole widget'. Apple developed a design ethic that involved giving users what they wanted, whether the user knew they had that desire yet or not, in the sense that Apple often designed what it thought were the right products and then released them. Apple also developed the related principle of closing devices off so that they could not be altered or tinkered with; after all, if Apple knew what you wanted and were the best designers to deliver your desire, then there was no reason to alter your Apple device. This was not always the case – the Lisa computer was built to be repairable for example – but from the time the Macintosh was built in a way that ensured it could not be opened by its owners, through to the iPod/iPhone/iPad era of Apple, the design philosophy was primarily about controlling all aspects of the product being sold and excluding hobbyists or alterations other than the trivial (covers, for example) (Dormehl 2013: 168). Each new device builds the Apple enclosure and constantly nudges the user toward greater connectivity with Apple as, famously, Apple products work best with other Apple products. Even Bill Gates admitted that the 'vertical integrated model' of Apple had proven a success (Isaacson 2011: 554).

All these sources, infrastructures and design choices involve information dynamics. For example, the thinness required and the desire for design simplicity contributed to such choices as the lack of a USB connection in the iPad that forced reliance on WiFi connections through iTunes or iCloud or reliance on proprietary cables, reflecting Apple's commitment to an integrated design model that integrates users into Apple (Dormehl 2013: 444). The power of such an information product to produce further information and to integrate this into wider information connections seems clear. The iPad is a device that will help to wall users into the Apple garden and siphon off the extra information that can be gained by following what iPad users do in the garden, including tracking their apps, choices and so on. With a closed app market, quality control and censorship is conducted by Apple itself, as illustrated by Jobs' suggestion that the iPad was part of a revolution for freedom when, in an email to a critic, he claimed that Apple offered 'freedom from programs that steal your private data. Freedom from programs that trash your battery. Freedom from porn' (Tate 2010). Within this garden Apple will not only have the power to censor but also the power to draw profit from information flows through its 'magical' devices.

But all these words starting with 'i' take us a bit too far into the internal features of Apple. So far this case study has followed the design process of an astoundingly popular commodity that clearly draws on a number of information platforms, such as clouds; but the iPad also comes with other political connections that are opened up by the design process. For example, to produce the information environment that creates the possibility of recursions within Apple's walled garden, all those design choices have to be manufactured into products, and this generates, at least, two other political dynamics for the iPad: environmental and labour dynamics.

Toward the end of his initial presentation of the iPad, Jobs finished extolling the device and its various features, calling the iPad a 'great citizen' and touting its credentials as a 'green' device. He noted that the device was arsenic free, brominated flame retardant free, mercury free, and a PVC-free system whose case and screen were highly recyclable (iPad 2010). By the time of the launch of the iPad, Apple as a company had tried to establish its pro-environment credentials, after having previously been attacked by Greenpeace for a poor environmental record, particularly in its use of toxic chemicals and a lack of thought about recycling. Both problems were not uncommon among fast-growing information technology firms but both were also acute for Apple because of, on the one hand, its desire to build closed devices which can make recycling difficult and, on the other, its self-presentation as a radical company drawing on strong roots in the 1960s counterculture, putting it on the side of the empowerment of individuals. This makes the exploitation of the environment a particular issue for Apple, as was reflected in Jobs' characteristically strong rejection of criticism combined with an internal rethink that led Apple to launch a recycling programme and to reduce some of the most harmful chemicals it used, such as those touted as absent from the iPad (Kahney 2013: 248). The environment is a central and global political antagonism in the twenty-first century, one that is reflected in major environmental movements as well as faltering attempts by governments and corporations to deal with the degradation and the long-term future of the environment. While there is not the space here to lay out this antagonism in full, it can be seen that the issues of information politics intersect strongly with those of environmental politics through the iPad (Doyle 2005; Dobson 2007).

It is clear that Apple made efforts to 'green' the company, whether, as is often claimed, because of a recognition of the ethical importance of doing so or (and these are not mutually exclusive) because of critical campaigns such as 'Green My Apple' (AppleInsider 2006; Kahney 2013: 248–50). A range of initiatives, including reporting by Apple on its own green performance, shifted Apple's relationship to at least a public commitment on the part of the company to becoming greener. While the fact of some change seems undisputed, there remain questions about Apple's participation in the exploitation of the environment for company goals. In particular, its culture of secrecy creates a lack of transparency. For example, while Jobs and others at Apple have argued that the Unibody manufacturing process is highly favourable to recycling, they provide no information about what components of the iPad, because of the desire for lighter and thinner tablets, are glued in or attached in ways that make it impossible to separate them out and recycle them. Apple, in common with many other companies pursuing the miniaturisation of technology, rely on various rare earths for magnets and other components, and the extraction of these and their recycling cause significant environmental problems (Anon 2012).

Despite the lack of clarity from Apple about these and similar issues, the effort the company has made – for example, in the claim that MacBooks have become fully recyclable (Kahney 2013: 248) – suggests that it has engaged with environmental exploitation in ways that acknowledge and attempt to lessen its exploitation of the environment. However, this also to an extent misses a larger and, for the environment, troubling picture that results from the iPad's popularisation of the category of tablet computers. In the final quarter of 2012, the number of tablets shipped surpassed both laptop and desktop computers, with both of the latter beginning to show what looks like a slight decline. However, even with a small decline, when combined, the total number of tablets, laptops and desktops sold remains far greater, with the figure for desktops at around 35 million units, laptops at around 45 million, and tablets reaching 50 million then falling back to 35 million per quarter (Meeker and Wiu 2013: slide 45). The long-term future is uncertain, but at the end of 2012 it appeared that the small decline in laptop and desktop sales combined with a massive increase in numbers of tablets resulted in an extraordinary rise in the use of the environment to produce information technology. This implies a concomitant increase in the use of the environment to produce the power for such devices and to absorb them back when their life ends. Jobs' comment that a tablet would only be of interest to a 'rich guy' who could afford a third device now seems ironic, as tablets appear to be mainly additional to other computers for many people (and this is without counting smartphones as another recent and popular computer device). This wider context means there is a strong link between longer term environmental degradation and the rise of tablets (Williams 2011). The success of the iPad necessitates environmental exploitation.

Such radically increased environmental risk links closely to class issues, because someone, somewhere has to make all these tablet devices and while this lies at the core of environmental issues it also opens up connections to labour exploitation. There are three main connections to labour-capital disputes here; first through those who manufacture the iPad, such as the Foxconn corporation operating in China; second, through those who work within Apple in ways conceptualised by Neff as 'venture labour'; and, third, through the role the iPad plays in more general shifts in wider social divisions like those of work and leisure and home and factory in what can be called a new paradigm of design and work that is 'after the desktop'. The manufacture of so many iPads in such a short space of time, and often in addition to other devices, should focus attention not only on the environment but also on the factories that make them.

> We produced the first generation iPad. We were busy throughout a 6-month period and had to work on Sundays. We only had a rest day every 13 days. And there was no overtime premium for weekends. Working for 12 hours a day really made me exhausted. (Foxconn worker cited in SACOM 2010: 7)

Foxconn Technology Group made the majority of iPads, as well as manufacturing other Apple products and products from other companies such as Dell. In globalised capitalism the production process, as the most labour intensive part of a commodity's cycle from conception to consumption, is often moved to places that offer cheap and easily controlled labour. This is often thought to be a process particularly focused on the rise of information technologies as a product and the rise of China as a place of production (Qiu 2012: 177). Apple fully participates in this side of globalisation by sending the iPad to Foxconn, a Taiwanese company running large factories in China. These factories manufacture iPads in facilities of up to half a million workers that are characterised by low wages, long working hours, lack of worker organisation (at one point the head of Foxconn's publicity department was 'elected' head of the trade union), exposure to chemicals and stultifying repetitive work. Workers are often migrants from inner rural China who overwhelmingly live in dormitories provided by the company (Qiu 2012, 2011, 2009; SACOM 2010, 2011, 2012; Kahney 2013: 209).

Conditions and the super-exploitation of workers in Foxconn gained greater exposure with the suicide of 17 workers between January and August 2010, resulting in 13 deaths and four badly injured workers. Research into the exploitative working conditions revealed a factory so depressing that it had to have suicide nets installed to prevent its workers from jumping from its buildings (Qiu 2012; SACOM 2010, 2011, 2012).

Here the forces of global capitalism in relation to the rise of fast-growing information technology industries become focused on the bodies of the workers who manufacture the devices. This is exemplified by such details as the daily quota of a worker being to put 5,800 tiny screws into 2,900 Mac Superdrives (Qiu 2012: 175). Or we might consider the ability of Foxconn to suddenly recruit and layoff large numbers of workers. In March 2008, 100,000 of 500,000 workers were laid off, in December 2008 a further 10,000 were sacked, but with iPhone sales accelerating in March 2009 30,000 were recruited 'overnight' (Qiu 2012: 182). Finally, and as Qiu poignantly points out, the bodies of workers are centre stage in the enormous power and irony of the number of fingertips that are lost in Foxconn factories manufacturing the devices, like iPads, that are built to be used by fingertips because Jobs and his design team hated a stylus that could get lost, after all, they reasoned, you cannot lose your finger (unless you are making the device in the first place) (Qiu 2012: 173).

Qiu develops this picture by noting that the attraction of China for such work is not just because of low wages but rather comes from the emergence of what he calls a new networked working class that consists of super-exploited labour of the kind making iPads but also includes other kinds of labour.

> From the assembly line to call centers, from 'SMS authors' to gray-collar software testers, network labor is crucial to the ascent of Chinese informationalism. Responding to demands in the highly volatile global ICT market for a huge variety of products that need to be upgraded constantly and economically ... Chinese network enterprises ... have created a full range of programmable labor: workers who collaborate with self-programable and generic labor to become the foundation of China's new working class ... it is labor advantage based on the provision of an extraordinarily wide variety of blue-collar, gray-collar, and low-rank white collar employees. These workers take up millions of jobs that are programmed and simplified; skilled, semiskilled, or unskilled; in a highly stratified structure of working conditions that is indispensable to the Chinese model. (Qiu 2009: 236–7)

And these workers are indispensable to the massive sales of devices like the iPad which so many point to as success stories of information economies. This generation of a new kind of working class in China connects the information politics of recursion and network-protocols that exist within devices such as the iPad to the restructuring of class relations that has progressed at the same time as the rise to mass use of such devices. The massive profits generated by a company like Apple or Foxconn, and more widely China's rapid industrial and information development, are built on the exploited labour of workers who are driven at times to suicide by intense working conditions, militaristic management styles, underpayment and withheld payment for pensions and health checks, unsafe and unhealthy working environments and a closed system of dormitories ensuring social control. Such intensification of labour exploitation finds multiple routes. For example, Foxconn has entered into relationships with schools to provide mandatory 'internships' which require students to 'study' by working in Foxconn factories for little pay and with little if any relevance to the subjects students are studying (SACOM 2012). These are combined with a particular way of creating what Qiu calls the 'networked working class' based both on the state-sanctioned opening up of Chinese labour and on the inter-relation of different kinds of low-waged labour (Qiu 2012: 178).

Environmental exploitation and labour exploitation criss-cross in the factories that make the iPad, often safely out of view of those who see Apple as an inheritor of unconventional countercultural ethics. It is, however, not only about the labour to create the physical device in the manufacturing process but also involves the kind of labour that has become familiar in and characteristic of many creative industries and which, particularly in the Silicon Valley that is home to Apple, valorises the intense work of technology startups that Neff terms 'venture labour' (Neff 2012). This should not be understood as a kind of labour only available in startups or small independent projects but is a kind of labour that large corporations have attempted to inculcate, often with cultural markers like free high-caffeinated drinks or 'fun' working environments (Google has offices with a slide to move between floors, Microsoft's Redmond software factory is laid out like a University campus and is called a campus) (Jordan 2008: 112–7). Here is an account of the creation of the Apple Macintosh, often considered a revolutionary personal computer design with a graphic-user interface, mouse and so on, that was developed by a small team within the then already established Apple Corporation. This project was emblematic of the kind of labour often relied on, or at least seen as highly desirable, within technology companies and more widely in creative industries:

What really turned the Mac team on was the addition of a Defender arcade machine – which they would now no longer have to trek across the road to Cicero's pizza to play … If cocaine is God's way of telling you that you have too much money, then an atypically low score on Defender was His way of saying that your brain, your body, or both, were in the process of meltdown … Even then many of the team kept working. As far as Jobs was concerned, people would have the chance to go on vacation, have children, or raise families later on in life. But the Macintosh would ship only once. (Dormehl 2012: 212)

This kind of commitment, even to a project within an existing and wealthy large company that had the resources to fund a project fully, can lead to a kind of super-self-exploitation that often takes on the messianic tone of promising to 'change the world'. This phenomenon has been widely noted, from praising it as a new kind of work ethic and business strategy (Himanen 2001) to attacking it as the new form of voluntary labour from which capitalist businesses seek profit (Terranova 2004). This kind of labour is in a strange position in being paid but demanding such long hours from staff that the remuneration when calculated in terms of hourly pay may be quite small, and may not include the possibility of the 'lottery win' pay off of share options in a successful company. Such labour in creative industries has been a focus of discussion around issues of immaterial labour and uncertain working conditions, often based on projects that carry no long-term health or pension benefits and which disband on failure or completion leaving project workers unemployed while seeking the next job (Gill and Pratt 2008; Hardt and Negri 2000: 290–4; Hesmondhalgh 2007: 189–206; Banks 2007).

In her study of 'venture labour' in the context of information technology, Neff argues, based on following such information technology focused work in Silicon Alley in New York, that workers in these industries juggle two kinds of value: cultural and monetary. She notes how workers in her research were fully conscious of the risks they were taking in working long hours on projects that may fail or from which they may not see personal financial reward commensurate with the time and expertise they put in. But the meshing of cultural factors, like Apple's constant claims to have changed the world for the better, itself built on a connections to 1960s countercultures (Turner 2006), and the potential for monetary compensation, varying from a project surviving and keeping a worker going with a wage to the windfall of massive wealth, are managed by workers into an ethic in which they are willing to take the risk of undertaking this labour (Neff 2012: 153–6).

The collaborative joy of working with others on a project that may change the world, combined with the knowledge that riches may follow, is linked and managed through cultural capital and a conscious choice to take risks, but it also results, Neff argues, in a transfer of risk from businesses to workers (Neff 2012: 156). It may be remembered that when Apple 'floated' and became a public company, around 400 individuals were instantly made millionaires, though it is not as often remembered that only 40 of them were employees. Many other stories of similar wealth hang over the calculations made by venture labourers, not just the riches made by the billionaire poster boys like Jobs, or Brin and Page at Google, or Williams at Blogger and then Twitter but by those few who put the work into the startup that created a successful corporation (Defree 2013). This model of venture labour reflects a reversal of risk from capitalist enterprises to workers who venture their time and expertise, and it may be implemented beyond information technology companies and beyond startups through a 'project in a company' strategy. The cultures of these workers are built on projects that involve working with others like themselves and may be cloaked in high-minded ambitions that give them great urgency, behind which the glow of treasure chests may be glimpsed. As Neff shows, this is not a kind of false consciousness about their situation but a conscious and thought-through choice that weighs the risk of ending up with nothing against the benefit of gaining great wealth and of having a major cultural effect, while also accompanied by the perceived benefit of working in a team of like-minded experts, as opposed to the risk of being an 'office drone' (Neff 2012: 160–2).

Venture labour stood in for venture capital – both in the real sense of resources needed to build companies and in terms of seemingly being an accessible option for wealth accumulation of middle-class knowledge workers. This plays into the political right's rhetoric of the 'ownership society' that employs the middle-class dream of profiting from ownership. Whether from one's labour or one's home, the false dream of the ownership society promises that generating profits in a capitalist society is as easy as cashing a paycheck or paying the mortgage. (Neff 2012: 162)

Venture labour in Apple is the second of three dimensions of class politics in relation to the iPad; it addresses both many of the employees within Apple and those who look to it as one of the emblematic companies that should be emulated (Jobs at one point tutored Page and Brin about how to run Google) (Isaacson 2011: 511–2). If Foxconn workers risk their long-term health, their sanity and their lives, then the iPad's venture labourers risk their impoverishment through self-exploitation because that may result in either failure or success (as *Sir* Jony Ives might attest). The iPad also participates in a third dimension of change that engages class exploitations and contributes to shifts in gender politics. This can be summarised as being 'after the desktop', which may be understood along two linked dimensions. The first dimension is of changes in workplace practices that break down previously existing divisions between home and work and labour and leisure. The second dimension concerns the changes in the ways we interact with our information technology devices, with the 'desktop' metaphor of virtual files and folders on our computers changing to apps, clouds and mobility.

Near the centre of Melbourne, Australia, there is a monument with 888 at its top, celebrating and remembering the mid-nineteenth-century achievement of legislation based on the principle of eight hours work, eight hours sleep and eight hours play. This not only articulated a restriction on the number of hours workers could be required to work but also relied on a divide between work and 'other' spaces such as home, entertainment, sport and so on. The latter is collapsing for many workers in the twenty-first century, particularly immaterial labourers, whose engagement with information technology means their phones, tablets and home computers all connect their work and other spaces in ways previously hard to achieve (Hardt and Negri 2000: 290–4; Boltanski and Chiapello 2005: 245–51; Harvey 2010: 91–5). The iPad is one element of this breakdown, in particular with its creation of extra mobility combined with increased work capacity resulting from its larger screen over smaller smartphone screens. This mobility lines up with many other changes that lead to a wider change in labour to which the iPad contributes an information component. Flexibility in working hours for some workers also contributes to changes in gender roles in families supported by mobile information devices that are crucial in tethering the worker to their work while allowing them some freedom from the physical office. While often a white collar or information labour strategy, Qiu has seen similar issues of tethering emerging among the working class, with penalties in factories for workers who are not able to be reached remotely by their superiors (Qiu 2009: 186–91).

The iPad as a device adds information power to redrawn labour and gender relations in which the boundaries of home, work, leisure and entertainment have become highly permeable with many enticed into a constant connection to work, whether emailing on the weekend or checking updates while on holiday, in exchange for some flexibility in workplace and set working hours. The problem for many tethered to an iPad with a slogan like 'eight hours work, eight hours play, eight hours sleep' is that these divisions no longer clearly operate. Aspects of this change are sometimes called the 'social factory' where the focus is on the production of value, which may occur for some workers well beyond the physical confines of their office or factory, meaning such work relations have begun to permeate and structure all social life (Gill and Pratt 2008; Fuchs 2014: 117–8). While undoubtedly providing some insight, the change being referred to here in relation to the iPad is also importantly a gender change, reflecting ways in which women have been integrated into work while at the same time having to deal with patriarchal familial relations that seem to change all too slowly.

The iPad is a device in-itself and the populariser of a whole category of devices, tablets, that add information power to this restructuring of work and life. This is reflected not just in the iPad's use in relation to mobility and the workplace but also in relation to its dependence on various clouds and its participation in a more direct information shift in relation to interfaces. A number of the specific information shifts found here relate to the second dimension of being 'after the desktop', and two in particular are relevant to the iPad.

First, there is the sense that a computer world that once consisted of desktop and laptop computers tethered to wires and wireless points, sitting on desks and each individually loaded with various programmes, is moving to a world in which devices are lighter, multifarious and are connected to applications, such as word processors or spreadsheets, via the cloud. The difference can be represented as that between loading Microsoft Word onto a hard drive or accessing Googledocs over the internet. New devices appear that rely on cloud software, while the rapid spread of smartphones and tablets introduces many to this world. The rise of apps also fragments the World Wide Web with individuals no longer navigating across one information space via a browser but logging into and out of smaller, focused spaces each dedicated to one particular activity. The desktop is no longer the place where computing takes place, as mobility and variable devices spread the possibilities for information power to other physical spaces (Goggin 2010; Elliot and Urry 2010).

Second, the rise of apps also reflects the shift from a particular metaphor that dominated the organisation of the information space within computer interfaces. The organisation of access to files based on the metaphor of a writing desk, at which the computer user is imagined to be sitting, creates images that allow the user to control underlying computer processes through file systems, metaphors of 'opening' and so on. This is a complex area, involving arguments over how influential this metaphor really was and how different new app, touch and mobile based interfaces really are. For present purposes the key issue is not so much to define the 'before and after' of interface metaphors but to note there are two competing kinds of interfaces. There remains a keyboard and mouse based input system that is often connected to a metaphor of files and 'places', and there is a touch input and apps based system, usually present in smartphones and tablets, representing a different way of managing information flows that the iPad has been an important contributor to creating (Manovich 2013). Being 'after the desktop' sees this newer interface connected to the breakdown of distinctions between work, home and leisure.

With this return to the nature of information devices in the discussion of interfaces this case study moves from the criss-crossing battleground of the iPad to a focus on information power. I have by no means given a complete history or analysis of the iPad but the study has exemplified some of the connections that information as a political antagonism and form of exploitation has to other such antagonisms and exploitations.

No matter how 'immaterial' the iPhone culture seems to be, its material dimension is always indispensable, depending, first of all, on the physical labor of Foxconn workers. Labor is also integral to the research and development of the iPhone, the production, testing, and installation of its software, and even the consumption of the fingertip economy. Labor is not a thing. It is a perspective. (Qiu 2012: 186)

The perspectives of environment, labour and information power intersect across the iPad. My account has been generated by starting from information politics and then finding connections to other political antagonisms, but a different analysis could use similar material to start from another antagonism and then find the information politics that say class or the environment connect most strongly to. For example, starting from class politics could be done based on Qiu's connection of Foxconn to the rise of China's networked working class and could then extend to which products Foxconn was making leading to issues of information devices. This would point to a number of companies, including Apple, and from here consideration of the kind of devices and which elements of information politics are important to understanding the class basis of their production would be possible. This might be thought of as going in almost the reverse direction to the analysis conducted here, which sought out connections to other politics starting from the information aspects of the iPad's design and capabilities. However, the difference between them is not an inversion of the same but really marks different objects of analysis because they are framed by their political antagonism differently, even when dealing with very similar phenomena. My analysis can easily start from the information nature of the iPad because it is framed by the information politics of recursion, devices and network-protocols, whereas the briefly imagined class analysis even at this preliminary stage would be immediately focused on labour-capital relations which then result in seeing information connections where relevant. Neither analysis is more or less valid because each is a way of understanding a different kind of exploitation and liberation.

In addition, to create a more detailed case study, other political frames would need to be taken into greater account. For example, the divisions of gender around the use of iPads and around different types of labour (both in terms of different roles on the Foxconn factory floors and different roles in the male-dominated design divisions of Apple, operating under the random aggression of a manager like Steve Jobs) would need to be brought out more than is possible here, as would more detail about shifts in gender power flowing through changes in divisions between home and work. However, without minimising the importance of other perspectives that future research and activism may explore, it can at least be claimed that a case study of the iPad must include the perspectives of information, environment and labour. The dynamics of each can be respected while seeing their inter-woven role when focused on a single technological device.

This raises the issue of how relations between different forms of power may be understood, given that each antagonism must be abstracted to understand its own dynamics but must also be inter-related to see specific moments and conflicts. Only through a kind of abstraction can we identify major forms of exploitation like that of class or information, but only by inter-relating these dynamic forms can we understand the nature of specific exploitations, such as the iPad and Foxconn or the iPad and rare earth minerals. This analytic work can only be done through a complex and perspectival approach that allows differences and even contradictions to emerge while remaining conscious of which kind of object is being analysed and what its proper referent theories in terms of their abstraction should be. The issue of relations between forms of exploitation and how they connect to information power will be returned to after taking up two more case studies that will help extend the analysis away from what has been implicitly so far a technological perspective, focused on the materialised device of information power in the iPad.

This case study emphatically 'materialises' the iPad and its forms of information exploitation. Connected to the kinds of recursions, devices and network-protocols that flow through the iPad are clearly issues of class and environmental exploitation such that contributing information to the iCloud through an iPad is at the same time a product of and a reason for both the labour exploitations of Foxconn and the environmental exploitation that has individuals running simultaneously three or four different types of computer. But only by already having an abstract analysis of information power can the specifics of information and the iPad be both identified and connected to flows of power around labour and the environment.

8

Death and Gaming

The iPad might seem an obvious subject for a case study in information power – it is an influential information technology that has a known and controversial history in relation to labour. Focusing on a particular technology might then seem an easy or obvious way to examine information power. For a second way in which an information battleground can be explored, and connections between forms of power and exploitation be found, it will be useful to start not with a specific piece of technology but with a moment in an information complex, which can then be examined in terms of its inter-section of forces. In this case study, I will look at the moment in an online game when an avatar dies. One such moment will be described and then compared across a number of games from the same genre; from these descriptions the significance of the moment will lead to an examination of its information and other flows of power, particularly in relation to gender and race.

The following moments of death all come from massive-multiplayer online games (mmpogs or mmos), the most famous of which is World of Warcraft, though there are quite a number including Star Wars Galaxy, Guild Wars, Rift and so on. To play this particular genre a gamer must be sitting at a computer (primarily in 2014 still a laptop or desktop computer but consoles are being connected) controlling an avatar represented on their computer screen as a body of some kind. Pushing buttons, typing, using the mouse and so on are conducted by an out-of-game body that leads to the in-game body doing things that are capacities the game allows and which the gamer can initiate, such as firing fireballs, using a sword and so on. This is a relationship that appears to involve the control of one body over the other – the gamer over the avatar. However, the capacities of the in-game body also discipline the out-of-game body to perform in certain ways, such as using the keys 'wasd' for movement in combination with the mouse for turning instead of turning with an arrow key, because the latter makes the avatar much slower to turn. There are then senses in which the avatar and its capacities discipline the gamer-body at the keyboard (Jordan 2013a: 84–6). In addition, these are spaces in which multiple avatars can exist at the same time and can interact, within the capacities the game gives them. Finally, avatars can be controlled by software as well as by gamers, meaning there are avatars in-game that may look similar to avatars being managed by a gamer but are instead running according to pre-set software rules. These different kinds of avatars mean that there can be play that is player versus player (pvp) or player versus the environment (pve), with environment understood as being software controlled avatars.

The first moment of death I will recount is from an older game than Warcraft called Dark Age of Camelot (DAOC). It was popular in the early 2000s but lost out when World of Warcraft (and Everquest II) was launched in late 2004 and early 2005, though Dark Age continues to be played with a small player base. The following death was experienced by an avatar controlled by myself, a troll called Krill who was running by himself in a region of the game where he could be attacked by other players. To do this, I was sitting at a computer, hands on keyboard and mouse, navigating my avatar through a gate which, once passed, I knew would make being attacked by other players possible, and then down a road, along which I knew there was a good chance any players looking for a fight might be watching. The road appeared on my screen as sunk in a valley flanked by snow covered hills. 'Krill and I' were doing this knowingly, inviting the attack to create a possible one-to-one combat, which we found when a member of an opposing army (Umilard) attacked me. It was a close battle (honest! I have pictures to prove it!), and the two characters having bashed at each other – my opponent with a trident and myself with hammer and shield and both of us using various magic spells – were both near to losing all their hit points[1] which were needed (even just one) to stay 'alive'. This is when death happened: zero hit points were reached 1 minute and 3.16 seconds into the fight, in between frame 1580 and 1581 of my film of the fight.[2]

My health bar shows the merest sliver of orange, seconds earlier I was still alive but showing no orange at all – the normal health regeneration

---

1. As in many games, my avatar's ability to 'do' things in the world is measured by my 'health' which has a number of points or 'hit points' and is represented on my screen as an orange bar that reduces as I lose hit points. See Peterson 2012 for a history of 'hit points' within games.
2. The film was taken at 30 frames per second. It was created using a screen capture programme that I trigger as soon as the fight starts leading to a full recording of the event.

had led to a small amount of hit points returning just when I might need them. My opponent's health bar is non-existent as well but he is also still standing upright. He must be down to such low health, as I was, that the graphics cannot register it, but the database in the background recording his health still awarded him at least a point. The next damage must see one of us fall; we are both far, far too hurt to take even the weakest blow and survive. That is when it happens – 1 minute and 3.16 seconds since I was first jumped by Umilard the Minstrel, Krill the Thane's hit points reach zero. Not that dying is unusual, either for Krill or for players of Dark Age, but this was so close, as close as can be.

On my screen Krill falls. In frame 1580 my avatar is standing, hammer raised to hit while holding a shield to guard myself. Sitting at my computer I view this all from the typical camera angle of just above and behind the avatar; my gamer-body at the computer is effectively looking at the back of my avatar-body on the screen and a bit over his shoulder. Then in 1581 Krill has been wrenched from my control: no matter what buttons I press nothing I do can affect my avatar and my view has shot up as if I am leaving the avatar-body behind and moving skyward. As a Thane[3] of Midgard, the realm I fight for in Dark Age, I am going to Valhalla. Frame 1583 arrives and though Krill's body is still upright, his arms have dropped with hammer and shield now down and shoulders slumped; the knees have not buckled but neither is there any strength in them conveyed by the image. From here the death is orchestrated as each frame from 1583 until 1597 holds an image of Krill as a lifeless yet upright avatar, but each second or third frame shifts the view a little higher. Not only is Krill out of my control but he is getting farther away from me, the horror of death represented as the conscious guiding spirit being removed from the body and dragged upward. Then in frame 1598 Krill's head slumps forward and he falls, dropping to the ground, unmistakeably, totally dead. In a final jerk or spasm of loss, frame 1622 drops Krill away from me much further than any previous drop and then his arms jerk out to the side in three frames moving first out and then back in until finally Krill is lying on the ground completely immobile. Gallingly, on the film I have my near-dead opponent walks past and away.

The fall of Krill happens like a cut-scene, it is an animation that is out of control of the player, and each time an avatar reaches zero hit points it will

---

3. Thane is the class Krill ascribed to and my opponent Umilard was a Minstrel. These classes define different kinds of capacities for in-game action that avatars can take.

be triggered. In real time, the fall is quick, taking seconds, and somewhat sudden and shocking. As I can do nothing, a sudden stillness falls over what had been a bare minute and a half of tension, fun and furious button pushing. What happens next? Resurrection of course. In this case, Krill and I will have lost time. I/we will be resurrected automatically once I request it from the game by typing /release, but I/we will be placed some distance away from where we fell. The only other way would be if a fellow avatar/ gamer passed by and resurrected me, in which case I would come alive again at the same spot and be ready to start again. Dying has at times had other penalties such as a reduction in the quality of my armour that I would have to use in-game currency to pay to repair, but in this case the penalty is loss of time, measured by the distance to return, a blow to pride for having failed (which is public as within the region everyone will have seen a message 'Krill killed by Umilard'), and frustration at having performed poorly. The animation is then attached to certain game functions and to a set of cultures and technologies. What happens between frame 1580 and 1581 is an information moment that can be multiplied not only with other zero hit points experiences in Dark Age but across other games with related visualisations and gameplay meanings. Looking at some of these other games and their combination of visuality and gameplay at the moment of zero hit points will help explore this moment further.

The game that came after Dark Age, at least for me and many others, was the hugely popular World of Warcraft (Chen 2012). Here zero hit points has some similarities and differences to Dark Age. Again the gamer loses control of their avatar and has to view the avatar fall to the ground to lie motionless. This time the view does not shoot up above the avatar nor does it move further away or toward the sky, with its implication of ascension. Instead, one just sits there looking at a once lively avatar that is now a crumpled pile of inert pixels, from the same perspective as when the avatar and its pixels were lively. Within seconds the gamer is offered the chance to click on a button called 'release spirit', which also notes that in a certain number of minutes the spirit will be released without the gamer's intervention. Again, if another avatar/gamer is around they might resurrect me, which is crucial if one is playing with a group and some people die and others remain alive. However, if I click on 'release spirit' I am then moved to a place nearby graphically modelled on a graveyard where I will appear before a winged angel clad in white. My avatar will still be dead and this is marked by it being transparent and all the land around having its colour removed and appearing only in white-blue shades. If I ask (that is, click on) the angel it will offer me the chance to be resurrected on the spot, with some extra penalties, and if I do so I will return to full colour and capabilities along with the landscape. However, I can now only control my avatar to move it, none of the other capabilities of combat or spell casting are available, but if I run my avatar back to where it died, I can be resurrected automatically there with lesser penalties.

After World of Warcraft, I followed my group of friends to a game called Rift. There death came in what may begin to feel a similar way. Zero hit points leads to loss of control of the character allied to graphics in which the avatar drops to the ground, with death also marked by the colours all turning black and white. Like in Warcraft, a button appears asking whether I want to 'respawn' and if I am not resurrected by another player and I click this button then my avatar will be ported to a graveyard nearby and come alive automatically with no choice to run back. Penalties here are as little as the time it takes to get back to wherever it was the avatar had gotten to and spending some in-game currency to repair my damaged soul.

Finally, I also began playing an older game, NeverWinter Nights, first released in 2002, that some friends had resurrected by restarting a multiplayer world that they had some years ago lovingly designed. Here the graphics were less advanced than in Rift or Warcraft but gameplay was interesting in a player-created world. Here death follows a similar visual and gameplay script: when the bar of hit points is empty, my avatar falls suddenly onto his back, makes one feeble attempt to rise and then lies in a pile of inert pixels. A menu appears offering the following choices: to wait for a resurrection, log out of the game or to 'respawn'; if I choose the latter my character will appear at whichever point I had 'bound' his soul (there are only certain places this can be done). But I will also have been given a penalty reducing the experience points I have gained which can undo some of the time I have spent destroying other avatars to gain points (this kind of penalty also exists in Dark Age of Camelot pve but not in its pvp). These forms of experience lead to a character gaining greater powers as they move through the 'levels' that define each avatar (at the time of writing these were: Dark Age of Camelot 50, Warcraft 90, Rift 60, NeverWinter Nights 40). Losing experience points can make progression slower, meaning this is a greater penalty than that of the extra time needed to return to where death happened, and often leading to different playing strategies.

The moment of death across these four cognate games, all massive multiplayer with level progression, sociality and combat against both human and software controlled avatars, has common characteristics related to visuals and to gameplay. In relation to the visual, all present a view of the fallen avatar and some reference to another world that the avatar passes through before coming 'alive' again. NeverWinter Nights had the least reference to this other world, simply a loading screen with a picture on it relevant to wherever the avatar was to be resurrected. Dark Age and Warcraft had more extensive visualisations, with Dark Age's 'ascension' and Warcraft's use of both an angel and a complete change in visual tone. In terms of gameplay, these visuals are closely linked to the loss of control of the character, which can only be fixed by being resurrected by another player at the place where one died or being moved to a respawn point somewhere else. The penalties for death ranged from the minimal in small amounts of lost time and pride through some in-game currency cost to a loss of experience.[4] These two aspects of visuality and gameplay need to be joined together to see the information content of the moment between frame 1580 and 1581.

The terms 'dead' and 'alive' have been used above and they are nearly universally adopted to describe the moment when an avatar reaches zero hit points, but a key point in information terms here is that the issue is not really about death or life but about resurrection. Zero hit points, or death, is simply the trigger for various visual and gameplay moments that lead through resurrection to life again, and it is the nature of the resurrection that defines the meaning of life and death in this information moment.

The visual dramatises the moment of reaching zero points but there is no information carried by the animation once it has been seen once, as it is exactly the same each time; it is only the context of the visualisation of death and resurrection that carries a difference. To understand this it will help to introduce the technical background to nearly all these games – which may have somewhat different implementations but nearly all share the following basic characteristics. The animations are generally stored on the local computer, my desktop for example, and are triggered by my button pushing or commands relayed from a central server that is 'serving' out the current game state of each avatar to all the computers that are connected and, in terms of visuality, those that have avatars close enough

---

4. Gamers may use these characteristics in unexpected ways, for example dying may be the quickest way to get from one place to another, and particularly if the penalty is minimal and mainly consists of the time needed to return from the respawn point to the place of death. If one wishes to move to a place near to the respawn point it becomes logical to seek out a quick loss of hit points and use that as an instant port.

to each other to be seen. Thus a hammer blow, a shield smash, the casting of a firebolt or falling to the ground are animations that are called from each local installation of the game and in visual terms alone they carry no information – there is no difference since the animation is the same each time. What they reflect is that the databases and software protocols in the central servers keep track of such things as the number of hit points or the effectiveness of a particular action and then issue the relevant command. The visual is then something of a screen, an often engaging and dramatic one, for what are essentially moments in databases that track gameplay and ensure the right visualisation is triggered.

The gameplay, however, seems to produce key differences, e.g. Krill died and Umilard ran away, which are information and which enter through devices into further recursive relationships in which information is channelled and built. Recursions here are reflected to the game company that often reviews and changes gameplay to further engage players or correct difficulties. A game-breaking problem such as one class of avatar being overly strong will be recursed to the game owners and designers as they find the numbers of that class increasing and can see from their correlations the damage this is doing to a sense of equal gaming. So-called 'fotm' (flavour of the month) classes are common in games, when a type of play is perceived by players to be much more powerful than other types and so gamers rush to adopt it. Such recursions within the information flows of an mmpog will be reflected by information generated in forums and other ways of creating feedback to game designers, but it is the recursions that will tell the internal story and they are not available to players.

Resurrection is then an information moment from which recursions may be harnessed and which is supported by the devices (keyboards, monitors, hard drives, locally installed software, internet connection) and the network-protocols (log in required to the game, internal protocols defining who can see and talk to whom, internet protocols for passing data from local computers to central servers) that define each mmpog. Krill falling to the ground falls in information power.

Reflecting on resurrection as being key in this moment we can begin to explore the information power engaged by players and harnessed by game owners, who try to create a game that will compel more people to play and to pay, and connect it to other forms of power. Why is resurrection a key and recurrent moment in games? In theory, hit points do not have to be about life and death, nor do bodies have to fall so dramatically and be confronted with angels, the afterlife and resurrection. They could be teleported away or be frozen but untouchable for a set time. A common frustration in gaming is losing control of an avatar who is normally moved by the gamer, because it removes any sense of being 'in the game', in a sense it removes the reason for being a gamer in the first place. Being frozen would therefore be a 'loss' just as much as falling to the ground. Similarly, if the penalty for zero hit points is effectively being removed from the scene and the time needed to return then a simple teleport could work.

The answer might be thought to lie in 'playability', or the things that engross or engage a gamer, by offering ways of identifying with the avatar on the screen. Such ideas draw on the history of role-playing games. With the 'dungeons and dragons' history of the kinds of games that I am examining, there is clearly a sense in which the gamer, embodied in their chair with fingers hovering over keyboard and mouse, is enticed to identify with the avatar on the screen and to enter into the role of whoever they are playing (Peterson 2012; Ewalt 2013). For me, Krill was a fighter for the realm Midgard which was at war with Albion (Umilard was from Albion) and Hibernia. This was a made-up history and lore that explained to players why they are the avatars they are and why they take the actions they do (like trying to kill each other). Even this, however, though part of the answer, is questionable because players so often focus on game mechanics and not their putative role and its relevance to the lore and history of their realm. A quick look at any mmpog will find the numbers of players in role-playing environments is far outstripped by those who are not in such environments (Peterson 2012: Chapter 5; Chen 2012: 24–7; MacCullum-Stewart and Parsler 2008; Miller 2006).

A different kind of answer lies in what is called the masculine bias in such games in the ways they are structured ostensibly around combat and death. This focus on combat (which is entirely true of all the games examined so far), it is argued, produces a certain hegemonic gender bias in computer games. This immediately hits a major issue in gaming studies.

Video games are not the first medium to capitalize on the riveting power of violence ... Digital games did not merely continue inherited traditions of violent entertainment but drove them to new levels of technologically enhanced intensity. (Kline et al. 2003: 248)

Kline et al. identify three circuits of interactivity needed to analyse digital games, with one such circuit devoted to culture in which the key structure is the relationship between violence and variety in games (Kline et al. 2003: 246–68). Neither are they alone in identifying this embedding of violence, combat and death into games as a core dynamic of a masculinised and often misogynist culture (Cassell and Jenkins 1998; Kafai et al. 2008). This discussion should be distinguished from the 'effects' debate around digital games and violence, which addresses whether or not games have effects that may cause violence outside of games. The effects debate is also a considerable and difficult debate, but not the one under discussion here in relation to violence and zero hit points which addresses the kinds of actions taken within games.

Here the kind of information power that flows through the recursions, devices and network-protocols that create an mmpog platform and games like World of Warcraft (12 million subscribers at its peak) connects to wider issues of gender imbalance and the association of violence with a particular militarised masculinity. Mimicking some wider gender imbalances in relation to information technology, for example in analyses of hacking (Jordan and Taylor 1998), patriarchy in the form of environments hostile to women that are built around practices familiar to and which create a form of masculinity that valorises violence and brute competition are a key context for understanding why zero hit points equates with death. Backing such dynamics are not only visuals of death but also overt and stereotypical representations of gender appearance. A pertinent example of appearance is the controversy over the change of the graphics that made up the model for a new race in World of Warcraft. It is not unusual in games for human-looking male characters to look like successful body builders with exaggerated musculature. When looking to introduce a new race the designers at World of Warcraft initially tested a male blood elf who had a relatively slim build. The response from players was negative and the designers 'bulked up' the body, releasing a statement to players that they acknowledged the character was 'too feminine' and stated that 'the decision was made to increase the body mass to give them a more substantial, masculine feel' (Timsey 2006). This was then objected to for its implicit homophobia and for the way it revealed an underlying pandering to stereotypical versions of male and female (Langer 2008: 98–9).

Criss-crossing the information powers that draw gamers into an intimate relationship with an avatar that is, in some sense, 'them', is a set of exploitations based on gender that conceive of activity and strength in terms of violence associated with masculinity. This is not an echo of a simple essentialist account – it is violent and therefore it is made by and for men – but of the complexity of the construction of gender in mmpogs and how this is allied to exploitative constructions of gender outside of games in which male violence plays a central role. In this sense, the resurrection of an avatar that information power flows through should not be viewed as a simple reflection of patriarchy but of moments in which patriarchy is itself partially constituted and produced. It is a reflection of moments in which what it means to be a gender is performed and so brought into being through repeated practices (Butler 1999: 177–89).

There are also complications to this story in so far as much of the violence that mmpog players engage in is group violence. In particular, the ability to progress to the most difficult content in mmpogs often relies on the organisation of groups of players, in sizes between 10, 40, and in the case of Dark Age of Camelot hundreds. Without such organisation it is not possible to experience some of the most compelling and complex content or to complete the most difficult challenges (Chen 2012; Jordan 2013a: 93–103). This means that while the final aim remains violent confrontation and 'achievement' will mean some avatar(s) reaching zero hit points, there is also an enforced sociality that leads players to set up their own groups and clubs. Such guilds, as they are usually called, vary greatly and may exaggerate the kind of gender roles that I have suggested underlie violence and visuality or they may ameliorate or contest gender roles. Without diminishing the still central role of death and resurrection or the connections of these to what Kline et al. term 'militarised masculinity', mmpogs as a genre also demand from players forms of cooperation and of organisation requiring some accommodation of differences in others to be able to progress.

Some other characteristics of mmpogs further complicate too straight-forward an equation of mmpogs with patriarchy. For example, there is usually no difference in the capabilities an avatar has in-game whichever gender is chosen. That is, an avatar like a warrior will have exactly the same in-game capabilities whether the gamer chooses them to be male or female; the only difference will be in the way they look, which, however, will often be based on exaggerated stereotypes of gender differences (Corneliussen 2008). Connections here open up between information power and gender power and other politics. The point just introduced of avatars having the same in-game abilities despite being different visually as stereotyped genders is also relevant to issues of race, implicitly raised briefly above in the case of the introduction of a new race to World of

Warcraft that also brought out issues of sexuality and heteronormativity (Langer 2008: 98–9).

All the mmpog games I have mentioned have pre-set races that the gamer must choose between to form their character, and which are also related to the lore and history of the particular setting. Krill was a troll, for example, but could have been a dwarf, kobold, or norseman as these were the possible races to be a member of Midgard. In-game races may reference real-life races, for example Albion in Dark Age had a race called 'saracen' that was vaguely dark skinned, and also one called 'highlander'; or they may be fantastic, such as lurikeens in Dark Age. They may also be mixtures referencing both 'real life' and fantasy, such as the troll in World of Warcraft who is blue skinned but speaks with a cod-Jamaican patois (saying 'mon' nearly every sentence). Choosing a race sometimes has consequences in-game: trolls in Dark Age could have higher strength but lower dexterity affecting in-game performance, and in Warcraft and Rift different races are given a different ability (for example, dwarves in Rift used to be able to fall from greater heights suffering less damage, until damage from falling was removed entirely from the game). However, there is a strong tendency toward such differences becoming cosmetic or only at most marginally useful because any significant advantage in gameplay, that will make it easier to inflict zero hit points, often leads to more gamers taking on those races and the game's variety diminishing as increasing numbers of a particular race are played. A recursion may occur in which the information that a particular race is better is taken in by other gamers which may then be recognised by game designers as unbalancing the game, both in terms of gameplay and variety. Accordingly, racial characteristics have tended in mmpogs to move much closer to the way gender is handled, becoming almost entirely a cosmetic difference, which also essentialises the race because it becomes unmodifiable within itself. All trolls and all undead and all mathosians share the particular looks, speech patterns and abilities of their race, leading to race becoming something fixed and essentialised. As Galloway argues 'One cannot "play" race in *World of Warcraft*. One must accept it as such' (Galloway 2012: 118; Monson 2012).

As a number of commentators have noticed, this produces a version of race as something with essentialised characteristics. This is in terms of cultures of speech and appearance, for example different races in many games have different automated dances and cannot do the dances of other races. It is also based on gameplay abilities that are often trivially different between races. Gender and race, to the extent that they no longer provide information in relation to gameplay because there is no difference between the in-game abilities of different races and genders, become fixed in relation to gameplay while their visual representation remains significant – a male blood elf Mage looks different to an undead female Mage. This lack of gender and race as gameplaying information, while remaining consequential in terms of the look of a character and the sounds they make, produces race and gender as essentialised categories that have little consequence for competition and contest in the game (Tronstad 2008).

Race and gender develop in contradictory directions with, on the one hand, the essentialisation of both in terms of visual, sound and movement styles but, on the other hand, their trivialisation in terms of competition and gameplay. While Galloway and others are right to point out the worrying ways in which games suggest that races are clearly defined, different and unchangeable, at the same time the extent to which this essentialisation is confined to cosmetic factors renders race and gender as non-information and thus, in the information environment of an mmpog, as irrelevant to gameplay. This contradiction is exemplified by the way that in both Warcraft and Rift players may change race and gender as many times as they like through a paid service. Race and gender change may be seen as trivial by gamers, that is, changes do not affect gameplay or in-game competition, because they are more or less a purely cosmetic and visual change, even while the militarised masculinity of violence and organised killing permeates this very gameplay. At the same time, within each race and gender and once any change has been made, the essentialist visuals, sounds and movements reassert themselves: blue-skinned trolls in Warcraft will always say 'mon'. The effect is to assert that race is essentialised but then to obscure any attention to the significance of this conceptualisation by rendering it irrelevant to gameplay. In this way, race and gender in mmpogs share the problem of their essentialisation being asserted as 'normal' while the significance of essentialisation is obscured.

Beginning with the moment of death, I have pursued this case study and found connections between broad antagonisms of gender and race and those of information. We see not only how these connect and how the platform of an mmpog, relying on devices and network-protocols that feed recursions, may propagate and reinforce existing gender and racial stereotypes, particularly through the gameplay of violence and competition, but also how these can be trivialised and obfuscated by the need to focus on the information aspects of the game. This shows how closely information and gendered power may be connected in mmpogs as this gameplay is itself dependent on a stereotypical masculinity that competes through violence.

There is clearly further work that could be done here, just as the iPad case study could become a whole project in-itself. For example, it would be interesting to look at the racialisation and industrialisation of 'gold farming', which is the practice of playing a game to generate in-game currencies that are then sold to other players for real-world money. This is a complex area which would begin to extend the connections of information, gender and race already explored to further issues of labour and racialised globalisation, because it is often 'Chinese gold farmers' who are blamed by players for this practice. While there are gold-farming factories in China they also exist in a number of nations, but the idea of 'Chinese gold farmers' has taken hold and they are often perceived to be ruining a game by distorting the in-game currency and allowing 'pay to win' strategies. In this way an intense form of paid labour is racialised. There is not the space here to fully explore this but it marks out how further connections of information, gender, race and labour might be pursued in the information environments of mmpogs (Qiu 2009: 182–6; Nakamura 2009; Castranova 2005).

There is, however, one last point that that should be made. This is to note that this case study, by starting and focusing on the individual moment of death, has perhaps underplayed the 'multi' aspect of mmpogs. In doing so, it may also seem to be presenting gamers as working within information, gendered and racialised environments that they simply have to accept. Extending this case study further we would need to look more closely at how gamers utilise capabilities and start to flesh out the requirement for cooperation and the kinds of player-creativity and sociality that is important to such games. This would not contradict the analysis given so far – zero hit points still means resurrection whether one dies alone or dies with 40 friends. Chen has recounted what happened when his 40-person raid attacked Ragnaros in World of Warcraft:

> Imagine 40 people grouped together in a dark, hot, volcanic cavern deep beneath the earth … The apparent leader of this raiding party, the one who is summarizing roles and strategy, yells 'Get into positions!' and everyone spreads out, running to various parts of the large cavern … The raid leader … yells, 'ATTACK!' and a flurry of activity commences. Within moments, the raiders are all dead. (Chen 2012: 1–2)

Zero hit points came quickly and to 40 characters all together – and it is that 'together' that may have been under-emphasised so far. At the risk of repetition, the cooperation and planning required for 40 gamers to attack (and eventually defeat) Ragnaros does not mean that somehow the moment of death and the militarised masculinity underlying it is dissipated. On the contrary, it is an example of how the game progresses through dying not once but many times until a particular battle is won and it is Ragnaros who experiences zero hit points. It is a good example of how violence and resurrection are built into a core dynamic of gaming, what Juul calls the 'art of failure' (Juul 2013; Chen 2012: 173–5). Far from denying such an analysis, it is important to extend it, by recognising gamer activity and organisation as an important factor in mmpogs, which, after all, rely on there being enough players for the game to be 'playable'. This would extend the analysis into what Dyer-Witheford and de Peuter argue is a form of bio-politics that they find in World of Warcraft and that is relevant to many mmpogs.

> While an MMO's initial programming – code manufactured and owned by a corporate publisher – sets the constituted parameters for virtual existence, it is the constitutive bottom-up behavior of player populations, the interaction of thousands of avatars, that gives this form content, animates its parameters, and sometimes pushes against its preset limits. (Dyer-Witheford and de Peuter 2009: 127)

In information terms, the architecture created by a particular set of recursions, devices and network-protocols that brings into existence a World of Warcraft or a Dark Age of Camelot also brings into existence, and requires for success in both commercial and gameplay terms, sociality among players. It brings into existence a basis for bottom-up organisation and for what we might even call resistance to and manipulation of information power by those who have so far seemed largely subjected to such power.

In mmpogs we therefore find not just utilisations of pre-set capabilities but also the manipulation of these capabilities in new ways by gamers. We also find a requirement for sociality and mutual support and organisation that can develop in various forms. Taking account of such gamer activity in relation to gameplay means extending the analysis to examine how gamers react to and reproduce race and gender and seeing that such things may be reproduced in relation to multiple aspects of games – from the essentialisations recounted above to the possibility of guilds that counter sexist, racist and homophobic language and behaviour within their own organisation. The point here is that information power connects to racism and sexism in these contexts in complex ways. While a full analysis of this interaction of gamer activity and existing structures of exploitation is not possible within the space available here, two examples will help establish the range of possibilities.

In one example from my own gameplay, I once asked another player who I knew had a male body sitting at their computer why they always chose female avatars. His response was that as they played like most of us in a third-person view – meaning they viewed the back of their avatar moving through the virtual world environment – they liked looking at a pert female bottom. He used the gaming possibilities to continue widespread patriarchal practices of objectifying women and asserting idealised female forms.

In a second example, a straight male-gamer I knew started a male-avatar character called Alexander McQueer, who he played in a highly camp way. At first this seemed like it might be an objectification and trivialisation of homosexuality, but the player took their avatar outside the guild environment and into general chat, ensuring he created anti-gay statements which he then proceeded to confront and trouble, usually humorously but sometimes in angry exchanges. He also developed the in-game skill of being a tailor, meaning he could make clothes that other avatars could wear, allowing him to draw on a long tradition of double entendres in comedy. It was not unusual to hear Alexander touting for business with the cry 'Suits you Sir' or offering to 'Measure your inner thigh, Sir'. Once this style of play became known, the appearance of Alexander McQueer in-game would sometimes become a focal point not necessarily of abuse, though this happened, but of humour and of contestation of abuse where it occurred. For example, his presence prompted discussion of the all too frequent use of 'gay' as a term of abuse by gamers.

These examples demonstrate the point that further analysis needs to take forward Dyer-Witheford and de Peuter's contention that there are possibilities for bottom-up action within mmpogs; whether those possibilities are used to look at women's behinds or to contest homophobia. These points also relate to the extensive work demonstrating how the divide between producer and consumer has become complicated within video games, suggesting the creative and active touches gamers bring to games (Banks and Potts 2010; Bruns 2008). Cases of resistance discussed in the case studies so far, at least until Alexander McQueer was reached, have too often been implicit or reactive. The arguments that have been articulated up to this point are not wrong, but they are perhaps incomplete and give a view of information politics as one-sided, whereas the powers of recursion, devices and network-protocols are not one-sided and, just as there are feminists, anti-racists and black power activists, so there is the active production of a different world through a different use of information powers. As Postigo observes:

> the concept of participatory culture from Jenkins and others speaks of a culture of participation among subsets of content consumers. I would contrast this view of a participatory culture to the digital rights movement's notion of culture (the whole of shared meanings parsed through mass media and new digital technologies) as necessarily participatory. Culture for the movement is meaningless or increasingly alienated from citizenry unless that citizenry can participate in its production. (Postigo 2012: 9)

The final case study will turn to such information activism and the possibilities for producing a different liberated world, and will look at the way information power is part of such struggles that inevitably, due to the mess of the world, connect multiple forms of exploitation and multiple places of struggle and liberation. Gaming shows us how in one brief moment, in my case between frames 1580 and 1581, multiple politics connect to each other, including the politics of information. By considering in the next chapter an information resistance movement it will be possible to see more clearly the possibilities for resistance and liberation in the political antagonism of information.

9

Hacktivism: Operation Tunisia, Modular Tactics and Information Activism

The first case study of information power was focused on a technological device and the second on a specific information-saturated moment. It will be useful now to provide another contrast by examining a third type of case study to demonstrate how information power can be examined and related to other forms of power. To do so I will follow a movement and its activists. Activism in and through the internet has made many waves and is not hard to find, from the somewhat absurd attempt to suggest that Facebook and Twitter were responsible for the Arab Spring to the fear-inducing coverage of Anonymous's actions. To begin I will follow events that have gained the most attention in the early twenty-first century, namely Anonymous's actions during the Arab Spring, particularly its campaign Operation Tunisia, and then broaden discussion to the wider movement that has become known as hacktivism.

In the midst of the Tunisian revolt of late 2010 and 2011 activists in Tunisia were noticing that their Facebook pages were being blocked, and when they could access their pages they were finding their posts deleted or altered. Internet access outside of Tunisia also became throttled, tracked and sites blocked. Access to Wikileaks was cut off and most believed this was done because US State Department communications available on Wikileaks were both critical of the Tunisian government and revealed corruption. Bloggers began to report being arrested and tracked through the same means that were harvesting Facebook and other log in details and passwords (Anderson 2011; Ryan 2011). In the midst of this a number of activists within the broad umbrella of Anonymous decided to do what they could to help.

An early action was to try to halt the phishing of people's log ins and passwords. A hacktivist wrote a small programme that could run in a browser that had installed the Greasemonkey extension; once both were installed the programme returned control over their browser to the user (Olson 2012: 142; Anderson 2011; Galperin 2011; Howard et al. 2011: 8–9). Other Anons took up actions to attack Tunisian government websites, bringing them down and, in one case at least, loading an open letter of protest that appeared on the Tunisian Prime Minister's homepage demanding that oppression stop and access to the internet be opened up (Audenaerde 2014; Olson 2012: 142–3; Howard et al. 2011: 8–9). Further technologies were collected to be made available in what were called digital care packs, including the Greasemonkey script, programmes to install more secure communications using the TOR network, and other aids. Videos were transferred out of Tunisia to be uploaded and proxies maintained to allow Tunisians, media and others to see some of what was happening (Coleman 2013a: 216; Anderson 2011; Ryan 2011). By this time Anonymous had launched what they called Operation Tunisia, which drew together these different threads and would lead to similar efforts as other revolutions unfolded across the Arab Spring. Were these actions significant in the overthrow of the Tunisian government? They were certainly not the only or primary causes nor were they the key actions in the Tunisian revolution, but it seems clear that assisting information flows and organisation through these interventions was part of that revolution (Howard et al. 2011).

In information terms we see here circuits of information power being contested. The Tunisian government had constituted an internet whose protocols could restrict access outside Tunisia and that could automatically harvest accounts. Tunisian activist Aziz Amamay articulated this succinctly: 'Here we don't really have internet, we have a national intranet' (cited in Ryan 2011). Anonymous activists were able to bend this back, changing network-protocols by providing new devices – code, proxies – that reordered the information world. This then shifted flows of information such that provision of access to leaked US government cables supporting criticisms of the Tunisian government, information that could be conveyed by being able to see videos of what was happening, and/or the ability to access online organising and publicity tools safely again, were all available to an oppositional information politics as part of a revolutionary change. As this information was then recursed – for example, as someone's access to a video or a critical cable changed their viewpoint and was passed on to someone else either through discussion or sharing of links

– information powers can be seen as having been utilised by the Jasmine Revolution. Keeping avenues open allows information recursion, evidence for which can be seen in the spikes in Facebook and Twitter activity prior to major actions on the ground and in the key role online spaces played in spreading information from one revolution to another, both adding to the information and returning it to the revolutionary environment (Howard et al. 2011; Aouragh and Alexander 2011). Hacktivism here operated to try to bend information flows to ensure secure access to information, which then allowed that information into multiple different spaces, such as through the devices of social media, offering potential recursions promoting change.

It is important to emphasise that Tunisia was in revolt for a wide range of reasons and not simply because organising through electronic means had gained a wider audience via Facebook or because Anonymous and other hacktivists intervened to ensure information continued to spread. The revolution sprang from a range of causes and relates to broad political changes; Dabashi, for example, argues that in the Arab Spring colonialism and post-colonialism were both being overcome (Dabashi 2012). The fascination of much Western media with reducing these revolutions to Twitter or Facebook is undoubtedly incorrect, even if Twitter and Facebook both had roles to play in them (Howard et al. 2011; Aouragh and Alexander 2011). However, the overemphasis on social network media found in some mainstream Western media is not a reason to dismiss the actions of hacktivists in these struggles. Hacktivists were able to direct forms of information power as a part of these revolutions. We do not need to overestimate these actions or dismiss them. If this were an account of the Arab Spring no doubt what I have outlined as the role of Anonymous in Tunisia would be a minor factor, but in relation to the present arguments concerning information power these examples articulate some key forms of information activism.

Interventions through information power by activists outside of state, corporate or security agencies have a history through which we can follow one form of information activism. To show this I will outline what can be thought of, loosely, as three 'generations' or 'phases' of hacktivism as marked by the typical actions of hacktivists: a pre-generation in which two key resources for hacktivism emerged; a first generation in which two different types of hacktivist actions were established; and a second generation in which new actions emerged and existing actions were changed. These should also be understood not as successive generations in which one displaces the other, but instead as generations and actions that accumulate and co-exist.

The emergence of networked computer communication has involved politics of various sorts, but there are two kinds of traditions that, looking back, form the 'pre-history' of hacktivism. The first is what has become known as the 'golden age' of hacking, when by far the majority of phone phreaking and computer-break-in activities were done for the intoxication of exploring a new electronic world. Within these expertise-enabled groups of mainly young men there was an even smaller group who allied their ability to break into newly emerging computer networks to the desire to make political statements. These were isolated and occasional acts that did not create a movement but first explored the online world as a site of information action (Sterling 1992; Lapsley 2013). The second theme was that amid the widespread articulation of the new networked realm as a place, most often then called cyberspace, there emerged a political conception of what this place should be. In varying places and varying ways, some of which, like Levy's articulation of the Hacker Ethic, became world famous and others of which sank without a trace, there were attempts to develop the idea that social and cultural activity on global computer networks formed not just a new place or land but a place or land with a particular and innate kind of politics (Levy 1984; Jordan 1999b). The exploits of early hackers and the ruminations of early ideologists of cyberspace created actions and ideas that fed into hacktivism.

The golden age of hacking – beginning with phone-phreaking and its discovery of the phone network as an object of curiosity and ending with the increasing criminalisation of cracking as the internet came to be viewed as an essential social infrastructure – put into place many of the facets of illegal computer intrusion that are familiar today. Such facets have undergone significant change with the increasing connection of some cracking groups to organised crime in the early twenty-first century (Menn 2010; Glenny 2012; Poulsen 2011) and the increasing use by nation-states of cracking for both espionage and for plausibly deniable attacks on each other (Deibert 2013; Deibert et al. 2011; Morozov 2011). These more recent meanings of hacking can make it difficult to see the earlier post-phreaking phase in which breaking into computers might be plausibly likened by a hacker to an intellectual pursuit such as chess (Jordan and Taylor 1998; Sterling 1992). This has been called by some the heroic or golden age of hacking as cracking, though no systems administrator on the receiving end of a cracker's attention would call it that. The names were legendary: Eric Bloodaxe, the Masters of Deception, Kevin Poulson (by 2014 an editor of *Wired* magazine), Mudge, and the most emblematic figure of all in the first ever person accused of causing a billion dollars' worth of damage by cracking, Kevin Mitnick (Mitnick 2011; Littman 1997; Quittner and Slatalla 1995; Lapsley 2013). What makes this period important for hacktivism's history is what seems now to be its innocence: exploration was everything and economic, political or any other gain were at most secondary or were just as often simply absent.

This does not mean that the explorations of hackers breaking into computer networks were harmless, as each cracked computer or faked phone line would eventually lead to work for someone, and sometimes to accidental and occasionally deliberate erasures and damage done to systems. The point of calling cracking in this period exploratory is not to suggest it was harmless. It is however to note that it was done primarily to find out about systems, to use expertise to unpick the puzzles that online networks seemed to offer, and to conduct clever, if often also juvenile, tricks that demonstrated how an expertise-fuelled obsessive could gain control over systems built by such institutional behemoths as NASA or the US military.

From this intellectual and expertise-driven background emerged some of the most notable elements of hacking. Holding conferences to meet and share expertise marks out hackers' interest in intellectual engagement with each other (and their rather different attitude to secrecy to criminals or spies), one of the most notable being DEF CON, that began in 1993 and continues to this day. Journals such as *2600: The Hacker Quarterly*, first published in 1984 and continuing today, contain articles sharing the expertise central to exploring networks (Goldstein 2008). Some behaviour, such as breaking into a system and then contacting the system administrator to explain how the break-in was done and what should now be done to prevent future break-ins, also mark out this group as puzzle-interested explorers. Across these and other markers, it is important to see hacking in this phase as a community phenomenon with a diffused sense of purpose in its exploration of the virtual realm and its rejection on limits set by anyone but themselves to that exploration (Taylor 1999; Jordan and Taylor 1998; Sterling 1992).

The hacking community is based on the kind of informal mechanisms seen in collective identities more generally as there is no formal membership of any sort. Once individuals seek to become members of the hacking community they therefore become engaged with an ongoing problem, because this expertise-based community undertakes actions that are difficult to demonstrate to others except by showing them how to undertake the action themselves. Sometimes copies of documents or other information objects gained through cracking can be used to confirm hacking actions, but documents in this context are easily copyable and poor proof in helping sift through the claims made by individuals about what they have done. It becomes necessary for those individuals to teach at least some others to do what they have done to prove they have done what they claim they have. Teaching allows proof and creates connections to other hackers, often then leading to access to more secret chat rooms or fora, a willingness to meet at conferences, introductions to others and at times being vouched for as a real hacker. For these reasons once hackers engage with their community they must participate in widespread peer teaching because one characteristic of their core activities is that their conduct and so their identity as hacker can only be proven by teaching others to do what they have done (Jordan 2008: 27–33). What would emerge from such a community was a dynamic of peer education resulting from the sense of there being an information 'place' that could be explored. For example, the judge at a young Julian Assange's trial for hacking in 1994 stated that 'there is just no evidence that there was anything other than a sort of intelligent inquisitiveness and the pleasure of being able to – what's the expression – surf through these various computers' (cited in Katchadourian 2010).

Within this community, hacking for a political purpose was rare. The most famous example is probably that of the International Subversives, who were Australian hackers including Mendax or Julian Assange. This group launched a number of attacks on NASA in protest at projects to use nuclear reactors as engines on rockets, something the ecological movement was protesting at the time given the possibility of a rocket explosion in the earth's atmosphere. One action of the International Subversives was The Worm Against Nuclear Killers that infiltrated and spread throughout NASA's computer network, filling up screens with dire warnings that files were being deleted, though no actual deleting was being done, and signalling on a computer screen that the victim had been 'WANKed' while quoting a well-known environmentally supportive rock band (Dreyfus 1997). Yet this kind of connection of political action to the expertise gained for and from exploring online networks was rare and seems pre-hacktivist. Even while hacking explicitly as ethical hackers, it seems clear that politics were both a rare occurrence and secondary to the ethic of exploration.

Out of this period of hacking came a further factor worth emphasising in relation to the rise of hacktivism as a movement. This is a sense of there being a place or space that was in-itself worth exploring and in which many hackers felt themselves to be natives or in some sense 'at home'. This underlies a nascent 'politics of the internet' which ascribes a particular set of political principles and ethics to activities that are dependent on internet technologies.

At the same time as the age of the hacker as an expertise, or intellect, fuelled explorer emerged, the internet was beginning to attract increasing numbers of users in addition to its first home as a research network for computer scientists. Among these users would emerge a whole range of cultures, from lol to trolling, and, importantly for hacktivism, a range of thinkers and groups who began to trumpet the internet and its concomitant digital cultures as the basis for a revolutionary new stage in society. These groups also began to examine and discuss ideas of what this new space might mean. In this debate would be articulated a complex of ideas that have informed a politics of the internet. Turner's history of the emergence of cybercultures from countercultures traces one stream of this, but there were others, from the dramatics of ranting hackers to the grassroots ethic of the pre-internet global network Fidonet (Turner 2006; Jordan 1999a). A number of themes of an internet politics were articulated and these were echoed and promoted through online resources and print publications like *Mondo 2000* and *Wired*. Themes such as the right to secure access to all the world's information, the collapse of hierarchies in favour of networks, a libertarian and/or anarchistic approach to organisation, and a sometimes contested but, particularly in the USA, often evangelical belief in free markets versus the state – all these themes were repeated across different ways of thinking about a place called cyberspace that has its own sociality and own politics. Two of the most famous examples of this were John Perry Barlow's 1998 'A Declaration of the Independence of Cyberspace' (Barlow 1998) and The Mentor's 'The Conscience of a Hacker', written by a hacker shortly after being arrested and which declared:

> We make use of a service already existing without paying for what could be dirt-cheap if it wasn't run by profiteering gluttons, and you call us criminals. We explore ... and you call us criminals. We seek after knowledge ... and you call us criminals. We exist without skin color,

without nationality, without religious bias ... and you call us criminals ... Yes, I am a criminal. My crime is that of curiosity. My crime is that of judging people by what they say and think, not what they look like. My crime is that of outsmarting you, something that you will never forgive me for. (Mentor 1986)

Barlow's and the Mentor's manifestos are just two of the best-known articulations of a politics that mixes up many ideas but that repeats around the ideas of knowledge, curiosity and a right of access. Some interpret this freedom as consonant with or even requiring free markets and radical libertarianism, while others understood the kind of information freedom at stake in anarchist terms (Jordan 2001). Sometimes these ideas simply erupted in particularly acute contexts. One lesser known (outside the Fidonet community) example was the 1995 request to break the structure of governance of Fidonet, called 'The Fidonet Sysop Manifesto'. While the content of this manifesto had little effect, it is worth noting its claim that Fidonet's organisational structure was failing to promote 'a system of organized anarchy for the purpose of communication first, last and foremost' (Anon 1995; Jennings 1995).

Across a whole range of information and computer-networked contexts there emerged the sense of there being a 'there' on the internet accompanied by a politics of the 'there'. This forms an important cultural context for the rise of politically motivated hacking, and a range of other groups might have been mentioned in this context. For example, the cypherpunks were key in thinking through not only how to create encryption but also the importance of encryption and what it means in the context of a radically changed information environment (Levy 2001; Assange et al. 2012). The civil rights group the Electronic Frontier Foundation was not only fighting legal battles, conducting publicity and education and supporting the creation of tools, but also pondering what all this meant (Jordan 1999b). The Free Software Foundation was producing software accompanied by its source code and licenses to ensure this continued, and also working out what 'free culture' meant (Williams 2012; Jordan 2008: 42–65). The Chaos Computer Club in Germany was beginning its long engagement with trying to ensure that 'broken' technologies might be fixed – broken, in their view, for a number of reasons, but including the lack of security and control for the user, with companies able to turn people's devices on and off (Blanc and Noor 2011). If Barlow and the Mentor drew attention with dramatic manifestos, then these and other similar groups were places in which ideas of information politics were being discussed, debated and developed.

These are two key cultures for hacktivism that had come into existence by the early 1990s: breaking into computer networks as a form of intellectual exploration, intellectual because cracking was primarily through expertise rather than hardware; and the rise of an ideology conceiving of computer networks as creating a place with its own politics, primarily that of freedom of information. At this time, explicitly political uses of the internet or other computer networks seemed isolated and rare, but thinking about such uses was beginning to emerge. The next phase picks up this thinking as hacktivism emerges as a movement.

What starts to appear is the idea and practice of political actions online, not just communication and organisation within groups and not just publicity for political causes, but that the virtual realm was itself a place for distinct political actions. The increasing migration of various institutions to cyberspace, whether corporate or government, opened up the possibility of connecting the idea of cyberspace as a place to the idea of de-institutionalised political action (Jordan and Taylor 2004; Jordan 2008). An early and influential political reading of this situation was offered by the Critical Arts Ensemble (CAE), when they argued for an electronic civil disobedience to match the already existing, though in their view obsolete, civil disobedience.

> CAE has said it before and we will say it again: as far as power is concerned, the streets are dead capital! Nothing of value to the power elite can be found on the streets, nor does this class need control of the streets to efficiently run and maintain state institutions. (CAE 1996: 11)

> Nomadic power must be resisted in cyberspace rather than in physical space ... A small but co-ordinated group of hackers could introduce electronic viruses, worms, and bombs into the data banks and programmes, and networks of authority. (CAE 1994: 25)

CAE's articulation of the necessity for online actions was one of the earliest. Ironically for its conceptualisation of electronic civil disobedience as being based on hacker attacks, the two types of online political action that emerged as hacktivism were unlike their suggested information bombs. Here we can see the influence of hacking as exploration at the time, because such explorations tended to reject harmful attacks on online resources. The two types of hacktivism were called by myself and Paul Taylor mass action hacktivism and digitally correct hacktivism (Jordan and Taylor 2004: 69).

Mass action hacktivism drew heavily on the suggested addition of 'electronic' to civil disobedience tactics. It focused particularly on artist-activism and converting street demonstration and sit-in tactics into online tactics (CAE 1996; Serafini 2014). The nature of such electronic demonstrations can be explained by one of the earliest ever online actions launched by the Italian hacktivist group Netstrike. This action consisted of a date and time at which everyone participating was requested to enter a particular URL and then repeatedly click the reload button on their web browser. Enough people clicking repeatedly might produce enough requests to gag the targeted site by overwhelming it with information (Jordan and Taylor 2004: 43). Later protests would automate this process in two ways. First, they would allow one request to be automatically repeated rather than the protestor having to manually reload a targeted page by repeatedly clicking and, second, in some attacks one request would be multiplied several times (in one protest against the WTO meeting in Seattle there was a choice of being multiplied either three or six times) (Jordan and Taylor 2004: 74–9). However, such automation needed limits because otherwise it would be impossible for a protest to mirror the participation of many people that in some sense confers a political legitimacy on a mass protest, just as one person attending a demonstration does not convey the same politics as one million.

Here are the key elements of mass actions online in the 1990s and early 2000s. First, internet technologies had to be impaired in the sense of not functioning to their full possibilities to ensure that a claim could be made for mass participation. Rather than promoting the full powers of information by recursing them in ways that feed the production of more information, these information powers were deliberately curtailed. Second, this is a 'modular' tactic that can potentially be used by nearly any kind of political agenda, in particular there is no necessary connection between this tactic and the kind of information politics these ideologists of the internet were articulating. In fact, such protests were largely the preserve of activists closely associated with the alter-globalisation movement, in particular among groups supporting the Zapatista uprising in Mexico. A third facet of mass virtual action is the connection to artist-activism, which was a marked feature of the end of the twentieth century in the alter-globalist movement. This was put into practice by trying to make some kind of performance out of each political action, such as the elaborate puppets that became a feature of alter-globalist demonstrations (Serafini 2014; McDonald 2006). For example, the Electronic Disturbance Theatre used the internet error message 404 (meaning content not found) during an electronic sit-in to generate a string of messages such as 'Error 404: human rights not found on this site' or 'justice not found on this site', when the targeted site would make this a political statement by claiming there was no justice found on the site of, for example, the President of Mexico. Mass action hacktivism was (and is) a form of political protest that involved targeting someone's information presence and restricting it. At the same time a different set of ideas and actions emerged that constituted digitally correct hacktivism.

Digitally correct hacktivists developed an activist form of action on the internet that was necessarily connected to the nature of information technologies. The primary actions undertaken within this variant of hacktivism were to ensure secure access to information over the internet, and this primarily meant providing tools that sometimes maintained features of the internet that were under threat or sometimes altered the nature of the internet where it was seen to be restricting secure access to information. This form of activism was often closely connected to human rights activism, arguing that in providing various tools that evaded government censorship or surveillance it was providing tools that enabled human rights (Jordan and Taylor 2004: 90–115). This form of activism clearly draws on and seeks to implement different kinds of devices embedding within them network-protocols that promote information flows.

Possibly the best-known and ongoing action was the creation of the TOR network. TOR is a grassroots supported and implemented computer network that secures traffic over the internet from being surveilled 'end to end'. That is, TOR blocks tracking of someone's internet traffic from where it begins and where it goes to, making it impossible to map the connections that person is creating across the internet. It was widely known that there was a security problem that allowed such a mapping, even if the content of what was sent was secured and could not be read, and an earlier unimplemented tool called Peek-a-Booty had been developed in the 1990s to address this problem (Jordan and Taylor 2004: 100–11). TOR is created by individuals installing TOR servers on their computers and volunteering some of their bandwidth so that TOR users can bounce their messages between TOR-enabled computers. It is in this sense a grassroots network as it relies on individual volunteers who add to TOR purely for the promotion of a more secure internet. The programming for TOR is open source so it is open to grassroots intervention, though it was also produced initially with the US military in the shape of the Naval Research Laboratory (Jordan 2008: 262–70).

There are a range of other similar tools, some of which offer ways of hiding information from surveillance, but TOR remains possibly the most long-lived and significant. It demonstrates clearly the way a tool can offer a more secure form of access to information and to communication, how such tools are often built on grassroots action both in the programming of the tool and in its implementation, how ideas about information freedom are manifested in these online actions, and how the actions undertaken alter the possibilities for users of internet technologies, in a sense altering the internet itself. Though more cracker-like tools were not unknown within this kind of action – for example Back Orifice (a tool for cracking Microsoft operating system based networks) or Stacheldracht (a tool that can be used for individual denial of service attacks or for testing system vulnerabilities) – they became less prominent as digitally correct action progressed and these hacktivists articulated ever more clearly their desire to protect secure access to information over the internet (Jordan and Taylor 2004: 111–4).

This kind of hacktivism contradicts mass action because while the former believes primarily in the right to secure access to information, the latter employs tactics that restrict access to information (in attempts to 'sit in' on sites in ways that remove them temporarily from the internet). They are also distinguished by their political connections. Mass action hacktivists were closely connected with political causes other than the internet, the most prominent connection being to the alter-globalisation movement though many other causes were taken up, whereas digitally correct hacktivists were primarily concerned with the nature of information access and the internet. Despite these connections, both generate modular techniques that could be used by many different ideologies.

These two themes within hacktivism constitute its first generation and their characteristic sets of actions – from the Electronic Disturbance Theatre's year-long Floodnet performance, which also produced one of the first ever state-based online attacks when the US government sought to prevent a mass action that was part of Floodnet, to the coalition called Hacktivismo that actively sought out programming to secure the internet and to hide information from state surveillance. Both these movements developed actions that could be taken only over the internet and that were clearly creating a grassroots or de-institutionalised popular movement for change. From these two variants of hacktivism, it would then take only the first ten years of the twenty-first century to see a new generation of hacktivists who would alter and re-conceive hacktivism into its second generation.

Just as the pre-hacktivist generation blended into first generation hacktivism, with many groups such as EFF and the Chaos Computer Club continuing throughout, so the second generation of hacktivism blends into and co-exists with the first generation. Mass virtual actions continue to take shape and an information infrastructure politics such as TOR has seemed only to grow in importance and scope, but at the same time a new series of tactics have arisen in campaigns such as Anonymous' Operation Tunisia. This action, described above, and other Anonymous actions will be used as examples here to follow the way information power has been bent in different directions. Three of these changes are key: denial of service attacks, the hack as leak, and internet infrastructure.

Fully powered denial of service attacks using sometimes only a few people to target and take down a site have become part of the armoury of hacktivism, whereas previously, while not completely unknown, they were rejected by both of the main trends in first generation hacktivism. Mass action hacktivists rejected the anti-democratic nature of using software to multiply flows of information instead of using many people, while information infrastructure hacktivists rejected the limitation on free flows of information. But in the second generation, denial of service attacks were prosecuted with full information power. This did not mean that a sense of mass participation was absent. At the height of Operation Payback's denial of service attacks on companies that had cut off their services to Wikileaks there were over 7,000 people in the chat room that promoted the attacks (Coleman 2012b: 28). However, each participant was also using a software programme (the now infamous Low Orbiting Ion Cannon or LOIC) to multiply their one click into a stream of data and, in addition, some attacks were conducted by botnets through which one or a few people could direct cracked computers from thousands of locations to simultaneously and suddenly fire data at a targeted site (Coleman 2013a: 4–12; Olson 2012: 74–5, 115–20). One example of such an attack was that used to shut down various Tunisian government servers during Operation Tunisia. Instead of restricting the capabilities of information on the internet this tactic fully exploited the available recursions through a range of devices. Botnets may particularly be seen as a linked set of recursions; each computer turned into a bot and attached to the botnet has the same device or programme illicitly placed inside it which is then linked and connected through its network-protocols. Turned on suddenly, the command to one device moves throughout the network to power on a flood of data, capable of drowning, at least for a short time, many websites (Olson 2012: 110–24).

Breaking into other people's and organisations' networks has also become part of the armoury of hacktivism. Whereas the first generation largely avoided, or dismissed as inappropriate, the idea that CAE proposed of hackers breaking into systems, the second generation began to exploit it. In particular, this was connected to the idea of leaking as a political act, again in the tradition developed early in online politics of seeing the internet as a key arena for free flows of information. Here the manipulation of network-protocols to access illicitly other computers is used to copy information and then release it. This was a key tactic that emerged when Anonymous developed operations in support of the Arab Spring, and found its full flowering in the emergence of the group Lulzsec who set about using their cracking skill to break into and often leak information of various sorts (Olson 2012). Leaking is a tactic of its own whose tradition is not necessarily one of computer intrusion but which was connected by hacktivists to cracking into systems. WikiLeaks and the Snowden revelations are clearly both attempts to release information to expose injustices (Sifry 2011; Harding 2014). Hacking as cracking into systems involves key moments of breaking into a network by slipping past protocols or reordering protocols that aim to prevent access. As has been known since hacking in the golden age, this then allows the copying of documents that the re-ordered protocols allow access to (Jordan 2008: 17–41). Once these documents are copied they can then be leaked.

The third tactic of second generation hacktivism is already familiar in digitally correct hacktivism's altering of the internet's infrastructure to promote secure flows of information. This internet infrastructure politics continues during this phase with the digitally correct hacktivist tactics not changing while also becoming linked to new networks of action. Whereas hacktivists such as those in the Hacktivismo project, which began in 2002 and whose last announcement was in 2008, had rejected cracking and denial of service attacks, the new generation simply added defending and extending secure internet infrastructures to their array of actions. The digital care packages of Operation Tunisia are clearly part of this and demonstrate the connections this generation of hacktivists were able to make between different ways of manipulating information forces to generate oppositional actions.

The second generation of hacktivists both takes tactics from the first, partially reordering their meaning in the case of information infrastructure, and develops new tactics. The first generation and its tactics continue to operate; mass actions continue to be called as virtual sit-ins and changes to internet infrastructure to secure information continue to emerge. The rich information tactics of hacktivism all offer ways for de-institutionalised political actors, the grassroots or the social movement of the internet to form information forces into effective forms of protest.

Hacktivism across its generations is an example of the struggle against corporations and governments for a populist politics of the internet. Such political actors provide another case study of the way information as a political antagonism creates its own politics while at the same time providing tactics that may be taken up in the politics of other political antagonisms. Whereas when looking at the iPad and then at death in mmpogs I was able to identify key alternative political antagonisms, the story of hacktivism is slightly different for there are two clear effects here. First, hacktivism in part directly addresses the grassroots politics of information as an antagonism. Information politics is here an activist politics in-itself. Second, hacktivism connects the politics of information to all such grassroots struggles because its information politics provide tactics that may be taken up by nearly any struggle.

The latter point is important as it brings to the fore the way information connects by being used within many different political antagonisms. In this case, hacktivism as an information politics provides a range of tactics that can be taken up, each tactic itself representing a particular way of putting together recursions, devices and network-protocols. In this case study it has then been easy to identify connections in particular examples, such as colonialism and dictatorship in Tunisia and the Arab Spring, but more generally when talking about hacktivism as a movement it is not clear whether there are some political struggles that connect to it more strongly than others. Rather, it is the ability of hacktivism to provide tactics that can be used in many other struggles that seems obvious. In this sense, the connections the first wave alter-globalisation movement had to the first hacktivist generation and the second wave alter-globalisation movement had to the second generation can be seen as historically contingent.

Hacktivism also identifies information politics as a struggle in-itself, as a particular kind of grassroots or popular struggle, and it does this most clearly in its attempts to implement a particular relation to information by altering internet infrastructures. What we see here is that because information forces can be turned into political tactics, the politics of information will flow into and affect struggles that take up such tactics. Understanding the nature of information as a political antagonism is then important for understanding the role of information in any political struggle in the twenty-first century. This does not in any way make information politics the 'master' or primary politics of the twenty-first century, but it does mean that the peculiarities of information power will need to be taken into account by many struggles. There is here also an inverse effect, as issues such as gender (as seen already in gaming) or class (as seen in manufacturing the iPad) need to take account of the way they may structure information politics in particular actions. Concrete actions are the places this will need to be done as political antagonisms are not all evenly connected all the time, but rather are unevenly connected in specific struggles. The overall point is to recognise that antagonisms must take account of each other but only on the basis of their own specific dynamics and only through the specificity of particular connections.

The tangible specificity of information in relation to exploitation and struggle, and the varying ways in which information connects to many forms of exploitation and struggle, have been explored through three case studies. It is now possible to turn to consider the general meaning of information liberations and exploitations. Having begun these case studies with the class, information and environmental exploitations so clearly embodied in the iPad, and ended them with an account of activists' attempts to take back control of their nations, their information and their lives, it is now time to conclude by surveying what these arguments about information as a political antagonism tell us about liberation and oppression in the twenty-first century.

Conclusion:
Information Exploitation and Information Liberation

To understand information exploitation and information liberation it is important to return to the theory of politics as a multi-pole field of many interacting political antagonisms as the general framework for understanding information as a politics. Linked exploitation(s) and liberation(s) are the central dynamic of each antagonism constituted in and through recurrent patterns of interaction between groups. In such interactions, something that enriches one group and impoverishes the other is shifted repeatedly between groups. What it is that enriches and impoverishes is itself constituted in these interactions and can be a wide range of things or relations. What is being exchanged may then be taken as the origin of this antagonism; often it will then be naturalised as the inherent property of one group over the other – such as in claims that women are 'naturally' family makers or black people have a lower IQ – however it is only through such performative processes that what it is that impoverishes and enriches is constituted and can then be taken as the reason for these relations in the first place.

Each such antagonism exists in relation to other antagonisms such that their dynamics, as opposed to their effects, appear primarily when they are abstracted through intellectual work that delineates the specificity of a dynamic of exploitation. In the struggles of the everyday, multiple antagonisms inter-weave and affect each other. The only way to see exploitation and liberation in particular moments is then to have some understanding of the different dynamics of exploitation and include in that understanding the specific ways in which antagonisms interact. There has to be an interplay between the specificity of exploitations and the mess and connections found in political struggle.

The final part of this analysis of information as a politics with its own recurrent dynamics of exploitation and liberation will draw together the analyses and try to understand how the dynamics of recursions, devices and network-protocols come together in repeated patterns that define struggles between informationally defined groups and between information and other political antagonisms. To begin, a key difference between information exploitation and other exploitations will be focused on through the question: What is it that may be struggled over within information politics that may enrich and impoverish groups and in so doing constitute them?

Information Rivalry: Citizens not Subjects

If I start briefly with Marx's analysis of exploitation, then we can see that, in a sense, he specifies class exploitation as the transfer of working time. Put overly simply, Marx identifies that a worker can produce a certain amount of value during a working day but the payment for work they receive can be less than the value they have produced, the difference then falling into the lap of the controller of that production process. The intelligence, sweat and muscle that a worker uses over time is transferred unseen, and what the worker loses the capitalist gains. Another example would be domestic labour, when a woman labours in the home, reproducing life, and this is used in a patriarchal system to sustain men in positions of power, then this gendered division is produced in patriarchal relations in which women lose immaterial and material labour that cannot be reclaimed and which benefits their Other. Another example is that of heteronormativity, created, at least partially, on the invisibility of other sexualities. For one sexuality to be normalised it is made visible all the time, while other sexualities have their potential visibility absorbed by heterosexuality. Each of these antagonisms could also be understood through multiple such relations, and I have so far focused on a key dynamic in these examples solely for clarity. For example, it could be argued that racism is constituted by multiple relations, including visibility when 'white' is asserted as 'normal', by the transfer of racialised labour power, and by the essentialisation and biologisation of characteristics, allowing the definition of certain roles in society as only possible for certain races, and so on.

In each of these examples of exploitation we can see how the specific relationship is patterned and sustained across large collectives that are themselves defined through the relations of exploitation. Those very relations may then be taken as the reason for differences between collectives. In this way, exploitation and liberation may take many forms.

The key characteristic of these exploitations is that in the transfer from one group to another what is transferred is lost by one side to the gain of the other; the time of labour is lost to workers, races and women; visibility and normality is lost to sexualities and races and so on. It is also essential to the relationship that one side is more powerful, richer and dominant because something is gained by them that is lost to the other side of the exploitative relationship. Powerful definitions of exploitation and liberation are based on impoverishment and enrichment because in the transfer between groups one group is enriched while another is necessarily impoverished.

This 'zero sum' game in which one side gains only by another losing is, however, not necessarily the case with information. As is well known, information is, to use the term drawn from economics, a 'non-rival good' whose possession by one does not exclude simultaneous and full possession by another. It is only with artificial means that information can be treated as a rival good. For example, information can be made rival by imposing some kind of technical restrictions on access, such as only allowing some information to be accessed as a book that must be purchased, putting digital information behind a pay wall, putting digital rights exclusion technology on information and so on (Gillespie 2007; Berry 2008: 83–5). This aspect of information is often discussed within the largely economic frame of public, rival and non-rival goods which seeks to define the efficiency of markets and how society and economy can benefit from managing such goods (Benkler 2006: 30–8). Information as a non-rival good can be held by several at once and can, if anything, increase in value from being held by more people. Information is then a different kind of entity to those underpinning the understandings of exploitation given above, such as the necessary loss of labouring time by the worker in order for the capitalist to benefit, in which both cannot possess the labouring time simultaneously.

Further, this capability of information should be conceived positively, not as economists do as 'lacking rivalry' but for its potential for simultaneous complete use. The three terms 'simultaneous complete use' capture the way information can be used at the same time by many, and all who are using it can, potentially, fully benefit. There is a sense in which conceptualising information as a lack or a negative embeds in that concep-tualisation the view that information does not allow exclusive ownership, which positions exclusion as the norm from which information deviates, whereas this 'lack' is precisely a more active capability of information. Information should not be conceived through lack or loss, but through its potential for differentiation and multiplicity. While it might seem a little ungainly, I will therefore use 'simultaneous complete use' to refer to this aspect of information.

This quality of information, that it can be simultaneously available to all to use to the full benefit of that information, is like many being able to simultaneously and fully hear a song without the number of people hearing it diminishing the quality of the experience of listening to the sonic information. This quality lies at the core of struggles over piracy and digital rights mechanisms in the twenty-first century and hence is often located as part of legal issues. However, it is important to see that the legalities of information are a result of the quality of information, in particular that it can be made available for simultaneous complete use. Further, this quality is more fully realised when information is digital and moves in the context of the internet. When information was primarily materialised in formats that restricted simultaneous complete use, for example in books that only one person can read at a time or on vinyl records that can only be heard in one space at a time, then the potential conflict between the distribution potential of simultaneous complete use and restrictive legal forms was ameliorated. Now that any digital form of such media-objects as a song or a book can be made available simultaneously to all to read or hear, legal issues have become a core battleground of information politics. However, though there is no question that these legal issues are important, the key is to see that such issues as those Gillespie traces in relation to copyright or Postigo in relation to digital rights or that are core to Free Software and distributive licenses, result from the nature of information. At this point in conceptualising the theory of information politics, it is important to put aside these legal debates and focus on the quality of information, in order to ensure consideration of how this quality relates to exploitation or liberation (Gillespie 2007; Postigo 2012; Weber 2004).

An important starting point is then that information cannot simply be conceived of as the exclusive possession of an individual that may be taken from them or bargained by them. Analyses of social media networks or of clouds that see the taking of an individual's personal data and the recursing of it as a straightforward form of exploitation are assuming that the users' knowledge about themselves that they input and that is then recursed along with others' similar data is these users' exclusive private property. This is why, when discussing clouds and social media networks earlier, it was clear that some kind of transfer of control over information was occurring and that this was related to the imposition of a particular conception of information as exclusive property, which allowed individually provided information to be channelled into a platform that then gifted recursions to the platform controller. But at the same time it could become unclear whose information is whose, for example when analysing who owns recursed information, because although it is new information created by the platform the recursion was only possible on the basis of the users' input of information. Understanding information as an exclusive property that can be exchanged underpins and allows the idea of a contract – free information for free services – that results in exploitation in the recursing of data and the transformation of leisure or sociality into free immaterial labour.

On the one hand, it is clear that platforms like Google and Facebook have massively profited from recursing individuals' data and this seems an obvious inequity. But, on the other hand, seeing this as an inequity embeds a notion of information as exclusive property within the analysis that sits uneasily with the potential of information to offer itself in multiple ways. Further, such an interpretation of information means that because recursions are themselves new forms of information, then to be consistent in seeing information as the exclusive property of the one who produces it (such as the user who provides it to a platform) the recursions resulting from the use of users' personal information should be seen as the platform owners' rightful property because the platform has produced that new information. What might seem an obvious exploitation in the vast profitability of some cloud and social media networks, because they use devices and network-protocols to privately recurse data that is given them or exchanged to them for free services, is undermined by starting from a view that anyone's information about themselves – their age, gender, location, sexuality – is their exclusive property profiting from which is a transfer equivalent to that of domestic labour to men or surplus labour to capitalists. Information as simultaneous complete use needs to be taken account of in information exploitation, and this means that ideas of information as property need to be handled carefully or they may embed in analysis the very ideas of information ownership that many major information corporations want to assert: that information should be made into a rival good (Gillespie 2007).

This is a key difference in understanding exchanges involving information that constitute exploitation. It is not that in labour, domestic labour, visibility and so on the nature and quality of these substances that are extracted in exploitation do not have to be formed. All have to be created as certain kinds of property in order for the exploitations they are part of to materialise; but information is the non-rival property that has to be made rival. Even if I offer my labour for free or for a community, I can still only offer, say, one hour of my sweat and muscle, but my information can be kept by me and taken by many others unless it is created as exclusive. If I labour in a factory or a kitchen then the value that my labour produces in the hours I work cannot be taken by both me and my boss – only one side of this divide can benefit from goods that only offer non-simultaneous incomplete use. In social media networks my likes, pokes, posts and chats all have to be conceived as a property of the particular network so that these networks can privatise the recursions that produce the extra information that leads to targeted advertising and other sources of profit.

What is clear in the preceding case studies and platform analyses is that forming recursions, devices and network-protocols in particular ways can mean creating information as a particular kind of property. The divide identified by the Free Software movement between information as a distributive property and as an exclusive property is at play here. As is well known, the Free Software movement inverts exclusive property by writing software licences that enforce the right to distribution, so that anyone using software licensed in this way is also forced to keep it open so that others may use it and alter it (Weber 2004: 16). In 2014, the Free Software Foundation defined four freedoms that define whether software is free or not in the following way.

A program is free software if the program's users have the four essential freedoms:

- The freedom to run the program, for any purpose (freedom 0).
- The freedom to study how the program works, and change it so it does your computing as you wish (freedom 1). Access to the source code is a precondition for this.
- The freedom to redistribute copies so you can help your neighbor (freedom 2).
- The freedom to distribute copies of your modified versions to others (freedom 3). By doing this you can give the whole community a chance to benefit from your changes. Access to the source code is a precondition for this. (FSF 2014)

Software is only free if there is open access to the information, the source code. This enforcement of distribution is however predicated on an assertion of an exclusive property right, it then inverts that exclusion by asserting rights to access and distribution (Jordan 2008: 59–64; Coleman 2012c: 69–70). Information as distribution is part of the simultaneous complete use of information because then the benefits that are available to all are made available to all simultaneously – in Free Software's case, fixes and improvements to software are available and can be included in the experience of all users and makers of such software. Within a legal system based on property as exclusion, the Free Software Foundation's use of exclusion to create distribution can be seen as an important tactical choice to preserve information as simultaneous complete use. In principle, however, what is key is not this tactic but the possibility of simultaneous complete use of information. In principle, why impair information by focusing on its lack?

Understanding information as simultaneous complete use points then to understanding the benefits of information: Who benefits from information propagated as simultaneous complete use or from information owned as a rival good? Clearly social media network platforms that are created for profit benefit from conceiving information as non-simultaneous incomplete use, thereby creating the exchange of personal information for services and securing private ownership of recursions. The Facebook user may have the scraps from the table in likes, pokes and posts, while the major shareholders of Facebook may have the riches of recursions turned into advertising. In contrast, the community of free software users may have the improved software that distribution provides and importantly they may contribute to the benefit they gain in ways that automatically contribute to the benefit others gain; they may become in Postigo's sense digital citizens because participation in making is possible.

What is the meaning of the digital rights movement, and what does it show us about technology for society as a whole? What it shows primarily is that as various forms of consumption are increasingly mediated through technologies that can increasingly control our levels of access and involvement, it becomes important to seize that very same technology for the opportunities it may afford us to become participants in the making of cultural goods. This capture requires not a tacit acceptance of the means provided for us by media companies, but rather a consideration of how we might actively design technologies for ourselves ... media consumption should be a form of intervention into the manufacture of cultural goods, and the technologies we choose to mediate content should have those affordances. (Postigo 2012: 178)

Postigo's argument also makes clear that consumption has conceptually and practically broken down when it only makes sense through production in participation. Digital citizens being defined by their participation in digital culture also implies the often discussed collapse of the divide between production and consumption (Bruns 2008; Banks and Pott 2010). Underlying and implicit within this conception of citizenship is information as simultaneous complete use, because only when we have information in this form can we fully utilise it to produce further information that is always available to others for further making. If information becomes a rival good we become subject to its owners; only if information's capacity for simultaneous complete use is realised do we become active. We may then become digital citizens not digital subjects.

Moreover, this is a relationship of exploitation and liberation. Information cannot be both open to simultaneous complete use and be a rival good, it has to be formed as one or the other. Once information is conceived as non-simultaneous incomplete use it can then exclusively benefit one group by being drawn off from another group. Within information terms this means that the production of differences and their movements can be placed within the hands of particular groups, where they allow both initial information capture and the restriction of the benefits of recursion, but this can only occur if information is degraded from simultaneous complete use. Information's ability to act with simultaneous complete use or to be made into a rival good is core to the relationship of information exploitation because information has to be in some sense exclusive for it to become transferable in a way that makes some rich by making others poor.

The first principle of information as a political antagonism is digital citizenry, not digital subjection. Information as simultaneous complete use opens up the widest mutual possibilities, whereas information as a rival good opens up hoarding and digital kings and queens. The theory of information as differences that move and their effectuation in the times of digitisation and the internet through the dynamics of recursion, devices and network-protocols means information exploitation and liberation can be seen in the fundamental difference between rival goods and simultaneous complete use. As we have seen in relation to platforms and battlegrounds, these two possibilities are materialised in specific ways. Exploring the meaning of platforms in terms of exploitation and liberation is the next stage in theorising information as exploitation and liberation.

Information Platforms: Differentiation and Enclosure

It has been a repeated point in this analysis that recursion, devices and network-protocols are dynamics that are formed into different architectures in which patterns of relations between them create different types of platforms. The nature of some specific platforms were explored, but how does materialisation of recurrent inter-relations between the three dynamics or bodies of information power feed into information exploitation and liberation? One starting point is the contrast between information as simultaneous complete use and information as a rival good, which shifts the focus to the benefits coming from information use and the issue of whether there can or should be ownership of information at all. The path to seeing how materialisation into platforms connects is to consider the benefits that follow. This can be done by looking at the key moments of information in platforms and how these are produced and managed.

Two different kinds of information need to be distinguished, as will be familiar from previous discussion. First, there is the kind of information that a user provides, or that is mined from them, which seems to come from their singular nature: name, email address, gender, age, etc. Second, there is information made from already available information. In the abstract this is too fine a distinction because someone's information about their individuality is also information about information; my age is a numerical difference derived from my date of birth embedded in an information system of years, days, months. As a difference that moves there will always be some sense in which information is about other information because information that is the same information is no information – there is no differentiation. The particular kind of difference at stake here is more specific and makes sense when seen in the context of two moments in the movement of information through recurring groups of recursions, devices and network-protocols. The first moment is defined not by being the origin of information but by being provided by an individual and, in its individuality, being as yet un-related to other relevant information in the context in which it is provided. When someone provides their age in a particular information moment they do not relate it to the ages of others who have already provided their details because each 'provider' does not have access to that information. The second kind of information emerges when such bits of information provided in isolation are inter-related and produce new kinds of information. Each kind of information is thus involved in a different kind of differentiation.

Information that appears individualised appears so because it is fetishised to the actant that provides it. Information about an individual that is a definite difference is fetishised as a quality of the individual, it may appear to the provider as their property because it derives from their self and their singularity. However, information about anyone or any thing is only made into a property by certain social relations. Information is by nature available for simultaneous complete use and is only made in differentiation, meaning that information must always relate to other information. My age is only available as information because it is different to many other people's age, yet when I give my age to register on a site I am interpolated to see that age as something that I give in exchange for services. What I have sometimes previously called 'first order' information is produced at that performative moment when someone, a user of some kind, offers up information that appears to be about their individuality that was not previously available to a platform of some sort. In that moment, this information is performed as a property inherent to the user offering it up, and is then also available to be the reason this exchange was happening in the first place. This issue is easiest to identify when thinking of sites that demand information in return for services and in this context it is often about turning information into an exclusive property to enable the exchange.

Exchanges of information do not stop once someone has offered information about their identity for use by a platform, because their already provided information may be connected to whatever services they use and how they use them and the user is likely to continue providing more information about themselves. This produces more information which now enters a greyer area because, while it may well seem to the user to be first order, because it appears to be about their identity and so is theirs to dispose of, to the platform it only exists because of the platform and so seems to fall to the platform.

The distinction between first and second order information in relation to platforms also occurs in relation to non-proprietary platforms. Even when signing up for a collectively produced forum – for example among a group of gamers who are friends and wish to communicate outside the game – in which the users may provide all the infrastructure themselves and so create a collectively run service, each user will in some way identify themselves to the system. Users here may have to provide commonly identified information, and though it may be minimal, perhaps no more than an email address, the relationship of an identity offering information about itself to a platform is repeated. The extreme position does not address distinctions between profit or not-for-profit, or privately or communally owned platforms, but relates to anonymity. If a user of a site is entirely anonymous then information about identity as an exclusive property is not possible. Even if being entirely anonymous is difficult, with sites that allow anonymous posting often requiring some kind of exchanges of information about a user and even if no information is requested users can often be identified by the IP number they connect with, it remains that there is at least the possibility of being entirely anonymous which short circuits first order information. Anonymity eliminates the fetishism of thinking that information about one's identity is already one's own and is formed in isolation to other information as the property of that identity. However, this is an extreme and difficult to maintain state. Even in a case where offline and online identities are radically disconnected and the offline identity is anonymous, the style of communication a user develops may identify them as a particular person even if that is disconnected from their 'offline' identity, creating forms of online identity that might be exchanged. In this broad sense, first order information or information fetishised as one's identity is near inescapable and so provides a possible basis for exchange.

What has been called 'second order' information is consequent on a platform of some sort that allows identification of significant differences that may be co-related and recursed producing information on information. Second order information appears always in relation to the platform it is part of and gains its sense as a property depending on the formation of the platform which itself results significantly from the nature of first order information. If first order information is a property available for exchange for services then information on information – which can include both co-relations of first order with other first order information and recursions – appears almost naturally as the property of the platform. The more voluminous the first order information the more information on information may be generated as the property of the platform. Moreover, first order information does not stop being produced at entry to the platform, creating the possibility of a confused area of information between first and second order contributions. A platform may continue to ask the user for extra information, perhaps to open up other services, and depending on the platform this may confuse what appeared at first to be clean divisions of performatively produced 'original' information that is then offered for services that produce subsequent information.

The key point, however, is not to lay too much emphasis on making too fine distinctions within information processes in a platform; and that between first and second order is broadly enough, rather the importance of this division is that it dramatises that a platform has to enclose information in such a way to make the information consistent enough to be co-related and recursed or the information on information cannot be produced. Age as a bit of information may seem obviously simple, but it must be held in any platform in a form such that information is able to be co-related and to be recursable, whether as a date in words, numbers or some other format, whether it has day first then month or in reverse order, and so on. The point about the fetishisation of information as individual property is that it partly derives from the fact that the platform requires information to be exchanged in forms that are consistent enough to make creating information from information possible.

This is the case even if the platform is 'everything', as we saw with securitisation. Here users of the internet had first order information formulated and removed without their knowledge (including the interesting idea that various platform owners such as Google or Yahoo had 'their' information taken) with the resulting recursions and co-relations kept secret as well. The pursuit of all knowledge follows the division of first and second order information, leading to some of the outrage resulting from exposure of these security practices being fuelled by the protest that 'taking our information' without knowledge or consent was an exploitation. Further, the fetishisation of information as a property of identity allows the creation of this massive enclosure of information which can then be profiled, again relying on the identification of information with an individual's singularity as their property, and ultimately returning it to individuals in terms of discarding them as innocent or targeting them as guilty of having the wrong profile. Even if 'all knowledge' is the platform, a platform still needs to place information in relation to other information by ensuring each is consistent with the other.

Such enclosures are sometimes taken to be comparable to the great enclosures of land that occurred at the dawn of capitalism, which decimated the commonwealth on which many relied (Marx 1976: 885–94). This well known, indeed foundational, capitalist exploitation needs to be rethought in relation to information, since the enclosure of land relies on rival goods whereas information allows simultaneous complete use. The enclosures of information platforms need then to be examined not so much in terms of the fact of enclosure of a property from another, in the sense of a transfer of property, but in terms of the benefits that are drawn from the enclosure of information that could potentially be available to many at once but which actually may only be available to the platform controller. We need to see that platforms are necessary for different kinds of information riches to be generated and that the platform will involve the codification of information to allow some form of comparability of information resulting in the possibility of the creation of information on information, but we can also assert the need to see who is benefiting from an enclosure of something that all could share in.

Platforms create differences on differences but each platform creates only certain differences on certain other differences. What is produced informationally from this moment then is a richness of information that may exponentially create complex information environments and goods. If the fact of a platform is not at stake, who or what benefits from a platform must always be at stake.

If a platform has to enclose this does not mean that it has to form information as an exclusive property. Platforms may homogenise information to create recursions in ways that promote information as simultaneous complete use. The possibility of enclosure as commons opens here, with an information commons based on information as simultaneous complete use for all. Such ideas clearly relate to the debate around the commons, particularly as Berry and Hardt and Negri have articulated it, in which it is argued that 'practices of the common in our world provide conditions that make possible a project for the creation of a democracy based on free expression and life in common' (Hardt and Negri 2005: 202; Berry and Moss 2005). These words of Hardt and Negri's are not related to the specific context of information as a politics as theorised here, indeed Hardt and Negri seem more concerned with reordering the multiplicity of politics by integrating political struggles under the sign of the Empire and the Multitude. But they do articulate the idea of a commons that is under collective control beyond the corporation and the state. Addressing similar concerns, Coleman reminds us to be careful of lumping together disparate forms of digital activism, but she also stirringly points out in relation to free software coders and their new technologies that:

> what makes these projects so interesting is not how they engender democracy writ large, or fundamentally change the warp and woof of economic and social structures, but that collaborators make technology at the same time that they experiment in the making of social commonwealth; it is there where the hard work of freedom is practiced. (Coleman 2012c: 210)

If these ideas can be applied to platforms as articulated herein they will only work if information is not treated as an exclusive property. The most mutually beneficial power of information is its capacity for simultaneous complete use, and this can underpin a platform in which information is formed and recursed in such a way that the benefits are available completely and simultaneously to all who have access to the platform.

Interpretations of information commons are often objected to as meaning not the work of democracy, free expression and life in common, but the destruction of income for information creators and the loss of rights of authorship, both of which, it is claimed, destroy the motivation for producing information. There can be no doubt that freedom is an important factor in the debate about enclosures, the commons and information in the twenty-first century. For example, in the name of creativity and the commons, the Libre Culture Manifesto asserts the potential of a 'creative field of concepts and ideas that are free from ownership' (Berry and Moss 2005). But the conception of information as simultaneous complete use does not preclude the possibility of forms of information being exchanged in different ways, including through payment, whether in kind, services or some other currency. Information can be made freely available and be paid for, just as many give money to the foundation that makes LibreOffice software even while that software is available to freely download. Similarly, simultaneous complete use does not block specific bits of information having authorship attributed to them. Ways of making non-exploitative exchange and ways of allowing those who wish to be identified as the producers of certain information forms are issues that may be resolved within platforms while still allowing the information to be treated as simultaneous complete use. Such problems of resourcing information creators or attributing credit for new information will have to be articulated in ways that accord with simultaneous complete use because this principle is foundational for any platform intended to implement liberatory forms of information politics. A platform must enclose the information that forms it, but that leaves open the issue of whether the platform is an exclusive enclosure or a distributive commons. Only a distributive commons can give full rein to information as simultaneous complete use available to all who can benefit from that information. But, as just noted, a distributive commons does not preclude authorship being attributed to new differences or the introduction of non-exploitative forms of exchange to support such authors.

Platforms can codify information and not treat it as exclusive property, because codifying means a homogenisation that allows information to be related to other information rather than requiring it to be treated as exclusive property. A distributive commons can still ensure co-relation and recursion. This may overlap with the kinds of issues of the common at stake in keeping the World Wide Web protocols collectively and non-profitably owned, or in the way Free Software projects return the information they make to their makers and users, but it invokes a wider issue that may be more challenging and may help address the nature of the collectivity in information politics. Berry argues that the underlying politics of the Free Software movement has a kernel of radical politics embedded within a moderate, social democratic view of politics. Coleman draws attention to the Free Software programmers' general lack of a broader political affiliation while also noting the radical challenge they pose by defamiliarising such things as exclusive property and practising forms of democratic making. It is these kernels of radicalism that are relevant here in their articulation of simultaneous complete use by a collective (Berry 2008: 192; Coleman 2012c: 196–210).

The argument I am making is that the connection of information as simultaneous complete use to the necessity of platforms that define co-relations and recursions defines a liberatory information environment. This also suggests that it is the platform that holds information and protects it as simultaneous complete use, no matter who or what contributes information. This returns the discussion to the rights of the networked as a network that were raised when discussing privacy and publicness in social media. That discussion progressed to the point of considering whether the user or individual actant had the right to withdraw information they had already provided to the network and we can begin to see the issue that arises when any information created in a platform is protected by the platform to ensure that the information is available for simultaneous complete use. It is then to the rights of the networkers as a network that I need to turn to further understand the principled issues of platforms of differentiation.

Networkers as Networks

Analysis of information liberation and exploitation points first to information as simultaneous complete use and second to information's incarnations in platforms. I now turn to a third issue concerning the complexity that results from whether information is in some sense held by users or whether the network holds and propagates the information on it. When discussing two different kinds of divisions between public and private, I identified a divide based on the form of internet communication that reverses a number of communicative practices that are so familiar most people take them for granted. To understand the potential kinds of benefits that information politics both produces and is used to pursue it is important to broaden this point and identify two intersecting and contradictory ways in which information is communicated.

The two different kinds of conception of information, as exclusive property or as simultaneous complete use, can be related to the ways of dividing public and private discussed above when analysing social media networks. I argued there that one public-private divide revolves around the conception of identity as something that an individual has the right to control and disclose only as they see fit, which is close to the conception of information about an individual being their property. The second public-private divide revolves around the way that becoming a member of a virtual community means being heard by others on the network and being recognised through styles of communication rather than being recognised as an identity that authorises messages. The reversal is from communication in which meaning can be sent because the identity of the author of a message is recognised through various cultural and technological means, to communication in which meaning can only be sent when those who receive it can recognise the style of the sender and so it becomes the receivers of messages who both stabilise a communicative system that allows meaning to be transferred and who authorise what a communicative identity is in such a system (Jordan 2013a). Bringing these ideas of information as property and information in communication together will identify two contradictory and co-existent ways in which users and networks flourish or fail.

On one continuum, information relates to the identity of a user, individual or actant who is understood as the author of their information. This continuum stretches from the utility of protecting individuals and defining their rights – for example, not to have their webcams spied on or their personal information traded by others because that information is their property – to the problems already discussed of platforms that impose a conception of identity as property in order to trade it for services and then convert sociality and entertainment into free labour. This can be summarised as the politics of information as a right. The second continuum relies on information as simultaneous complete use, even when it is about a user or individual's identity, which locates information as always-already part of webs and interconnections to which this information contributes and from which it gains its 'sense', its difference. This continuum stretches from the demand for openness and access to all information, because that information is a constitutive part of a collective identity, imagined community or social network (in the broadest sense), to the archive of all information created which refuses withdrawal of information, both in principle because it is part of the making of collective life and because the information space has become so vast and so often replicated that it is impossible to know if information can be removed. This continuum might be summarised as the politics of information as a responsibility. And the final complexity of these two continuums of information rights and responsibilities is that they exist simultaneously even though they contradict each other.

If we consider information as a right then a politics emerges concerning what a user or individual actant may call their own and what they can base their claims on. The liberatory potential is that grassroots or dein-stitutionalised information citizens have a clear basis on which to make claims and take action. In this conception, it is clear that information can be 'stolen' and used improperly because it was not a corporation or nation-state's information in the first place. In MacKinnon's phrase, the 'consent of the networked' is a powerful basis for action that contests the rights of large institutions (MacKinnon 2012). Yet, this conception is also easily understood as a claim to the property of the self, an easy move to make in which information about one's self is closely identified with the nature of that self – my age and the information of what my age is are, after all, different. Once information about the self is held to be the property of the self it becomes alienable and available for trade. Here, as already discussed, the way is opened up for many institutions to promote the idea that information is property so that it can be owned because it can then be collated and traded. Here the individual user is just that, individualised, with collective anger and action diminished and needing to be created on the basis of each individual's rights. This is of course possible, but it also underpins some of the clearest exploitations in which the possibility for an individual to not enter into the bargain offered by a platform is often undermined. In the early twenty-first century, is it possible to not be a member of some social network platform? Or not to use some form of search which operates by collating and recursing individual actant's data? Can one not be a user of such information platforms, any more than one could not use the telephone or a hundred years ago not use letters? The hallucinations of the unabomber or the practice of the techno-luddite are difficult to sustain for billions (Jones 2006). When there is no choice but to use a platform in which information is conceived as a personal property based on identity, this also means having to give up that identity in some form to gain access to platforms. Yet, at the same time, there remains the possibility that platforms could be created whose benefits go to many based on many individuals' rights to their information about their identity.

The way platforms can be difficult to avoid, unless one is excluded or seeks exclusion from the information sphere altogether, also invokes information as a responsibility; that is, information as collectively held and our responsibilities as members of information collectives to those collectives. Information as simultaneous complete use means information cannot be seen as individualised 'bits' but as inter-related and gaining its being as a piece of information from its place in a web of differentiations. If the web of differentiations shifts and the differences of a piece of information change then that information disappears in favour of new information. In communicative terms, if one has to be heard to exist then having one's style changed by related pieces of information being removed or altered is equivalent to having one's identity altered. This implies a politics of openness and access. The right to have information is not just about an individual's 'bits' but about the right to protect the meaning of information in the webs of differentiation, and this can only exist at a collective level: the web of differentiation can only be owned by itself and is always in this sense damaged by any lesser ownership.

The politics of Free Software and the common expresses this kind of politics (Coleman 2012c; Berry 2008). Such a politics allows and underpins claims to access, to openness and to participation; information is making differences, and to be able to make differences that move necessarily means having access to and using webs of differentiation. In Postigo's sense, this participation is what makes a digital citizen and not a subject or in Berry's sense this is the '*freedom to tinker*' that places on the political agenda the control of technology and who forms the nature of technology for who's interests and, finally, this is Coleman's practice of coding freedom (Coleman 2012c; Berry 2008: 197; Postigo 2012). Openness, access and making result from seeing information as already collectivised and available to all. Yet there is also the question of integration into this collectivisation. Can anything ever be rightfully withdrawn from the webs of differentiation? What harm is done by any deletion and what, if any, justification could there be to delete? This is an issue Rheingold articulated early on, as mass use of the internet began to grow, through the question of whether, in principle, anyone has the right to delete their contributions to online communities. If a virtual community is built from the information contributed, co-related and recursed, then, in information terms, removing what has already been made begins to unmake that community (Rheingold 1994: 34; Jordan 1999a: 97–8). At the same time, everything is archived and our differences are available to be tracked whether in frenzies of securitisation or commercialisation. When information is a responsibility because it is a collectively held web of differentiation, then we are made responsible to the collective; we can call on that web of differentiation and we can be subject to its requirements.

In summary, the politics of information of identity as personal rights offers both a basis for grassroots movements and a basis for the conversion of our selves into exchange values. The justification of the information individual's rights will always be tempting and can be effective, but it will also always be a way of limiting information and will always base its effectiveness on a language that easily feeds the desires of corporations and governments. The politics of information as simultaneous complete use and as a responsibility offers both a basis for openness, access and making and a basis for a total archive of information that demands differences never be removed. And the final component of these possibilities for exploitation and liberation is their interaction, for at all times they co-exist and contradict each other. There are two aspects of this that are important: contradiction and obfuscation.

The two continuums are contradictory and clash; this is not a dialectic with the hope of synthesis. As such, each continuum will not only produce its own sense of liberation as personal control or as openness, access and making, and its own sense of exploitation as commodified identities or as a total and endless archive; it will also tend to contradict itself within each liberation and exploitation. Information about identity understood as a private self that turns information into property contradicts information as simultaneous complete use; the two produce liberations that criticise and demand change from each other. For example, as the Creative Commons develops licenses to mediate copyleft with artistic control, how do you both support the artist as owner of their information product and promote the kind of collective ownership of copyleft? Exploitations contradict each other as the enclosures of commodified information seek to wall themselves off from a full commitment to webs of difference that are total. Digital citizens and subjects are formed and reformed through such conflicts as when Google dislikes Facebook erecting a wall against it as it can no longer integrate all that information into its webs of difference; but Google also dislikes the security agencies tapping into their network when securitisation seeks an all-encompassing web of differences.

To build liberations and to fight exploitations will require negotiating between these conflicts and resolving through struggle the most liberatory possibilities in a situation that is inherently complex. This raises the second point because for both liberatory potentials obfuscation is evil. Obscuring the nature of identity information as property will utterly undermine the liberatory potential of information as rights and it will make exploitation able to be implemented much more easily. Obscuring the information landscape and what is available to become part of it undermines openness and access and so damages and diminishes making. All the well-known tactics of obfuscation are exploitative. From the EULAs and TOS that are written in impenetrable styles and go on interminably, but which can be agreed to with a single mouse-click, to the massive secrecy of the security agencies and corporations who never make clear their algorithms or the results of their co-relations and recursing, and at every deliberately manufactured moment of fear, uncertainty and doubt in between; all these are exploitative.

This complex field of possibilities needs to be considered in relation to the two points raised earlier about the liberatory potential of simultaneous complete use and the construction of platforms as distributive commons. Promoting simultaneous complete use does not mean ensuring an abstract sense of access of all information to all information but of the production of simultaneous complete use within particular platforms and their specific instantiations. The platform also makes a transition between the principle of information as open, accessible and makeable and the application of this to a particular kind of openness, access and making. In that transition, particular attention has to be paid to actors' capabilities being produced in ways that prevent the possibility of subjection of actors to the requirements of the platform. Such a subjection remains the potential dark side of simultaneous complete use, which will need to be mediated by the nature of platforms and their benefits. It will be important to implement platforms in ways that promote simultaneous complete use and that understand under which conditions withdrawal of information may be possible and may even, in its guarding against total surveillance, offer benefits to a community. It is in the nature of the platforms that these possibilities can be mediated, which means that above all the nature of platforms themselves must be open, accessible and makeable. The rights of the network need to be implemented across multiple platforms and each time in ways that mediate the contradictions of information as rights and as responsibilities.

Information treated as an individual's property because it is about their self will always be a tempting political base. However, the effectiveness of this tactic is based on speaking the same language of exclusive property that allows the exploitation of recursions in privatised platforms and the profiling of selves. The power of individual rights is based on the same logic of property as the exploitations of information corporations and securitising intelligence agencies. As such they can only be used tactically, as passing moments when an assertion of information of the self to be inherently an individual's right may be effective in a specific moment of struggle. In the longer run, information liberation must eschew the individual and their rights and run the danger of the total archive by forming multiple platforms offering openness, access and making.

A third part of information as a political antagonism produces both complexity and contradiction in the struggles for liberation though contradictions based on repeated and genuine interests that cannot be made consistent. It also makes clear that mystification will always serve those who exploit. An emphasis on digital citizenship not subjection, platforms of differentiation, and the rights and responsibilities of information can form the basis for a map of information liberation and exploitation. But it will remain a partial map until the inevitable, lived connections between information as a politics and other vital forms of liberation and exploitation are also analysed.

Connections

There are three different aspects of the kinds of connections between information and other political antagonisms that can be drawn from the case studies of the iPad, death in gaming and hacktivism. First, information carries its political dynamics built on recursions, devices and network-protocols wherever it connects. Second, these dynamics of information power often provide tactics that can be utilised in other struggles. Third, connections are often conjunctural and hard to comprehend outside of concrete struggles. Looking at these in turn allows an understanding of connections and information in the field of many political antagonisms.

As has been argued throughout previous chapters, information as a political antagonism has specific dynamics that structure its liberations and exploitations, just as other antagonisms have their own specificities. These dynamics themselves constitute one connection between antagonisms because where information connects to other exploitations so its dynamics will have to connect with other dynamics and create new political formations in those contexts. The first point is that the analysis of information as a political antagonism has relevance to other political antagonisms because it is imported into them as and when it connects to them, and with the opposite being just as true. At the points where antagonisms connect, the analysis of information conflicts must take account of these other dynamics, just as when analysing the iPad it would be wrong to focus only on information and ignore class issues of labour exploitation. This is not to claim in principle superiority in any direction, only that antagonisms must take account of the specificities of each other.

We can see this if we consider universality. In any political conflict there are bound to be issues of sexuality, labour, gender, information, the environment and so on; these are universal factors that are also key political antagonisms of our time. But this does not mean that all are equally connected in every struggle; rather, it means that connections are always possible but only in conflict will the variable importance of particular antagonisms to each other become clear. It also does not mean that one antagonism integrates others within itself. As already argued, this could only mean interpreting integrated antagonisms through the integrator, which would entail discarding the specific dynamics of each antagonism. The specificity of antagonisms disappears if all struggles are integrated into one antagonism. Further, such a claim suggests exploitations and liberations could be doubly subjected not just within their own antagonism but also to their integration within another struggle that may not be their own.

The second point about information follows, namely that if information politics are carried into other antagonisms in specific contexts, and vice versa, then a key connection that makes this process happen lies in the tactics that different struggles can offer to each other. Here information politics will be carried into other struggles as they use various forms of communication and platforms. It was notable that as the use of email began to increase within British activism, activists who were moving away from letter, telephone trees and 'zines experienced not only a more horizontal, many-to-many form of communication but also suffered under information overload as they became weighed down by their email lists (Gillan et al. 2008: 142–5). Information-specific tactics like hacktivist virtual sit-ins are available to any cause, just as are street demonstrations and other forms of civil disobedience. Infrastructure politics are also available to all kinds of activists, with encryption techniques or apps to track police movements during demonstrations and other such devices all being relevant to many kinds of struggle.

The point here is that a host of tactics are available from information politics and each device or network-protocol that is integrated will bring some of the same information politics into other struggles. In this sense, the use of information technologies means that many struggles may need to consider the effect on them of information power and try to identify where they might be contributing to different information exploitations – just as information struggles have to consider if they are contributing to other exploitations. Gerbaudo has noted the use of mass social media networks like Facebook in alter-globalisation struggles and shown how this is important because it connects activists to a mass audience. If such struggles had located themselves in more activist focused devices, such as Diaspora pods, then they would have secured their information environment but would also have cut themselves off (Gerbaudo 2012). However, even accepting Gerbaudo's argument, it seems clear that Dean's critique of activism's contributing to communicative capitalism would apply simultaneously. The recursions of activists on Facebook still feed a mainstream social media and fuel communicative capitalism, even if the differences are being moved by activists opposed to capitalism (Dean 2012: 123–33). It is possible for liberation struggles in one antagonism to fuel exploitations elsewhere, and there is a need in analysis to ensure these connections are examined and critiqued.

Information politics may have its own dynamics but it may also embed and promote other exploitations through these dynamics. The case of online gaming and 'militarised masculinity' has already been discussed. This, however, also points to one of most difficult issues in that the theorisation of a multi-pole politics as the overall radical political environment refuses a totalisation of all struggles together. This refusal means that connections between the dynamics of struggles will most powerfully be made in more concrete than abstract analyses and struggles. This is the final and third point about connections because it is often difficult to say much generally and abstractly about them except, as I have done, that they will exist and that they do not easily and simply fit together. Analyses like those of platforms and battlegrounds given above are far more able to grasp and connect different antagonisms than a more abstract theory of an antagonism's dynamics, precisely because the main reason for such abstract theories is to do the necessary work of identifying a specific dynamics of exploitation and liberation. In following connections, then, it is crucial to ensure both that their specific dynamics are respected and their functioning identified while also seeing where such dynamics interact.

Connections do not constitute a jigsaw puzzle of pieces that fit together neatly to create one picture. Rather, connections each themselves constitute an empirically identifiable picture of a particular struggle in which specific dynamics of exploitation and liberation will shift as they connect to, fuel and contradict other such dynamics. The mess of the world is primary when connecting antagonisms.

Conclusion: Dynamics of Information Politics

The dynamics of information power are recursions, devices and network-protocols that are formed into platforms and appear in the political struggles and conflicts of our times. These three linked dynamics are always present in the arguments given in this book because it is their nature, argued in previous chapters and explored in platforms and battlegrounds, which constitutes the way information power is understood and underpins how exploitation and liberation in the politics of information are here conceptualised.

These arguments map out and analyse a theory of information exploitation and liberation as the defining dynamics of information as a political antagonism in the twenty-first century. It is a theory that follows other theories and that will be contested, modified and developed in its turn. Very few of the political antagonisms are as dominated by one theory as class is by Marxism, and even within class studies there is a rich and complex variety of Marxist interpretations, as well as alternative theories such as those derived from Weber, which when taken together make for a vast and not necessarily consistent theoretical and empirical corpus. Similarly, feminism, black power and anti-racism, queer and other theoretical complexes dealing with an antagonism are made up of many different intersecting and contesting complex conceptualisations and material studies. The politics of information is no different and this book does no more than contribute, but it does claim to have contributed. The arguments here conceptualise a theory of the dynamics of information in recursions, devices and network-protocols, and in four aspects of information exploitation and liberation that build on many existing ideas and arguments of information politics and will hopefully affect those to come.

Four points make up this theory of information exploitations and liberations as the mechanics of information as a political antagonism. Being a citizen and not a subject means seeing information as simultaneous complete use. Platforms, with their enclosures of information, are necessary so that information can be consistent and so able to be recursed. Platforms must be analysed with regard to the nature of the benefits of their enclosures and recursions and to who gains from them. Platforms that create digital citizens promote openness, access and making, particularly in relation to the nature of the platform itself, where restriction of openness, access and making attempts to channel benefits to platform controllers. Focusing on the rights of the network tempts us to base information liberation on a right to control information about one's self, which may have tactical efficacy or may be important in the connection to another political antagonism, but which pays for its efficacy by confirming the basis for privatisation of what could be collective information benefits. The responsibilities of information in platforms argues for information collectives that create real possibilities to make and use information which recurses further benefits back to the collectives, but each platform must also mitigate and address the dangers of the total archive that refuses any information withdrawal. Finally, information exploitations and liberations always exist in the mess of the world connected to other antagonisms, and can most clearly be seen in those messy webs. Information politics is imported into other struggles, particularly through the use of information as a tactic and will in turn be affected by the dynamics of other political antagonisms.

The dynamics of recursions, devices and network-protocols were seen through the abstract architectures of platforms and in the complexities and intersections of particular battlegrounds. Shifting back out from the mess of the world, draws these arguments into an understanding of information exploitation and how we might be liberated. Information liberation means creating platforms of recurrent patterns of recursions, devices and network-protocols that prize information for its capacity for simultaneous complete use that delivers benefits through openness, access and making to all information citizens.

Bibliography

Abbate J. (1999) *Inventing the Internet* (Cambridge MA: MIT Press).

Agamben G. (2005) *States of Exception* (Chicago: University of Chicago Press).

Anderson N. (2012) 'Google Cut Off Megaupload's Ad Money Voluntarily Back in 2007', *Arstechnica*, available at http://arstechnica.com/tech-policy/2012/01/google-cut-off-megauploads-ad-money-voluntarily-back-in-2007 (last accessed August 2013).

— (2011) 'Tweeting Tyrants Out of Tunisia: Global Internet at Its Best', *Wired*, available at http://www.wired.com/threatlevel/2011/01/tunisia (last accessed February 2014).

Andrejevic M. (2013) *Infoglut: How Too Much Information is Changing the Way We Think and Know* (London: Routledge).

Anon (2013) 'What effect will Monday's US Congressional hearing have on price?', *Bitcoin Forum*, https://bitcointalk.org/index.php?topic=335113.40 (last accessed December 2013).

Anon (2012) 'Rare-earth mining in China comes at a heavy cost for local villages', *Guardian*, available at http://www.theguardian.com/environment/2012/aug/07/china-rare-earth-village-pollution (last accessed February 2014).

Anon (2011) 'Jam Echelon Day', *Hack Story*, available at http://hackstory.net/Jam_Echelon_Day (last accessed January 2014).

Anon (1995) 'The Fidonet Sysop Manifesto', *Fido News*, Vol. 12, No. 24, available at http://fidonews.ca/issues/FIDO1224.NWS (last accessed August 2012).

Aouragh M. and Alexander A. (2011) 'The Egyptian Experience: Sense and Nonsense of the Internet Revolution', *International Journal of Communication*, Vol. 5.

Apple Corporation (2013) 'iCloud Terms and Conditions', available at https://www.apple.com/legal/internet-services/icloud/en/terms.html (last accessed August 2013).

AppleInsider (2006) 'Greenpeace Forced Out of MacExpo', *AppleInsider*, available at http://appleinsider.com/article/?id=2179 (last accessed February 2014).

Armbrust M., Fox A. Griffith R., Joseph A., Katz R., Konwinski A., Lee G., Patterson D., Rabkin A., Stoica I. and Zaharia M. (2010) 'A View of Cloud Computing', *Communications of the ACM*, Vol. 53, No. 4.

Arthur C. (2012) *Digital Wars: Apple, Google, Microsoft and the Battle for the Internet* (London: Kogan Page).

— (2011) 'iPhone Keeps Record of Everywhere You Go', *Guardian*, available at http://www.guardian.co.uk/technology/2011/apr/20/iphone-tracking-prompts-privacy-fears (last accessed April 2011).

Aspray W. (1990) *John von Neumann and the Origins of the Modern Computer* (Cambridge MA: MIT Press).

Assange J. with Appelbaum J., Muller-Maguhn A. and Zimmerman J. (2012) *Cypherpunks: Freedom and the Future of the Internet* (New York: OR Books).

Audenaerde E. van (2014) 'You Got WANKed: Hactions of Political Hacktivism', *YL Magazine*, available at http://www.global1.youth-leader.org/2011/05/you-got-wanked-hactions-of-political-hacktivism (last accessed February 2014).

Auletta K. (2010) *Googled: The End of the World as We Know It* (New York: Penguin).

Balkin J. (2008) 'The Constitution in the National Surveillance State', *Faculty Scholarship Series*, paper 225, available at http://digitalcommons.law.yale.edu/fss_papers/225 (last accessed September 2013).

Ball J. (2013) 'Xbox Live Among Game Services Targeted by US and UK Spy Agencies', *Guardian*, available at http://www.theguardian.com/world/2013/dec/09/nsa-spies-online-games-world-warcraft-second-life (last accessed January 2014).

Bamford J. (2009) *The Shadow Factory: The Ultra-Secret NSA from 9/11 to the Eavesdropping on America* (New York: Anchor Books).

Banks M. (2007) *The Politics of Cultural Work* (Basingstoke: Palgrave Macmillan).

Banks J. and Potts J. (2010) 'Co-creating Games: A Co-evolutionary Analysis', *New Media and Society*, Vol. 12, No. 2.

Barabási A.-L. (2011) 'Introduction and Keynote to A Networked Self' in Papacharissi Z. (ed.) *A Networked Self: Identity, Community and Culture on Social Network Sites* (London: Routledge).

Barad K. (2007) *Meeting the Universe Halfway: Quantum Physics and the Entanglement of Matter and Meaning* (Durham NC: Duke University Press).

Baraniuk C. (2013) 'Prism and the UK: Nothing to Fear?', *Prospect*, available at http://www.prospectmagazine.co.uk/blog/prism-hague-surveillance-uk-data/#.Usr39rRuSP9 (last accessed January 2014).

Barlow J.P. (2011) *Twitter*, available at http://twitter.com/#!/jpbarlow/status/10627544017534976 (last accessed June 2011).

— (1998) 'A Declaration of the Independence of Cyberspace', available at http://w2.eff.org/Censorship/Internet_censorship_bills/barlow_0296.declaration (last accessed August 2012).

Bateson G. (1972) *Steps to an Ecology of Mind* (Chicago: University of Chicago Press).

Baym N. (2010) *Personal Connections in the Digital Age* (Cambridge: Polity).

Baym N. and boyd d. (2012) 'Socially Mediated Publicness: An Introduction', *Journal of Broadcasting and Electronic Media*, Vol. 56, No. 3.

Benkler Y. (2006) *The Wealth of Networks: How Social Production Transforms Markets and Freedoms* (New Haven: Yale University Press).

Berardi F. (2009) *The Soul At Work: From Alienation to Autonomy* (Los Angeles: Semiotext(e)).

Berners-Lee T. (2000) *Weaving the Web: The Original Design and Ultimate Destiny of the World Wide Web* (New York: HarperCollins).

Berry D. (2008) *Copy Rip Burn: The Politics of Copyleft and Open Source* (London: Pluto).

Berry D. and Moss G. (2005) 'The Libre Culture Manifesto', *The Free Software Magazine*, available at http://www.freesoftwaremagazine.com/articles/libre_manifesto (last accessed April 2014).

Blanc S. and Noor O. (2011) '30 Years of Political Hacking', *Owni.EU: Technology Politics Culture*, available at http://owni.eu/2011/11/08/30-years-of-political-hacking (last accessed February 2014).

Bloor D. (1997) *Wittgenstein, Rules and Institutions* (London: Routledge).

Boltanski L. and Chiapello E. (2005) *The New Spirit of Capitalism* (London: Verso).

Booth K. (ed.) (2005) *Critical Security Studies and World Politics* (Boulder CO: Lynne Rienner Publishers).

boyd d. (2011) 'Social Network Sites as Networked Publics: Affordances, Dynamics and Implications', in Papacharissi Z. (ed.) (2011) *A Networked Self: Identity, Community and Culture on Social Network Sites* (London: Routledge).

— (2006) 'Friends Friendsters and Top 8: Writing community into being on social network sites', *First Monday*, Vol. 11, No. 12, available at http://firstmonday.org/ojs/index.php/fm/article/view/1418/1336 (last accessed January 2014).

Bonnington C. and Ackerman S. (2012) 'Apple Rejects App that Tracks U.S. Drone Strikes', *Wired*, available at http://www.wired.com/dangerroom/2012/08/drone-app (last accessed February 2014).

Brand S. (2003) 'Founding Father: Interview with Paul Baran', *Wired*, available at http://archive.wired.com/wired/archive/9.03/baran_pr.html (last accessed May 2014).

Brevini B., Hintz A. and McCurdy P. (eds.) (2013) *Beyond Wikileaks: Implications for the Future of Communications Journalism and Society* (Basingstoke: Palgrave Macmillan).

Britton D. and Williams C. (1995) '"Don't Ask Don't Tell Don't Pursue": Military Policy and the Construction of Heterosexual Masculinity', *Journal of Homosexuality*, Vol. 30, No. 1.

Browning C. and McDonald M. (2011) 'The Future of Critical Security Studies: Ethics and the Politics of Security', *European Journal of International Relations*, Vol. 19, No. 2.

Bruns A. (2008) *Blogs, Wikipedia, Second Life and Beyond: From Production to Produsage* (New York: Peter Lang).

Butler J. (1999) *Gender Trouble: Feminism and the Subversion of Identity* (London: Routledge).

— (1997) *Excitable Speech: A Politics of the Performative* (London: Routledge).

Buzan B., Wæver O. and de Wilde J. (1998) *Security: A New Framework for Analysis* (Boulder CO: Lynne Rienner Publishers).

CAE (1996) *Electronic Civil Disobedience and Other Unpopular Ideas* (New York: Semiotext(e)).

— (1994) *The Electronic Disturbance* (New York: Semiotext(e)).

Cassell J. and Jenkins H. (eds.) (1998) *From Barbie to Mortal Kombat: Gender and Computer Games* (Cambridge MA: MIT Press).

Castells M. (2012) *Networks of Outrage and Hope: Social Movements in the Internet Age* (Cambridge: Polity).

— (2009) *Communication Power* (Oxford: Oxford University Press).

— (2000a) 'Materials for an Exploratory Theory of the Network Society', *British Journal of Sociology*, Vol. 51, No. 1.

— (2000b) *The Rise of the Network Society*, second edition (Oxford: Blackwell).

Casti J.L. and DePauli W. (2000) *Gödel: A Life of Logic* (Cambridge: Basic Books).

Castranova E. (2005) *Synthetic Worlds: The Business and Culture of Online Games* (Chicago: University of Chicago Press).

Chen M. (2012) *Leet Noobs: The Life and Death of an Expert Player Group in World of Warcraft* (New York: Peter Lang).

Chomsky N. (2000) *The Architecture of Language*, edited by Mukherji N., Patnaik B.N. and Agnhotry R.K. (New Delhi: Oxford University Press).

— (1975) *The Logical Structure of Linguistic Theory* (New York: Plenum Press).

Coleman G. (2013a) *Anonymous in Context: The Politics and Power Behind the Mask*, Internet Governance Paper Number 3, available at http://www.cigionline.org/publications/2013/9/anonymous-context-politics-and-power-behind-mask (last accessed May 2014).

— (2013b) 'Anonymous and the Politics of Leaking', in Brevini B., Hintz A. and McCurdy P. (eds.) *Beyond Wikileaks: Implications for the Future of Communications Journalism and Society* (Basingstoke: Palgrave Macmillan).

— (2012a) 'Our Weirdness is Free. The Logic of Anonymous – online army agent of chaos and seeker of justice', *Triple Canopy*, Vol. 6.

— (2012b) 'Am I Anonymous?' *Limn*, Vol. 2.

— (2012c) *Coding Freedom: The Ethics and Aesthetics of Hacking* (Princeton: Princeton University Press).

— (2010) 'What it's Like to Participate in Anonymous' Actions', *The Atlantic*, available at http://www.theatlantic.com/technology/archive/2010/12/what-its-like-to-participate-in-anonymous-actions/67860 (last accessed February 2014).

Collins R. (2010) *Three Myths of Internet Governance: Making Sense of Networks Governance and Regulation* (Bristol: Intellect).

Constine J. (2013) 'Facebook Removing Option to be Unsearchable by Name Highlighting Lack of Universal Privacy Controls', *TechCrunch*, available at http://techcrunch.com/2013/10/10/facebook-search-privacy (last accessed January 2014).

Copeland B.J. (ed.) (2004) *The Essential Turing: Seminal Writings in Computing Logic Philosophy Artificial Intelligence and Artificial Life* plus *The Secrets of Enigma* (Oxford: Clarendon Press).

Corneliussen H. (2008) 'World of Warcraft as a Playground for Feminism', in Corneliussen H. and Rettberg J. (eds.) *Digital Culture, Play and Identity: A World of Warcraft Reader* (Cambridge MA: MIT Press).

Corneliussen H. and Rettberg J. (2008) (eds.) *Digital Culture, Play and Identity: a World of Warcraft Reader* (Cambridge MA: MIT Press).

Dabashi H. (2012) *The Arab Spring: The End of Postcolonialism* (London: Zed Books).

Daly M. (1978) *Gyn/Ecology: The Metaethics of Radical Feminism* (Boston: Beacon Press).

David M. (2010) *Peer to Peer and the Music Industry: the Criminalization of File Sharing* (London: Sage).

Davis M. (2000) *The Universal Computer: The Road from Leibniz to Turing* (New York: Norton).

DeAgonia M., Gralla P. and Raphael J. (2013) 'Battle of the Media Ecosystems: Amazon Apple Google and Microsoft', *ComputerWorld*, available at http://www.computerworld.com/s/article/print/9240650/Battle_of_the_media_ecosystems_Amazon_Apple_Google_and_Microsoft?taxonomyName=Personal+Technology&taxonomyId=229 (last accessed August 2013).

Dean J. (2012) *The Communist Horizon* (London: Verso).

De Beauvoir S. (2010) *The Second Sex* (London: Vintage).

Defree S. (2013) 'Apple IPO Makes Instant Millionaires December 12 1980', *EDN Network*, available at http://www.edn.com/electronics-blogs/edn-moments/4403276/Apple-IPO-makes-instant-millionaires--December-12--1980 (last accessed February 2014).

Deibert R. (2013) *Black Code: Inside the Battle for Cyberspace* (Toronto: McClelland and Stewart).

Deibert R., Palfrey J., Rohozinski R. and Zittrain J. (eds.) (2011) *Access Contested: Security Identity and Resistance in Asian Cyberspace* (Cambridge MA: MIT Press).

Deleuze G. (1994) *Difference and Repetition* (London: Athlone Press).

— (1983) *Nietzsche and Philosophy* (New York: Columbia University Press).

Derrida J. (1988) *Limited Inc* (Evanston Ill: Northwestern University Press).

— (1973) *Speech and Phenomena and Other Essays on Husserl's Theory of Signs* (Evanston: Northwestern University Press).

Dobson A. (2007) *Green Political Thought* (London: Routledge).

Dormehl L. (2013) *The Apple Revolution: The Real Story of how Steve Jobs and the Crazy Ones Took Over the World* (London: Virgin Books).

Doyle T. (2005) *Environmental Movements in Minority and Majority Worlds* (Rutgers: Rutgers University Press).

Dreyfus S. (1997) *Underground: Tales of Hacking Madness and Obsession on the Electronic Frontier* (Kew: Mandarin).

Dyer-Witheford, N. (1999) *Cyber-Marx: Cycle and Circuits of Struggle in High-Technology Capitalism* (Chicago: University of Illinois Press).

Dyer-Witheford N. and de Peuter G. (2009) *Games of Empire: Global Capitalism and Video Games* (Minneapolis: University of Minnesota Press).

Dyson G. (2012) *Turing's Cathedral: The Origins of the Digital Universe* (Harmondsworth: Penguin).

Elmer G. (2004) *Profiling Machines: Mapping the Personal Information Economy* (Cambridge MA: MIT Press).

Elliot A. and Urry J. (2010) *Mobile Lives* (London: Routledge).

Everett D. (2009) *Don't Sleep There Are Snakes: Life and Language in the Amazonian Jungle* (London: Profile).

Ewalt D. (2013) *Of Dice and Men: The Story of Dungeons and Dragons and the People Who Play It* (New York: Scribner Book Company).

Facebook (2014) 'Facebook Privacy Help: Choose Who You Share With', *Facebook*, available at http://www.facebook.com/help/459934584025324 (last accessed January 2014).

Feuz M., Fuller M. and Stalder F. (2011) 'Personal Web Searching in the Age of Semantic Capitalism', *First Monday*, Vol. 16, No. 2, available at http://firstmonday.org/ojs/index.php/fm/article/view/3344/2766 (last accessed March 2014).

Floridi L. (2011) *The Philosophy of Information* (Oxford: Oxford University Press).

— (2010) *Information: A Very Short Introduction* (Oxford: Oxford University Press).

Foucault M. (1985) *The Use of Pleasure: The History of Sexuality Volume Two* (New York: Pantheon Books).

— (1977) 'Nietzsche Genealogy History', in Bouchard D. (ed.) *Language Counter-Memory Practice: Selected Essays and Interviews by Michel Foucault* (Ithaca: Cornell University Press).

FSF (2014) 'The Free Software Definition', *Free Software Foundation*, available at https://www.gnu.org/philosophy/free-sw.html (last accessed March 2014).

Fuchs C. (2014) *Social Media: A Critical Introduction* (London: Sage).

Galloway A. (2012) 'Does the Whatever Speak?', in Nakamura L. and Chow-White P. (eds.) *Race After the Internet* (London: Routledge).

— (2004) *Protocol: How Control Exists after Decentralization* (Cambridge MA: MIT Press).

Galloway A. and Thacker E. (2007) *The Exploit: A Theory of Networks* (Minneapolis: University of Minnesota Press).

Galperin E. (2011) 'EFF Calls for Immediate Action to Defend Tunisian Activists Against Government Cyberattacks', *Electronic Frontier Foundation*, available at https://www.eff.org/deeplinks/2011/01/eff-calls-immediate-action-defend-tunisian (last accessed February 2014).

Gerbaudo P. (2012) *Tweets from the Streets: Social Media and Contemporary Activism* (London: Pluto).

Gill R. and Pratt A. (2008) 'In the Social Factory?: Immaterial Labour Precariousness and Cultural Work', *Theory Culture and Society*, Vol. 25, Nos.7–8.

Gillan K., Pickerill J. and Webster F. (2008) *Anti-War Activism: New Media and Protest in the Information Age* (Basingstoke: Palgrave Macmillan).

Gillespie T. (2014) 'The Relevance of Algorithms', in Gillespie T., Boczkowski P. and Foot K. (eds.) *Media Technologies: Essays on Communication Materiality and Society* (Cambridge MA: MIT Press).

— (2010) 'The Politics of Platforms', *New Media and Society*, Vol. 12, No. 3.

— (2007) *Wired Shut: Copyright and the Shape of Digital Culture* (Cambridge MA: MIT Press).

Gillespie T., Boczkowski P. and Foot K. (eds.) (2014) *Media Technologies: Essays on Communication Materiality and Society* (Cambridge MA: MIT Press).

Gleick J. (2012) *The Information: A History, A Theory, A Flood* (London: Fourth Estate).

Glenny M. (2012) *Dark Market: How Hackers Became the New Mafia* (London: Vintage Books).

Goldstein E. (ed.) (2008) *The Best of 2600* (Indianapolis: Wiley Publishing).

Goggin G. (2010) *Global Mobile Media* (London: Routledge).

Google (2013a) 'Facts About Google and Competition', available at http://www.google.com/competition/howgooglesearchworks.html (last accessed August 2013).

Google (2013b) 'Google Terms of Service', available at http://www.google.com/policies/terms (last accessed August 2013).

Greenberg A. (2012) *This Machine Kills Secrets: Julian Assange, the Cypherpunks and Their Fight to Empower Whistleblowers* (New York: Plume Books).

Gruener W. (2010) 'Did Steve Jobs Steal The iPad? Genius Inventor Alan Kay Reveals All', *Tom's Harware*, available at http://www.tomshardware.com/news/alan-kay-steve-jobs-ipad-iphone10209.html (last accessed February 2014).

Guardian (2014) 'The NSA Files', available at http://www.theguardian.com/world/the-nsa-files (last accessed January 2014).

Hachman M. (2012) 'Google: The Fifth Largest Server Vendor?', *Slashdot DataCenter*, available at http://slashdot.org/topic/datacenter/google-the-fifth-largest-server-vendor (last accessed August 2013).

Halavais A. (2008) *Search Engine Society* (Cambridge: Polity).

Halbert D. (2009) 'Public Lives and Private Communities: The Terms of Service Agreement and Life in Virtual Worlds', *First Monday*, Vol. 14, No. 12, available at http://firstmonday.org/ojs/index.php/fm/article/view/2601/2405 (last accessed August 2013).

Hall K. (2006) 'Shooters to the Left of Us Shooters to the Right: First Person Arcade Shooter Video Games, the Violence Debate and the Legacy of Militarism', *Reconstruction: Studies in Contemporary Culture*, Vol. 6, No. 1, available at http://reconstruction.eserver.org/061/hall.shtml (last accessed February 2014).

Hansell S. and Markoff J. (2006) 'A Search Engine That's Become An Inventor', *The New York Times*, available at http://www.nytimes.com/2006/07/03/technology/03google.html?_r=1&ei=5088&en=11ad7f241098c6e2&ex=1309579200&adxnnl=1&partner=rssnyt&emc=rss&adxnnlx=1151888719-NxrsEO+IzRvSa28feeFzfw&pagewanted=all&pagewanted=all (last accessed July 2012).

Haraway D. (2008) *When Species Meet* (Minneapolis: University of Minnesota Press).

— (1991) *Simians Cyborgs and Women: The Reinvention of Nature* (London: Free Association Books).

Harcourt B. (2007) *Against Prediction: Profiling Policing and Punishing in the Actuarial Age* (Chicago: University of Chicago Press).

Harding L. (2014) *The Snowden Files: The Inside Story of the World's Most Wanted Man* (London: Guardian Books).

Hardt M. and Negri A. (2005) *Multitude: War and Democracy in the Age of Empire* (London: Penguin).

— (2000) *Empire* (Cambridge MA: Harvard University Press).

Harvey D. (2010) *The Enigma of Capital and the Crises of Capitalism* (London: Profile Books).

Hauser M.D., Chomsky N. and Fitch W.T. (2002) 'The Faculty of Language: What Is It? Who Has It? and How Did It Evolve?', *Science*, Vol. 298.

Hesmondhalgh D. (2007) *The Cultural Industries*, second edition (London: Sage).

Hilbert M. and Lopez P. (2011) 'The World's Technological Capacity to Store Communicate and Compute Information', *Science*, Vol. 332.

Hillis K., Petit M. and Jarrett K. (2013) *Google and the Culture of Search* (London: Routledge).

Himanen P. (2001) *The Hacker Ethic: A Radical Approach to the Philosophy of Business* (New York: Random House).

Hjorth L., Burgess J. and Richardson I. (eds.) *Studying Mobile Media: Cultural Technologies, Mobile Communication and the iPhone* (London: Routledge).

Howard P., Duffy A., Freelon D., Hussain M., Mari W. and Mazaid M. (2011) 'Opening Closed Regimes: What Was the Role of Social Media During the Arab Spring?', *Project on Information Technology and Political Islam: Working Paper 2011.1* available at http://pitpi.org/index.php/research/publications (last accessed February 2014).

Hughes N. (2013) 'Apple Has Sold 170M iPads to Date Implying Sales Near 15M in Sept. Quarter', *Apple Insider*, available at http://appleinsider.com/articles/13/10/23/apple-has-sold-170m-ipads-to-date-implying-sales-near-15m-in-sept-quarter (last accessed February 2014).

iPad (2010) 'Apple iPad Mobile Computing: iPad Launch Event', *Design History Timeline*, available at http://designtimeline.cias.rit.edu/timeline/apple-ipad (last accessed February 2014).

Isaacson W. (2011) *Steve Jobs* (New York: Simon and Schuster).

Jeffreys A. (2011) 'In Which Eben Moglen Like Legit Yells At Me For Having Facebook', *Blog: News Gossip and Intel from Silicon Alley 2.0*, available at http://www.betabeat.com/2011/12/13/

in-which-eben-moglen-like-legit-yells-at-me-for-being-on-facebook (last accessed January 2012).

Jennings T. (1995) 'Infestation of Manifests', *Fido News*, Vol. 12, No.24, available at http://fidonews.ca/issues/FIDO1224.NWS (last accessed August 2012).

Jones S. (2006) *Against Technology: From the Luddites to Neo-Luddism* (London: Routledge).

Jordan T. (2013a) *Internet Society and Culture: Communicative Practices Before and After the Internet* (London: Bloomsbury).

— (2013b) 'Information as a Politics', *Culture Machine*, Vol. 14, available at http://www.culturemachine.net/index.php/cm/issue/view/25 (last accessed February 2014).

— (2011) 'Troubling Companions: Companion Species and the Politics of Inter-relations', *NORA-Nordic Journal of Feminist and Gender Research*, Vol. 19, No.4.

— (2008) *Hacking: Digital Media and Technological Determinism* (Cambridge: Polity).

— (2002) *Activism!: Direct Action Hacktivism and the Future of Society* (London: Reaktion).

— (2001) 'Language and Libertarianism: The Politics of Cyberculture and the Culture of Cyberpolitics', *Sociological Review*, Vol. 49, No. 1.

— (1999a) *Cyberpower: The Culture and Politics of Cyberspace and the Internet* (London: Routledge).

— (1999b) 'New Space New Politics?: Cyberpolitics and the Electronic Frontier Foundation', in Jordan T. and Lent A. (eds.) *Storming the Millennium: The New Politics of Change* (London: Lawrence and Wishart).

— (1995) 'Collective Bodies: Raving and the Politics of Gilles Deleuze and Félix Guattari', *The Body and Society*, Vol. 1, No. 1.

— (1994) *Reinventing Revolution: Value and Difference in New Social Movements and the Left* (Avebury: Ashgate).

Jordan T. and Lent A. (eds.) (1999) *Storming the Millennium: The New Politics of Change* (London: Lawrence and Wishart).

Jordan T. and Taylor P. (2004) *Hacktivism and Cyberwar: Rebels With a Cause* (London: Routledge).

— (1998) 'A Sociology of Hacking', *Sociological Review*, Vol. 46, No. 4.

Juul J. (2013) *The Art of Failure: An Essay on the Pain of Playing Video Games* (Cambridge MA: MIT Press).

Kadushin C. (2012) *Understanding Social Networks: Theories Concepts Findings* (Oxford: Oxford University Press).

Kafai Y., Heeter C., Denner J. and Sun J. (eds.) (2008) *Beyond Barbie and Mortal Kombat: New Perspectives on Gender and Gaming* (Cambridge MA: MIT Press).

Kahney L. (2013) *Jony Ive: The Genius Behind Apple's Greatest Products* (London: Portfolio Penguin).

Katchadourian R. (2010) 'No Secrets: Julian Assange's Mission for Total Transparency', *The New Yorker* available at http://www.newyorker.com/reporting/ 2010/06/07/100607fa_fact_khatchadourian?currentPage=all (last accessed February 2014).

Kelty C. (2008) *Two Bits: The Cultural Significance of Free Software* (Raleigh: Duke University Press).

Kline S., Dyer-Witheford N. and De Peuter G. (2003) *Digital Play: The Interaction of Technology Culture and Marketing* (Montreal: McGill-Queen's University Press).

Kot G. (2009) *Ripped: How the Wired Generation Revolutionized Music* (New York: Scribner).

Kravets D. (2012) 'Feds Tell Megaupload Users to Forget About Their Data', *Wired*, available at http://www.wired.com/threatlevel/2012/06/feds-megaupload-data/ (last accessed March 2014).

Langer J. (2008) 'The Familiar and the Foreign: Playing (Post) Colonialism in World of Warcraft', in Corneliussen H. and Rettberg J. (2008) (eds.) *Digital Culture, Play and Identity: A World of Warcraft Reader* (Cambridge MA: MIT Press).

Lapsley P. (2013) *Exploding the Phone: The Untold Story of the Teenagers and Outlaws Who Hacked Ma Bell* (New York: Grove Press).

Latour B. (2005) *Reassembling the Social: An introduction to Actor-Network Theory* (Oxford: Oxford University Press).

Leavitt D. (2007) *The Man Who Knew Too Much: Alan Turing and the Invention of the Computer* (London: Phoenix).

Lessig L. (2009) *Remix: Making Art and Commerce Thrive in the Hybrid Economy* (London: Bloomsbury Academic).

Levy S. (2011) *In the Plex: How Google Thinks, Works, and Shapes Our Lives* (New York: Simon and Schuster).

— (2006) *The Perfect Thing: How the iPod Shuffles Commerce, Culture and Coolness* (New York: Simon and Schuster).

— (2001) *Crypto: Secrecy and Privacy in the New Code War* (London: Allen Lane).

— (1984) *Hackers: Heroes of the Computer Revolution* (London: Penguin).

Littman J. (1997) *The Watchman: The Twisted Life and Crimes of Serial Hacker Kevin Poulsen* (New York: Little Brown and Company).

Livingstone S. and Helsper E. (2007) 'Gradations in Digital Inclusion: Children, Young People and the Digital Divide', *New Media and Society*, Vol. 9, No. 4.

MacCullum-Steward E. and Parsler J. (2008) 'Role-play vs. Gameplay: The Difficulties of Playing a Role in World of Warcraft', in Corneliussen H. and Rettberg J. (2008) (eds.) *Digital Culture, Play and Identity: A World of Warcraft Reader* (Cambridge MA: MIT Press).

McDonald K. (2006) *Global Movements: Action and Culture* (Oxford: Blackwell).

McKay G. (ed.) (1998) *DIY Culture: Party and Protest in Nineties Britain* (London: Verso).

MacKinnon R. (2012) *Consent of the Networked: The Worldwide Struggle for Internet Freedom* (New York: Basic Books).

McMillan R. (2012) 'Google: We're One Of The Largest Hardware Makers', *Wired*, available at http://www.wired.com/wiredenterprise/2012/06/google_makes_servers (last accessed August 2013).

Maher J. (2012) *The Future Was Here: The Commodore Amiga* (Cambridge MA: MIT Press).

Manovich L. (2013) *Software Takes Command* (London: Bloomsbury Academic).

Marx K. (1976) *Capital: A Critique of Political Economy Volume One* (Harmondsworth: Penguin).

May T. (1994) 'The Cyphernomicon' available at http://groups.csail.mit.edu/mac/classes/6.805/articles/crypto/cypherpunks/cyphernomicon/CP-FAQ (last accessed December 2013).

Mayer J. (2009) *The Dark Side: The Inside Story of How the War on Terror Turned Into a War on American Ideals* (New York: Anchor Books).

Mayer-Schoneberger V. and Cukier K. (2013) *Big Data: A Revolution that will Transform How We Live Work and Think* (London: John Murray).

Meeker M. and Wiu L. (2013) 'Internet Trends D11 Conference', *D11 Conference*, available at http://www.slideshare.net/kleinerperkins/kpcb-internet-trends-2013 (last accessed February 2014).

Mell P. and Grance T. (2011) *The NIST Definition of Cloud Computing: NIST Special Publication 800-145* (Gaithersberg MD: US Department of Commerce), available at http://csrc.nist.gov/publications/nistpubs/800-145/SP800-145.pdf (last accessed August 2013).

Menn J. (2010) *Fatal System Error: The Hunt for the New Crime Lords Who Are Bringing Down the Internet* (New York: Public Affairs).

Mentor (1986) 'The Conscience of a Hacker', *Phrack*, Vol. 1, No. 7, available at http://www.phrack.org/issues.html?issue=7&id=3&mode=txt (last accessed August 2012).

Miller J. (2006) 'Role Playing Games as Interactive Fiction', *Reconstruction: Studies in Contemporary Culture*, Vol. 6, No. 1, available at http://reconstruction.eserver.org/061/miller.shtml (last accessed February 2014).

Mitnick K. (2011) *Ghost in the Wires: My Adventures as the World's Most Wanted Hacker* (New York: Little Brown and Company).

Monson M. (2012) 'Race-Based Fantasy Realm: Essentialism in the World of Warcraft', *Games and Culture*, Vol. 7, No. 1.

Montfort N. and Bogost I. (2009) *Racing the Beam: The Atari Video Computer System* (Cambridge MA: MIT Press).

Morozov E. (2011) *The Net Delusion: How Not To Liberate The World* (London: Allen Lane).

Mueller M. (2010) *Networks and States: The Global Politics of Internet Governance* (Cambridge MA: MIT Press).

— (2002) *Ruling the Root: Internet Governance and the Taming of Cyberspace* (Cambridge MA: MIT Press).

Nagel E. and Newman J.R. (2001) *Gödel's Proof*, revised edition (New York: New York University Press).

Nakamura L. (2009) 'Don't Hate the Player Hate the Game: The Racialization of Labor in World of Warcraft', *Critical Studies in Media Communication*, Vol. 26, No. 2.

Nakamura L. and Chow-White P. (eds.) (2012) *Race After the Internet* (London: Routledge).

Neff G. (2012) *Venture Labor: Work and the Burden of Risk in Innovative Industries* (Cambridge MA: MIT Press).

Neill E. (2001) *Rites of Privacy and the Privacy Trade: On the Limits of Protection of the Self* (Montreal: McGill-Queen's University Press).

Norris P. (2001) *Digital Divide: Civic Engagement Information Poverty and the Internet Worldwide* (Cambridge: Cambridge University Press).

Oakes C. (1999) 'Monitor This Echelon', *Wired*, available at http://www.wired.com/politics/law/news/1999/10/32039 (last accessed January 2014).

Olson P. (2012) *We Are Anonymous: Inside the Hacker World of Lulzsec, Anonymous and the Global Cyber Insurgency* (New York: Little Brown and Company).

Papacharissi Z. (2011) 'Conclusion: A Networked Self', in Papacharissi Z. (ed.) (2011) *A Networked Self: Identity, Community and Culture on Social Network Sites* (London: Routledge).

— (2009) 'The Virtual Geographies of Social Networks', *New Media and Society*, Vol. 11, Nos. 1–2.

Papacharissi Z. (ed.) (2011) *A Networked Self: Identity, Community and Culture on Social Network Sites* (London: Routledge).

Pasquinelli M. (2008) *Animal Spirits: A Bestiary of the Commons* (Rotterdam: NAi Publishers-Institute of Network Cultures).

Peoples C. and Vaughan-Williams N. (2010) *Critical Security Studies: An Introduction* (Abingdon: Routledge).

Peterson J. (2012) *Playing at the World: A History of Simulating Wars, People and Fantastic Adventures, from Chess to Role-Playing Games* (San Diego: Unreason Press).

Petzold C. (2008) *The Annotated Turing: A Guided Tour through Alan Turing's Historic Paper on Computability and the Turing Machine* (Indianapolis: Wiley).

Postigo H. (2012) *The Digital Rights Movement: The Role of Technology in Subverting Digital Copyright* (Cambridge MA: MIT Press).

Poulsen K. (2011) *Kingpin: How One Hacker Took Over the Billion-Dollar Cybercrime Underground* (New York: Random House).

Quittner J. and Slatalla M. (1995) *Masters of Deception: The Gang that Ruled Cyberspace* (London: Vintage).

Qiu J. (2012) 'Network Labor: Beyond the Shadow of Foxconn', in Hjorth L., Burgess J. and Richardson I. (eds.) *Studying Mobile Media: Cultural Technologies, Mobile Communication and the iPhone* (London: Routledge).

— (2011) 'Deconstructing Foxconn', available at http://vimeo.com/17558439 (last accessed February 2014).

— (2009) *Working-Class Network Society: Communication Technology and the Information Have-Less in Urban China* (Cambridge MA: MIT Press).

Rainie L. and Wellman B. (2012) *Networked: The New Social Operating System* (Cambridge MA: MIT Press).

Rheingold H. (1994) *The Virtual Community: Surfing the Internet* (London: Minerva).

Rich S. and Gellman B. (2014) 'NSA Seeks to Build Quantum Computer That Could Crack Most Types of Encryption', *Washington Post*, available at http://www.washingtonpost.com/world/national-security/nsa-seeks-to-build-quantum-computer-that-could-crack-most-types-of-encryption/2014/01/02/8fff297e-7195-11e3-8def-a33011492df2_story.html (last accessed January 2014).

Roberts P. (2014) 'CERF: Classified NSA Work Mucked Up Security For Early TCP/IP', *Veracode Blog*, available at http://blog.veracode.com/2014/04/cerf-classified-nsa-work-mucked-up-security-for-early-tcpip (last accessed April 2014).

Rose N. (1999) *Governing the Soul: The Shaping of the Private Self*, second edition (London: Free Association Books).

Rowbotham S., Segal L. and Wainwright H. (1979) *Beyond the Fragments: Feminism and the Making of Socialism* (London: Merlin Press).

Rushe D., Ackerman S. and Ball J. (2013) 'Reports That NSA Taps Into Google and Yahoo Data Hubs Infuriate Tech Giants', *Guardian*, available at http://www.theguardian.com/technology/2013/oct/30/google-reports-nsa-secretly-intercepts-data-links (last accessed January 2014).

Ryan Y. (2011) 'Tunisia's Bitter Cyberwar: Anonymous has Joined Tunisian Activists to Call for End to the Government's Stifling of Online Dissent', *Aljazeera*, available at http://www.aljazeera.com/indepth/features/2011/01/20111614145839362.html (last accessed February 2014).

SACOM (2012) 'New iPhone Old Abuses: Have Working Conditions at Foxconn in China Improved?', *Students and Scholars Against Corporate Misbehaviour*, available at http://sacom.hk/reportnew-iphone-old-abuses-have-working-conditions-at-foxconn-in-china-improved (last accessed February 2014).

— (2011) 'iSlave Behind the iPhone: Foxconn Workers in Central China', *Students and Scholars Against Corporate Misbehaviour*, available at http://sacom.hk/islave-behind-the-iphone-foxconn-workers-in-central-china (last accessed February 2014).

— (2010) 'Workers as Machines: Military Management in Foxconn', *Students and Scholars Against Corporate Misbehaviour*, available at http://sacom.hk/workers-as-machines-military-management-in-foxconn (last accessed February 2014).

Schmid G. (2001) 'On the Existence of a Global System for the Interception of Private and Commercial Communication (ECHELON Interception System)', *European Parliament: Temporary Committee on the ECHELON Interception System*, available at http://cryptome.org/echelon-ep-fin.htm (last accessed January 2014), also available at http://www.europarl.europa.eu/sides/getDoc.do?pubRef=-//EP//NONSGML+REPORT+A5-2001-0264+0+DOC+PDF+V0//EN&language=EN (last accessed May 2014).

Schonfeld (2011) 'Apple is Tracking You to Build Something Very Valuable: Its Location Database', *TechCrunch*, available at http://techcrunch.com/2011/04/21/apple-tracking-location-database (last accessed April 2011).

Serafini P. (2014) 'Subversion Through Performance: Performance Activism in London', in Werbner, P., Webb, M. and Spellman-Poots, K. (eds.) *The Political Aesthetics of Global Protest: The Arab Spring and Beyond* (Edinburgh: Edinburgh University Press).

Serres M. (1982) *Hermes: Literature, Science, Philosophy* (London: Johns Hopkins Press).

Shenk D. (1997) *Data Smog: Surviving the Information Age* (San Francisco: HarperEdge).

Sifry M. (2011) *Wikileaks and the Age of Transparency* (New Haven: Yale University Press).

Singel R. (2010) 'Apple App Store Bans Pulitzer-Winning Satirist for Satire', *Wired*, available at http://www.wired.com/business/2010/04/apple-bans-satire (last accessed March 2014).

Smith N. (2004) *Chomsky: Ideas and Ideals*, second edition (Cambridge: Cambridge University Press).

So S. and Westland J. (2010) *Red Wired: China's Internet Revolution* (London: Marshall Cavendish).

SSCNSD (2005) 'Proceedings of the Standing Senate Committee on National Security and Defence, Issue 15 – Evidence April 30 2007', *Parliament of Canada*, available at http://www.parl.gc.ca/Content/SEN/Committee/391/defe/15evb-e.htm (last accessed March 2014).

Stark D. (2009) *The Sense of Dissonance: Accounts of Worth in Economic Life* (Princeton: Princeton University Press).

Steinert-Threlkeld T. (2011) 'Google Now The Largest Maker of Servers – Fried', *Security Technologies Monitor*, available at http://www.securitiestechnologymonitor.com/news/google-third-largest-server-maker-now-fried-27953-1.html (last accessed August 2012).

Sterling B. (1992) *The Hacker Crackdown: Law and Disorder on the Electronic Frontier* (New York: Viking).

Stryker C. (2011) *Epic Win for Anonymous: How 4Chan's Army Conquered the Web* (New York: Overlook Duckworth).

Sullivan D. (2013) 'Google Still World's Most Popular Search Engine By Far But Share of Unique Searchers Dips Slightly', *Search Engine Land*, available at http://searchengineland.com/google-worlds-most-popular-search-engine-148089 (last accessed March 2014).

Tate R. (2010) 'Steve Jobs Offers World "Freedom from Porn"', *Gawker*, available at http://gawker.com/5539717/steve-jobs-offers-world-freedom-from-porn (last accessed February 2014).

Taylor P. (1999) *Hackers: Crime in the Digital Sublime* (London: Routledge)

Terranova T. (2004) *Network Culture: Politics for the Information Age* (London: Pluto).

Timsey S. (2006) 'WoW Overwhelmed by Homophobes, Make Blood Elves Less "Feminine"!', *Gaygamer.net*, available at http://gaygamer.net/2006/10/wow_overwhelmed_by_homophobes.html (last accessed February 2014).

Travis A. (2014) 'Emergency Surveillance Bill to be Fast-Tracked Despite 49 MPs' Opposition', *Guardian*, available at http://www.theguardian.com/politics/2014/jul/15/emergency-surveillance-legislation-fast-tracked-parliament (last accessed June 2014).

Tronstad R. (2008) 'Character Identification in World of Warcraft: The Relationship Between Capacity and Appearance', in Corneliussen H. and Rettberg J. (eds.) (2008) *Digital Culture, Play and Identity: A World of Warcraft Reader* (Cambridge MA: MIT Press).

Turing A. (2004) 'On Computable Numbers with an Application to the Entscheidungsproblem (1936)', in Copeland B.J. (ed.) *The Essential Turing: Seminal Writings in Computing Logic Philosophy Artificial Intelligence and Artificial Life* plus *The Secrets of Enigma* (Oxford: Clarendon Press).

Turner F. (2006) *From Counterculture to Cyberculture* (Chicago: University of Chicago Press).

Vaquero L., Rodero-Merino L., Caceres J. and Lindner M. (2008) 'A Break in the Clouds: Towards a Cloud Definition', *SIGCOMM Computer Communication Review*, Vol. 39, No. 1.

Vercellone C. (2007) 'From Formal Subsumption to General Intellect: Elements for a Marxist Reading of the Thesis of Cognitive Capitalism', *Historical Materialism*, Vol. 15.

Vise D. (2005) *The Google Story* (New York: Random House).

Walton C. (2013) *Empire of Secrets: British Intelligence, the Cold War and the Twilight of Empire* (London: HarperCollins).

Wang L., Laszewski G., Younge A., Xi H., Kunze M., Tao J. and Fu C. (2010) 'Cloud Computing: A Perspective Study', *New Generation Computing*, Vol. 28, No. 2.

Wark M. (2004) *A Hacker Manifesto* (Cambridge MA: Harvard University Press).

Watson I. (2012) *The Universal Machine: From the Dawn of Computing to Digital Consciousness* (New York: Copernicus Books).

Weber S. (2004) *The Success of Open Source* (Cambridge MA: Harvard University Press).

Weintraub J. (1997) 'The Theory and Politics of the Public/Private Distinction', in Weintraub J. and Kumar K. (eds.) *Public and Private in Thought and Practice* (Chicago: Chicago University Press).

Weintraub J. and Kumar K. (eds.) (1997) *Public and Private in Thought and Practice* (Chicago: Chicago University Press).

Werbner P., Webb M. and Spellman-Poots K. (eds.) (2014) *The Political Aesthetics of Global Protest: The Arab Spring and Beyond* (Edinburgh: Edinburgh University Press).

Wikstrom P. (2010) *The Music Industry: Music in the Cloud* (Cambridge: Polity).

Wilkins J. (1694) *Mercury or The Secret and Swift Messenger or How a Man may with Privacy and Speed Communicate his Thoughts to a Friend at any Distance*, second edition (London: Rich Baldwin).

Williams E. (2011) 'Environmental Effects of Information and Communication Technologies', *Nature*, Vol. 479.

Williams S. (2012) *Free as in Freedom: Richard Stallman's Crusade for Free Software* (Cambridge: O'Reilly).

Woodward B. (2003) *Bush At War* (London: Pocket Books).

Wright S. (2002) *Storming Heaven: Class Composition and Struggle in Italian Autonomist Marxism* (London: Pluto).

XKeyscore (2008) 'XKeyscore Presentation From 2008', *Guardian*, available at http://www.theguardian.com/world/interactive/2013/jul/31/nsa-xkeyscore-program-full-presentation (last accessed January 2014).

Index

Printed in the USA
CPSIA information can be obtained
at www.ICGtesting.com
CBHW030458221124
17679CB00014B/50